Politics and State-Society Relations in India

T0386729

James Manor

Politics and State-Society

Relations in India

James Manor

With a Foreword by
Niraja Gopal Jayal

HURST & COMPANY, LONDON

First published in 2016 by Orient Blackswan Private Limited,
1/24 Asaf Ali Road, New Delhi 110 002

Published in the United Kingdom in 2017 by
C. Hurst & Co. (Publishers) Ltd.,
41 Great Russell Street, London, WC1B 3PL
© James Manor, 2017
All rights reserved.
Printed in India

Distributed in the United States, Canada and Latin America by
Oxford University Press, 198 Madison Avenue, New York, NY 10016,
United States of America.

The right of James Manor to be identified as the author
of this publication is asserted by him in accordance
with the Copyright, Designs and Patents Act, 1988.

A Cataloguing-in-Publication data record for this book is available
from the British Library.

ISBN: 9781849047180 *paperback*

This book is printed using paper from registered sustainable
and managed sources.

www.hurstpublishers.com

For my partners in crime (co-authors):

Richard Crook, Rob Jenkins, Surinder Jodhka,
Noushin Kalati, Anirudh Krishna, Marcus Melo, Njuguna Ng'ethe

and to the memory of

E. Raghavan *and* Gerald Segal

Contents

PART II
POLITICAL PARTIES

PART III
MANAGING POLITICAL AND SOCIAL FORCES

PART IV
CHIEF MINISTERS' STRUGGLES AT THE STATE LEVEL

TABLES

I t is a singular privilege and a pleasure to write a few words about the Collected Writings of Professor James Manor. When I first met Professor Manor in the mid-1990s, his was already a towering presence in the world of Indian political studies, and I was a young academic just embarking on a career in the same field.

It is scarcely possible to capture the essence of forty-four years of prodigious scholarship in one volume, let alone a foreword. I will therefore confine myself to identifying three especially distinctive aspects of James Manor's formidable *oeuvre*. The first of these is his sustained interest in studying leaders, for whom his preferred nomenclature is politicians. Leadership is a subject that political scientists have tended to avoid in post-behavioural times. The difficulty of studying this phenomenon and its problematic association with 'great men' theories of history and politics, have however meant that the baby has all too frequently been thrown out with the bathwater, leaving some gaping holes in political explanation, especially in phases of Indian political history when leaders have been perceived to be particularly strong or spectacularly weak.

With a salute to Machiavelli, James Manor has ventured out in these relatively uncharted waters. This neo-Machiavellianism is not merely descriptive but also normative, as his studies of chief ministers like Devaraj Urs and Digvijay Singh suggest that such politicians possess and exercise enormous power and have the ability to effect much good through new policy initiatives, welfare schemes, the superior implementation of centrally sponsored schemes and more effective methods of augmenting state resources. While this is in part a comment on the opportunities created—and seized by some chief ministers to attract investment for industrial development—by economic liberalisation, it also says something interesting about the changing nature of Indian federalism, which is the subject of several essays in this volume.

Manor acknowledges that this is a view of politics from above, or at least one that looks over the shoulders of politicians in power (mostly in the states). However, the focus in his recent work on local-level political fixers nicely complements the view from above and this is clearly his second distinctive contribution to the study of Indian politics. Political fixers, like political leaders, are indisputably an under-studied phenomenon. Manor's seven state survey of these 'political entrepreneurs' shows that, given the right environment, they can promote development by making government more responsive, transparent and accountable. They also enhance democracy by counteracting the tendency to centralise power and by undermining caste hierarchies.

It is the integration of these perspectives from below (the fixer) and from above (the chief minister) that makes this body of scholarship a compelling exemplar of the state-society framework. It provides an account of state-society relations in which the autonomous role of politics vis-à-vis society, of political leaders at the national and state levels, and of political functionaries in what Joel Migdal memorably called 'the trenches', all find their due place.

Thirdly, beginning with his early work on Karnataka, James Manor's scholarship has always manifested a substantive engagement with issues of caste and identity. This book contains his recent reflections on the changing dynamics of caste and power at the local level, and offers an explanation of why the questioning and unsettling of caste hierarchies has on the whole been accomplished by accommodation rather than violence, even if this may change in the future. The multiplicity and fluidity of identities in India makes it possible for citizens to sport identities that vary across time and context. While this can be challenging for political organisation and management it is also, Manor argues, a positive strength in that cross cutting social cleavages prevent any single cleavage from acquiring the power to destabilise the overall arrangement.

A special virtue of this book, frequently missing in such collections, is that each essay is prefaced by a short paragraph that helpfully dates it and places it in the original context of its publication. The volume brings together old classics like the article *How and Why Liberal Representative Politics Emerged in India* and glimpses of recent and new work such as a forthcoming book on the MGNREGS. Despite the fact that the selection does not include his writings on, for instance, the Prime Minister's Office (PMO) or on liquor, poverty and politics in Karnataka, this is unquestionably the definitive companion to James Manor's scholarship. The special (and non-poisonous) Karnataka brew that does find mention here is the Mysore coffee to which, as served at the legendary Koshy's in Bangalore, this volume contains a fittingly warm tribute.

Readers will be enriched by the range and quality of scholarship in this volume, which is sure to find a lasting place on the bookshelves of serious students of Indian politics.

Niraja Gopal Jayal
Professor
Centre for the Study of Law and Governance
New Delhi

PUBLISHER'S ACKNOWLEDGEMENTS

For permission to reproduce copyright material in this volume, the publisher wishes to make the following acknowledgements.

Wiley for 'How Liberal, Representative Politics Emerged in India', originally published in *Political Studies* 38 (1): 20–39, 1990.

Economic and Political Weekly for 'Anomie in Indian Politics: Origins and Potential Wider Impact', originally published in *Economic and Political Weekly* 18 (Annual Number): 725–35, 1983; and 'Pragmatic Progressive in Regional Politics: The Case of Devaraj Urs', originally published in *Economic and Political Weekly* 15 (5, 6, 7, Annual Number): 201–13, 16 February 1980.

Sage for 'Political Regeneration in India', originally published in *The Multiverse of Democracy*, by Ashis Nandy, pp. 230–41; '"Towel over Armpit": Small-Time Political "Fixers" in the Politics of India's States', originally published in *India and the Politics of Developing Countries*, by Ashutosh Varshney, pp. 60–84, 2004.

The Economist for 'Where the 1996 Gandhi Writ Doesn't Run', originally published in *The Economist* 283 (7237): 55–56, 15 May.

Taylor & Francis for 'The Congress Party since 1990', originally published in *Understanding India's New Political Economy*, by

John Harriss, Sanjay Ruparelia et al., pp. 204–20, 2011; 'In Part, a Myth: The BJP's Organisational Strength', originally published in *Coalition Politics and Hindu Nationalism*, pp. 55–74, 2005; 'Beyond Clientelism: Digvijay Singh in Madhya Pradesh', originally published in *Power and Influence in India*, by Pamela Price and A. E. Ruud, pp. 193–213, 2010; 'What Do They Know of India Who Only India Know?: The Uses of Comparative Politics', originally published in *Commonwealth and Comparative Politics* 48 (4): 505–16, November 2010.

Cambridge University Press for '"Ethnicity" and Politics in India', originally published in *International Affairs* 72 (3): 459–76, July 1996; 'Political Bargaining and Centre-state Relations in the Federal System', originally published as 'Centre-State Relations' in *The Success of Indian Democracy*, by Atul Kohli, pp. 78–102.

The Asia Society for 'India's Chief Ministers and the Problem of Governability', originally published in *India Briefing*, by Philip Oldenburg, pp. 47–74, 1995.

China Analysis for 'Politics and Experimentation in India: The Contrast with China', originally published in *China Analysis* no. 74: 1–29, June 2009.

— *one* —

Introduction

During a 2013 seminar in London for young researchers studying India, students expressed surprise when I stressed how dramatically politics there had changed since 1989. No party had achieved a parliamentary majority since then, so massive powers had flowed away from the Prime Minister's Office (PMO) to other institutions at the national level, and to the state level in the federal system. They were too young to recall the years before 1989 when powers had been radically centralised and prime ministers had dominated.

The students found my emphasis on that earlier era rather quaint. Surely that was 'ancient history': those days were gone, and no single party could now gain a parliamentary majority. But then the national election of 2014 gave just that to the Bharatiya Janata Party (BJP). At this writing, shortly after that election, a new prime minister is in a position to regain and exercise powers that have been unavailable to his predecessors for 25 years. That 'ancient history' has fresh relevance.

This book revisits studies of key themes during the years of prime ministerial dominance, and then assesses the transition through the post-1989 period of hung parliaments to the present day. It examines the democratic process and state-society relations during those two periods. It provides signposts as India navigates its way through a new phase which may turn out to resemble the era before 1989, or may not. Much has changed over the last 25 years. Many institutions at the national level have gained in substance, influence and autonomy—the courts, the Election Commission, Parliament and its committees, etc. So have state governments and the federal system. The media and civil society have grown more formidable. All of these institutions will interact with the executive in New Delhi differently from before 1989. We will not see an exact re-run of that 'ancient history', but we may detect echoes of it as the drama unfolds.

* * *

Each chapter in this book is preceded by a paragraph in italics which situates it both in the period when it was written and among other chapters in this book. (Many of these chapters were published outside India so that readers there may have missed them, and some have not yet appeared in print.) But to provide an overall guide, here is a survey of the main issues to be tackled in this book, and an account of the themes that arise in each of the five parts of this collection.

To understand what has happened and how things have changed over time, we need to consider how democracy first took root and then how powerful actors then responded to several major challenges. They had to deal with a political awakening among all sections of this hierarchical society—in which ordinary folk grasped the egalitarian logic of a system that gave every adult just one vote, conferred rights on even the humblest, and was meant to address the needs of all. Alongside the awakening, political decay threatened to undermine the capacity of state agencies and political parties' organisations to respond. These parallel trends— awakening and decay—posed grave dangers to the democratic order, but Indians eventually proved capable of developing a corrective: the regeneration of key institutions, especially after 1989. That regeneration did not fully reverse the process of decay, and it provided a less-than-satisfactory response to the awakening. But it averted collapse, and set in train a compelling drama which persists to this day.

Senior politicians—who exercise enough power to make them the main concern of many of these chapters—needed to find ways to integrate state and society, and the various levels in the political system from the apex of power in New Delhi and state capitals down through intermediate (district and sub-district) levels to the grassroots.

Those twin tasks became more difficult after 1990 when two kinds of identity politics emerged in strength. A decision by Prime Minister V. P. Singh to offer preferment to other backward classes (OBCs) forced politicians to cultivate broader social coalitions—including blocs of castes which leaders sought to mobilise in exercises that are often called 'social engineering'. That theme lives on as an ever-present reality, even though social and political volatility have made it hard to maintain solidarity within multi-caste blocs. Singh's actions then persuaded Hindu nationalists to counter with assertive efforts to mobilise the Hindu majority as a bloc which might cut across caste lines. That theme also lives on, even though Hindu nationalists have often had to shelve much of their agenda in order to win state and national elections.

These two changes accelerated the political awakening, made the problem of demand overload from below still more acute, and created dilemmas for political leaders of every stripe. To make matters worse, nearly all of their political parties had weak organisations. This combination of problems largely explained the excruciating difficulty of incumbent governments in gaining re-election. Between 1980 and December 2008, ruling parties (or coalitions) at the state level were ousted by voters at roughly 70 per cent of elections. If we remove West Bengal (where the Left Front was re-elected seven times between 1982 and 2011) from the calculation, the rejection rate approaches 90 per cent. At the national level, incumbent governments were thrown out at six of the eight general elections between 1989 and 2014.

These figures terrified politicians, and drove them to innovate in order to survive in office. Many began to stress 'development'—a word which acquired different meanings in different states and under different governments in New Delhi. Since most party organisations were too frail to deliver development, many leaders devised new government programmes that could be implemented largely through bureaucratic channels. And since the old politics of patronage distribution could no longer ensure re-election in the teeth of mounting demands, politicians sought to insulate these programmes from those who wished to divert resources for use as spoils. Patronage politics ('clientelism') did not end, but it was increasingly supplemented by what I call 'post-clientelist' initiatives. Some of these innovations made governments more responsive. In a minority of Indian states, politicians made greater use of other resources as well: elected councils at lower levels (*panchayati raj* institutions); and enlightened civil society organisations which had emerged in strength. In all states, two further resources proved helpful. The first was an army of political 'fixers'—small-time political entrepreneurs who forge links between their localities and government offices from which benefits from new programmes might be accessed.[1] Second and more crucially, after 2002, state and Central government revenues soared, thanks to economic growth and new approaches to tax collection. That gave governments far more money to spend on initiatives to cultivate popularity.

These themes arise repeatedly in these chapters, where we encounter the Indian state, interactions between state and society, and the democratic process in all of its complexity and ambiguity.[2]

---

[1]See chapter ten of this book. 'Fixers' were largely ignored in only a small number of states where—unusually—ruling parties possessed strong organisations that could penetrate to the local level.

[2]The chapters in this book cover a wide range of topics, but several themes which this writer has tackled over the years receive only limited attention in this collection. They include democratic decentralisation (a major preoccupation in which comparisons of Indian and other cases have loomed large) and the related topic of bottom-up, participatory politics and its promise and limitations; elections at state and national levels; prime ministers, as their office has evolved and interacted with other institutions and forces; India's presidents; the response of political and other institutions to major disasters; the political calculations that have underpinned economic liberalisation and kept it cautious and limited by international standards, and the political implications of liberalisation; and the Mahatma Gandhi National Rural Employment Guarantee Act (MGNREGA). Only

we see the Indian state here at its best, at its worst, and often as a tangle of contradictions.

* * *

Let us now consider the analyses in the five parts of this book. We have long heard ill-informed commentators from outside India describe the growth of its robust democracy as some sort of 'miracle'. Their theories tell them that democracy cannot flourish in a country with low levels of economic development and what we now call Human Development Indicators,[3] plus a daunting array of potential social conflicts. As early as 1966, one formidable India specialist in Britain sought to explain that it was not miraculous but logical that a liberal, representative system should take root—given India's recent history, socio-cultural resources, and the remarkable capacity for political bargaining.[4] Since the myth of the miracle refused to lie down, further arguments in that vein were needed. They can be found in chapter two which appeared in 1990.

I began studying India 44 years ago, just after the end of the first phase in its post-Independence history (1947 to the late 1960s) when the Congress Party exercised dominance. In its heyday, the Congress organisation was the most extensive network of regional political 'machines'—distributing patronage (goods, service, funds and favours) in exchange for political support—that the world had ever

---

chapter fifteen here focuses squarely upon caste, another topic on which much else has appeared. There is also relatively little in this book on the southern state of Karnataka which has absorbed this writer for 44 years.

[3] This yardstick combines a number of measurements: life expectancy, literacy rates, levels of education and per capita incomes, etc. It emerged from the United Nations Development Programme (UNDP) in 1990—thanks to the work of a team led by Mahbub-ul-Haq which included Sudhir Anand, Meghnad Desai, Keith Griffin, Gustav Ranis, Amartya Sen, Frances Stewart and Paul Streeten.

[4] W. H. Morris-Jones, 'India's Political Miracle', *Australian Journal of Politics and History* (August 1966), pp. 213–20; reproduced in his *Politics Mainly Indian* (Orient Longman, New Delhi, 1978), pp. 131–43. In that early period, his arguments were echoed in the pioneering work of Rajni Kothari and Myron Weiner.

seen or is likely to see. In that era, it was the country's most important political institution, and it contributed mightily to the emergence of democratic politics discussed in chapter two. It also integrated the two main sources of order in India: state structures (which acquired democratic substance) and agrarian social structures (which were then dominated by the landed castes, a minority of the rural population[5]). The landowning castes translated their dominance over village life into dominance of the Congress and of politics in nearly all Indian states. They got the lion's share of government benefits, although other groups received at least tokenism.

The party's organisation in those days also had the sinew and reach to integrate the various levels in the political system and to penetrate into rural areas where most of the votes were (and still are). Over time, however, the Congress organisation gradually ossified (as such institutions do) and was then fatally undermined by its leader, Indira Gandhi, who (bizarrely) regarded it, along with strong government institutions, as a threat to her personal pre-eminence rather than as an instrument through which to govern. By the early 1970s, the organisation's capacity to distribute patronage, to gather politically important information for its leaders, and to discipline errant members, had greatly diminished.

Many problems ensued. The disintegration of Congress's disciplinary power contributed mightily to the anomie (normless behaviour by politicians) which caused widespread popular dismay (for an assessment, see chapter three). Its inability to distribute patronage in a well coordinated manner damaged it further at a time when the political awakening was making voters (including those from disadvantaged groups) more impatient, more demanding, and thus less willing to be pacified by the distribution of spoils. Congress election victories at the state level ceased to be routine. The awakening was making India a more genuine democracy, but also a more difficult country to govern. Many began to ask whether the country was becoming ungovernable.

[5]Their dominance in rural areas later diminished markedly as the so called 'lower' castes increasingly refused to accept caste hierarchies (which were strong during that first phase). See chapter fifteen of this book.

That might have happened if awakening and decay had been the only trends that mattered. Democracy might eventually have collapsed, as it did in many other newly independent nations. But a third process offered a counterweight. Institutional regeneration gained momentum after 1989, as power drained away from the once dominant PMO and flowed to other institutions. These three great themes—awakening, decay and regeneration—are discussed in Part I.

Part II focuses squarely on political parties. It opens with a short paper (chapter five from 1982) on the self-inflicted problems which Indira Gandhi faced as a result of the destruction of the once-formidable organisation of her Congress Party—as she pursued personal (and ultimately, dynastic) rule. Although she did not realise it, by radically centralising power, she destroyed the information-gathering capacity of her party, so that she ended up flying blind. Flying blind is bad enough, but flying blind unknowingly is even worse. This analysis reminds us of a key point made elsewhere in this book: that the most effective way for leaders atop complex state and especially national political systems to make their influence penetrate downward is by pursuing bargaining and accommodation.

Chapter six then offers a detailed assessment of the Congress Party between 1990 and 2014—which governed alone or in ruling coalitions in New Delhi for 15 of those 24 years. It examines the party's response to three major challenges that emerged in and after 1990: efforts by some of its rivals to mobilise support from the OBCs; more assertive Hindu nationalism; and the rise of numerous potent regional parties. It discusses P. V. Narasimha Rao's efforts to shift the political agenda away from identity politics towards 'development', and his disastrous attempt in 1993 to rebuild the party by holding organisational elections. It also explains why the scarcely concealed chaos within the party's organisation creates a 'systemic need' for the dynasty which can act as the final arbiter in disputes. Today, when the efficacy of the dynasty has been called into question, this poses grave questions for the party.

The BJP's organisation—which is stronger and more democratic than those of most other parties—is then analysed in chapter seven. It argues that despite its strength, that organisation lacks the capacity to make its influence penetrate adequately below the district level and beyond urban centres, to the village level where nearly all elections are won and lost. As we saw in 2014, this does not mean that the BJP cannot obtain majorities. But to do so, it must rely on the strength of sister organisations and on effective, innovative campaign techniques such as those that it deployed in 2014.

Leaders at the national level have always had to find ways to manage relations with state governments in the federal system. That was not difficult in the period before the late 1960s, when the Congress Party was dominant at both levels. But since then— when opposition parties (and increasingly, regional parties) have headed governments in many states—it has often been a major headache. Prime ministers have varied in their approaches to this problem. Indira and Rajiv Gandhi (prime ministers for most of the years between 1967 and 1989) tended to adopt imperious postures, offering state governments few concessions. Between 1989 and the national election in mid-2014, when no single party could win a parliamentary majority, prime ministers have had to depend more on bargaining—even (or rather, especially) with regional parties that were allies in ruling coalitions in New Delhi.

There is, however, more to their management problem than that. Leaders at both the national and state levels are faced with the daunting task of dealing with political and social forces—not just political allies and adversaries, but interest groups that make heavy demands, and social forces that may come into conflict with one another and/or with governments. 'Management' sometimes entails stimulating certain conflicts. We saw this at the national level in 1990 when Prime Minister V. P. Singh sought to benefit disadvantaged OBCs, knowing that this would alarm 'higher' castes, and when Hindu nationalists responded with more assertive campaigns. At the state level, we have seen successive chief ministers of Uttar Pradesh foment suspicion between the different caste blocs on which they rely for votes. But for the most part, 'management' has entailed efforts to ease tensions between antagonistic interests—lest conflict lead to disorder which would call the authority of governments into question. Balancing these two objectives—stimulating and reducing inter-group tensions; dividing and uniting—is a delicate business.

The chapters in Part III consider this vexing set of 'management' tasks. As politicians tackle them, they first need to understand the social forces that they are dealing with in state- and national-level political systems. Chapter eight discusses a major impediment to such an understanding—the widespread use of the term 'ethnicity' to describe social forces. It is noteworthy that this term is often used by social scientists, but almost never by political practitioners in India. Practitioners who hear the word swiftly dismiss it. They sensibly recognise that it thrusts several very different and sometimes antagonistic things—language, religion and caste (each of which contains within it deeper complexities)—into a single category. Politicians know, instinctively and correctly, that the term confuses more than it clarifies—a point endorsed in chapter eight.

Chapter nine then focuses squarely on approaches to the management of 'Centre–state' relations within the federal system, but that discussion inevitably leads into a wider assessment of the management of political and social forces. One crucial theme that emerges (yet again) from chapter nine is that the best way for political leaders at the apex of national and state political systems to make their influence penetrate downward is by way of bargaining rather than *diktat*, beloved of Indira and Rajiv Gandhi. (This point also arises in chapters four, five and six.) Between 1989 and mid-2014, when no single party achieved a majority in Parliament, national leaders were compelled by circumstances to emphasise the politics of bargaining. It will be interesting to see whether that trend continues now that a government finally has a solid majority in the Lok Sabha.

In their dealings with social forces, senior politicians have certain advantages over their counterparts in other countries. Three are especially important.

The first is the unrivalled complexity of Indian society—which is both a problem for politicians charged with 'management' and, in some ways, an advantage. This is partly to do with India's massive size, but is more the result of the heterogeneities within heterogeneities that they encounter. India's regions vary greatly from one another, but within each region there are many further complexities—a welter of social groups pursuing divergent interests. For example, clusters of *jati*'s (endogamous caste groups) compete with one another, but within each cluster there is further contestation between individual *jati*'s, and between people from different interest groups based on class and other divisions. Religious groups—Hindus, Muslims and others—compete with each other, but are again divided by various sectarian cleavages. These and other social fissures within individual states impede the kind of regional solidarity that would fuel secessionist movements—as we see in chapters eight and nine. That makes the task of political management to maintain national unity less taxing than many in other countries.

The second advantage is the strong tendency of Indians to shift their preoccupations from one to another (and then another) of the many 'identities' that are available to them—often and with great fluidity. No other society offers people such a large number of such identities: three kinds of caste identity (*jati*, *jati*-cluster and *varna*); religious identities (including sectarian sub-identities)—plus linguistic; regional and sub-regional; urban and rural; gender, and class identities. Opinion surveys firmly indicate that the fluidity and frequency with which Indians shift their preoccupations has not diminished over time. For politicians who must manage social dynamics, this fluidity is a challenge but more importantly, a blessing. It is challenging because it makes it difficult to sustain social coalitions on which politicians rely to gain or retain power. But since it also prevents tension and conflict from building up for long periods along a single fault line in society—as in, for example, Sri Lanka—it makes conflict management easier.

The third advantage is a major democratic resource which India has generated in far greater measure than most other countries: an army of local-level 'fixers' who shuttle back and forth between their villages and government offices at higher levels, to obtain benefits for their neighbours (see chapter ten[6]). These small-time political entrepreneurs lubricate and enrich the democratic and development

---

[6]These people are also discussed in the works of Anirudh Krishna: for example, *Active Social Capital: Tracing the Roots of Development and Democracy* (Columbia University Press, New York, 2002). I call them 'fixers' while Krishna calls them *naya netas* (new leaders).

processes with their bargaining skills. And since many of them come from groups other than the traditionally dominant landed castes, they often deepen democracy. Amid many ambiguities, they enhance democratic competition, transparency and accountability—at and above the grassroots. They also serve as a partial antidote to anomie in Indian politics (see chapter three). They are a product of India's prolonged experiment with democracy, but they also help mightily to sustain it.

Part IV focuses on the state level which is immensely important to an understanding of how politics and state-society relations have changed over the years. It is at the state level and below that most of the actual governing occurs. State governments adapt centrally sponsored programmes in different ways, and they create many programmes of their own. One distinguished civil servant has said that the most striking change that he has witnessed in the last half-century has been the proliferation of central and state government programmes.[7]

The condition of the bureaucracy also varies across states—partly because different administrative traditions from the British period still have residual influence, but mainly because of what has happened since 1947. In some states, the bureaucracy is aloof and imperious while in others, it is more open and responsive. In some, civil servants have long been abused and browbeaten by politicians so that they lack autonomy and capability while in others they have retained relatively high morale, autonomy and operational capacity. So bureaucracies in different states implement programmes with varying degrees of effectiveness.

There are also marked differences in relations between the main political parties in various states. In some, their interactions are reasonably civilised, but in others quite caustic. In some (Rajasthan and Karnataka are examples), they compete for votes from roughly the same set of interests and social groups. In such states, different parties therefore pursue rather similar policies and when governments change, there is considerable policy continuity. In

[7]Interview with B. K. Bhattacharya, former Chief Secretary of Karnataka, Bangalore, 7 February 2010.

other states (Uttar Pradesh is the classic case), different parties seek support from quite distinct social bases. They therefore cultivate division and even spite between different social groups. And when governments change, the new regime tends to uproot the policies of its predecessor and start afresh—with so that policy continuity is largely unknown.

It is at the state level that state and society mainly interact. That is true not least because (speaking rather crudely) every linguistic region has its own distinctive caste system—which differs somewhat, or radically, from those in other regions. (There are, for example, no indigenous *Kshatriyas* or *Vaishyas*—major *varnas* or sub-divisions in the traditional caste system—in south India.[8]) And since state boundaries were redrawn in 1956, a large number of states conform roughly to individual linguistic regions (a theme examined in chapter eight).

So the state level, and variations across states, demand attention from anyone interested in politics and society in India. Part IV contains three chapters which examine state politics as it has changed since the 1970s—and chapter fourteen, which opens Part V, carries this further by assessing the state politics in very recent times.

In each case, state politics are examined from 'over the shoulders' of chief ministers who head state governments. There are of course other ways to approach state politics—from below[9]—but the view from the apex of power reveals a great deal, not least because chief ministers of states have immense influence. As I note below, they have had far too little attention from scholars who study India.

Part V brings us fully into the twenty-first century. It opens with chapter fourteen which extends the discussions of chief ministers in Part IV into the present. In very recent times, power has been

---

[8] I am grateful to the late M. N. Srinivas for educating me on this point, and on much else.

[9] That approach is used in R. Crook and J. Manor, *Democracy and Decentralisation in South Asia and West Africa: Participation, Accountability and Performance* (Cambridge University Press, Cambridge, 1998); and in R. Jenkins and J. Manor, *Politics and the Right to Work: India's Mahatma Gandhi National Rural Employment Guarantee Act* (Hurst/Orient BlackSwan/Oxford University Press, London/New Delhi/New York, forthcoming).

centralised—substantially or radically—in the hands of many (though not all) chief ministers. This is ironic because, as we have noted above, power has been *de*centralised away from the PMO in New Delhi since 1989—although after the 2014 national election, that may change. But at the state level, centralisation has proceeded to the point where nearly 60 per cent of Indians now live under state governments in which one person (the chief minister) exercises dominance or near-dominance.

Chapter fourteen provides those figures and explains how this has happened. It is not an entirely new development. After I interviewed Chief Minister N. T. Rama Rao at 5 am in 1984, G. Ram Reddy explained NTR's centralised approach by saying 'his is a government of heroes and zeroes, and the number of heroes is one'. There are many more such state governments today, partly because chief ministers can exploit opportunities provided by India's limited (and far from 'neo-liberal') economic liberalisation by using the formidable discretionary powers which remain in their hands to extract sizeable 'contributions' from industrialists. Centralising chief ministers limit the influence of their ministers and legislators. That reduces the leakage of funds into patronage networks, and facilitates technocratic and/or 'post-clientelist' programmes—some but not all of which are popular and make good developmental sense. But it also means that legislators cannot adequately represent or serve the people who elected them, so that the democratic process is constricted, sometimes severely.

Chapter fifteen then examines the implications for political dynamics at the rural grassroots of a fundamentally important social change: the declining acceptance of caste hierarchies by supposedly 'lower' castes. The institution of caste—if by that we mean *jati*, or endogamous caste group—remains strong. Indeed, *jati* is arguably the most durable pre-existing social institution in Asia, Africa and Latin America—not because it refuses to change, but because it absorbs it and adjusts to it. But hierarchies among *jati*'s are increasingly rejected at the village level in most regions. As we saw early in this introduction, the old hierarchies were one of the two main sources of order in India in the initial post-Independence period. As they crumble, new arrangements are needed, but they are hard to generate and in some (but not most) places, they have failed to emerge. Amid the shaking of the foundations of society, we might expect greater violence to occur, as formerly dominant castes kick against this change. But surprisingly, violence—which has taken lethal forms in some villages—has been less common than uneasy, grudging, tenuous accommodations between caste groups. This chapter offers an explanation for this, grounded in the Indian capacity for bargaining—a theme which often emerges in discussions in other chapters of politics at higher levels. But it also identifies trends which may make accommodations more difficult to achieve as further change occurs.

In recent years, India has witnessed a remarkable diversity of political and policy experiments, as senior politicians seek (assiduously and sometimes desperately) for ways to maintain their popularity and win re-election. Many experiments have originated at the national level, but state-level leaders have done even more of this, so that the federal system can be seen as a vast laboratory for experimentation. Chapter sixteen analyses how this happens. It does so by contrasting India with China where a great deal of experimentation has also occurred, but in markedly different ways. The contrasts between the two countries are mainly (and not surprisingly) explained by the dissimilarities between their political systems.

Further comparisons between India's democracy and political systems elsewhere take centre-stage in chapter seventeen. Several examples are discussed—to show that we India specialists learn crucial things about the country by comparing it with other cases. If we focus only on India, some of those things remain largely invisible and taken for granted as 'normal' and not especially important. But comparisons reveal that they are actually quite distinctive, and worthy of close examination. Of course, many India specialists—especially those who reside there—lack opportunities to undertake comparisons with other countries. But they still have a promising avenue for comparative analyses—comparisons between India's instructively diverse regions and states. Several chapters in this collection illustrate the promise of comparative studies of Indian states.

* * *

This book argues that politics matters. It is not 'epiphenomenal'—it is not something superficial that is dominated and determined by deep, underlying socio-economic forces. It is certainly shaped by them, as we see repeatedly in this book. But it also shapes them, and enjoys a significant degree of autonomy from them. The interplay of politics with society—with socio-economic and socio-cultural forces—is just that: *inter*play, in which each set of forces influence the others.

Nor can politics be ignored, as it sometimes is when technocratic commentators offer excessively tidy prescriptions for policy reform. Many of them view politics—even democratic politics—with distaste as an impediment to 'rational' policy making. They always misunderstand politics, and often ignore it—as if 'governance' could somehow be insulated from it. They fail to see that their technocratic proposals are deeply political—in their origins and their implications. They also fail to recognise that many of the most constructive policies to emerge in India have been responses to pressures from the democratic process.

Senior politicians feel and react to those pressures. They—especially chief ministers in India's states—loom large in this book. That does not mean that the 'great man' (or 'great woman') theory of history is being revived here. It is rightly discredited. But senior politicians demand our attention because they possess great power. They can do, and have done, immense good and immense damage. But they have been marginalised or ignored in many analyses which focus on other things—be they social forces, or political structures and processes, or technocratic blueprints. Those other things are important, and as many chapters here indicate, we need to pay close attention to leaders' engagement with them. But to ignore senior politicians is to give us Hamlet without the prince—and without *The Prince*, Machiavelli's study of statecraft which influences many of the studies here. Political 'agency'—the actions of politicians and bureaucrats—has had too little attention in many studies of India. This book offers a corrective.

It demonstrates, repeatedly, that political agency often trumps path dependency (a theme that is over-emphasised by some analysts). In other words, senior politicians are not always forced by constraints imposed by social forces or political routines to stick to the paths that their predecessors followed. We encounter numerous examples in these chapters of leaders who experimented[10] and innovated, who departed from well worn paths. Instead of clinging to old practices, they introduced changes which in turn induced change in society, in the economy, and in political dynamics. They have more autonomy, and room to manoeuvre and machinate, than many commentators concede. Far from being a case of 'same old, same old' stodginess, Indian politics—and the policy process—are actually quite dynamic. Politicians' actions have often made a major difference.

Note the emphasis there on 'actions'. The studies in this book assume and demonstrate that politicians' actions count for more than their rhetoric, their discourse, and the concepts that they bring to their work. Many of these chapters also stress the importance of materiality—the material forces that politicians encounter, and the material implications of their actions. These too count for more than do concepts and discourse. There is of course (as we often see here) an *inter*play between ideas and discourse on the one hand, and material realities and politicians' actions on the other. But the latter are uppermost in these chapters, because they count for more.[11]

Commentators who stress ideas and discourse, and others, sometimes lament the passing of an earlier generation of enlightened politicians in India. They yearn for the emergence of high-minded leaders who are inspired by humanitarian ideals, or by a progressive ideology. But ideologies count for little in India, and if we wait for humanitarian idealists to take charge, we will wait forever. Many studies in this book argue that we should rely instead on democratic institutions, on the vast army of local-level 'fixers' which democracy has spawned, and especially on thoroughly awakened and sophisticated voters who exert pressure on politicians to behave more constructively. These things are reliable because politicians have no choice but to grapple with them—since it is in

---

[10]See chapter sixteen of this book.

[11]For an example, my disagreement with T. N. Madan in chapter eight of this book.

their selfish interests to do so. There are several telling examples of this in these chapters.

* * *

Taken overall, the studies assembled here add up to a study in ambiguity. They provide plenty of good news about India's democracy, but it is presented here 'warts and all'. We must consider both sides of this story. Politicians and bureaucrats are often corrupt, callously complacent, and at times even brutish. But these things are often checked by potent counterweights—especially by the tendency of voters to reject wretched leaders and governments. Repeated rejections have compelled many powerful actors to restrain themselves, at least somewhat, and to seek ways of governing and of interacting with society more responsibly and responsively.

In this book, we often catch sight of the Indian state at its worst and at it best. When we consider the 'worst', corruption often dominates discussions. But there is another aspect to it which has had far less attention, but which does as much damage. Perceptive civil society analysts point to an acute allergy among politicians and bureaucrats to transparency and downward accountability. Those analysts regard that allergy as 'the defining feature of the Indian state'.[12] They are mistaken: it is not the only defining feature. But they are right to stress it. The allergy probably does as much damage as corruption, which it facilitates and which in turn facilitates it.

However, at other times, we encounter the state at its best. The most startling example of this emerged from a separate study of India's largest poverty programme, the Mahatma Gandhi National Rural Employment Guarantee Act (MGNREGA).[13] Its architects inserted into it formidable transparency mechanisms. They did so in the hope that transparency would reduce corruption, which it has done. But they knew that it would not end it. So the transparency mechanisms had one other key purpose. When corrupt acts— especially thefts from poor workers' wages—occurred, they would

[12]Discussion with three key civil society leaders, New Delhi, 7 December 2010.
[13]Jenkins and Manor, *Politics and the Right to Work.*

be visible to victimised workers. That visibility would inspire discontent among workers and make them more politically aware and proactive in defending their interests—so that what I call their 'political capacity'[14] would be strengthened and pressure would grow, from below, for probity and justice. No other government in the developing world—not even in extremely enlightened Brazil—is self confident enough and progressive enough to cultivate discontent among poor people. But the Indian state did that. Here we see it at its best.

Many of the constructive official actions discussed in this book are less dramatic than that, but they have had a potent impact. The restraint showed by India's leaders in the first phase after independence enabled the democratic process to take root (see chapter two). The regeneration of institutions after 1989 (chapter four) fortified that process. Accommodative approaches to 'ethnicity' and Centre–state relations fostered constructive ties between state and society (chapters eight and nine). Those ties were reinforced by the actions of small-time political 'fixers' (chapter ten). Nor should we overlook the enlightened initiatives introduced by pragmatic progressive like Devaraj Urs, Bhairon Singh Shekhawat and Digvijay Singh (chapters eleven to thirteen)—which included programmes that were insulated from those who wanted to divert resources to patronage networks.

Further, telling evidence of the state at its best emerges from an authoritative study which surveyed 41,554 households across India in 2011–12—the same households surveyed in 2004–05.[15] Investigators sought to determine whether economic growth in recent years had been 'inclusive'. Inclusion was a key objective of the Congress-led

---

[14]'Political capacity' is a term that refers to four things: people's political *awareness*; their *confidence* as political actors; the political *skills* that they acquire as they become more proactive; and their political *connections* to others, so that their collective leverage increases.

[15]It was made up of scholars from India's National Council of Applied Economic Research (NCAER) and the University of Maryland. The project was entitled 'The India Human Development Survey'. See www.ihds.umd.edu, accessed 11 May 2014.

government which sought to ensure, first, that rural dwellers were not left behind as urban centres boomed, and second, that poor people (rural and urban) made significant gains.

The study found that between 2005 and 2012, real average household incomes in rural areas had increased by 5 per cent annually—almost twice the increase of 2.6 per cent in towns and cities over the same period. When they adjusted their calculations to reflect household size, the growth of rural incomes was even more impressive: an annual average of 7.2 per cent. Government policies had clearly helped to make growth more 'inclusive' in rural-urban terms.

To examine variations among income groups, respondents were separated into various social categories. While per capita household incomes among high caste Hindus (the most prosperous group) increased by 4.6 per cent per annum, significantly larger gains were made by *all* other categories. OBCs saw per capita incomes increase by 7.3 per cent; Dalits by 7.8 per cent; *Adivasis* by 5.7 per cent; Muslims by 5.4 per cent. The last three of those groups include many of the poor*est* people in rural India who are notoriously difficult for policies to reach. Agricultural labourers, who are also very poor, saw their wages triple between 2004–05 and 2011–12.[16] This and various other examples, provided in these chapters, of the Indian state's better self provide a counterweight to the 'worst'.

The tensions between the 'best' and the 'worst' will of course persist, as India's great democratic drama unfolds. By recognising that both things are at work, we achieve a fuller understanding of this compelling spectacle than we find in accounts which merely bemoan the worst or celebrate the best.

---

[16]Ibid., and *The Hindu*, 30 March and 5 April 2014. See also an important forthcoming study which demonstrates rigorously that democratic de-centralisation (*panchayati raj*) has reduced poverty, an unexpected finding: H. P. Binswanger-Mkhize, S. S. Meenakshisudaram and H. K. Nagarajan, *Decentralization and Empowerment for Rural Development: The Case of India* (Cambridge University Press, Cambridge and New Delhi, 2014).

— t w o —

HOW LIBERAL, REPRESENTATIVE POLITICS EMERGED IN INDIA

India's success in developing a robust democracy with firm roots in society puzzled many observers in the West. This paper which appeared in 1990 was addressed mainly to them, although Indian readers may also find it interesting. It seeks to explain India's achievement by challenging Western theorists who argued that democracy could only emerge in countries with high literacy rates, substantial economic development and other things which India lacked in that early phase. It considers an array of factors—socio-cultural, historical and political—and the management of main sources of order in the first phase after independence in 1947.

How did India come to establish a liberal, representative political system[1] and how did it survive, take root and develop in the crucial first phase after independence in

[1] I have deliberately avoided the use of the more loaded word 'democracy' here. I take that term to imply very widespread participation by people with at least a rough understanding of the logic of the political and electoral systems and of the implications of their actions. I also take it to mean participation which is reasonably free of constraints by the more powerful elements in society. India's liberal, representative system—while never grossly undemocratic—has become much more democratic since

1947? This chapter seeks to answer these questions. Central to this discussion is the development of the Indian National Congress into a force capable of integrating the two main sources of order in post-Independence India—the institutions of state and the agrarian social order. It is necessary to consider a long span of years from the decision of Indian nationalists to take power at the provincial level under the British Raj in 1937 to the death of Nehru in 1964. With so much ground to cover, this chapter is bound to deal with virtually every issue in insufficient detail. But these questions are so important that they should not be ignored as—surprisingly—they largely have been. In tackling them, we need to look at India's culture and social structure, at the character of British imperialism there and of India's encounter with it. This will entail a brief assessment of the links and accommodations which the British forged with powerful groups in Indian society and which the nationalists first undermined, then captured and developed. We must also consider the process by which leaders in post-Independence India retained and adapted much of the institutional structure of the colonial state.

Culture and Social Structure

For *direct* contributions to the establishment and growth of a liberal, representative political system in India, we must look mainly to the British Raj and to India's encounter with it. But India's indigenous culture and social structure greatly influenced the nature of that encounter. Consider, for example, the place of politics in Hindu civilisation. Ashis Nandy has written,

> ... Indian society is organised more around its culture than around its politics. It accepts political changes without feeling that its very existence is being challenged, and with the confidence—often unjustified—that politics touches only its less important self.

Rajni Kothari has argued that, historically, Indians have lacked 'a strong identification with a given political order', that they tended to 'de-emphasize the importance of secular changes'. This helped to

---

the mid-1960s than it was before, thanks to a gradual political awakening that has altered the logic by which the system works.

insulate Indian society from traumas which originated as political crises. He adds,

> In historical societies with a more continuous secular tradition and in which the dominant identity was with the political order, such (secular, often political) changes have given rise to both prolonged resistance and a considerable sense of humiliation and futility when they eventually did come about.[2]

This was not the case in India. Indians often regarded the British presence as unpleasant, exasperating, even outrageous. But in most of India, where the Mughals had claimed to rule, this new regime did not seem markedly more alien or less accommodative than the one that had preceded it. In the eyes of most Indians, the coming of the British did not imperil their creeds, mores, culture or identities. It is therefore not surprising that the movement which arose to resist British rule was so free of spite, desperation and violence, or that it sought solutions that were less than drastic.

Consider also that Hindu civilisation neither generates nor offers broad acceptance to grand orthodoxies which might facilitate the rise of autocrats claiming either to be defending an orthodoxy against threats or to be imposing an orthodoxy for the purity and benefit of society.[3] India is emphatically not a univocal civilisation. It is not just that Hinduism 'lacks organizational integration in a unifying bureaucracy capable of providing authoritative guidance for orthodoxy and heterodoxy'. Nor is it only that we find in India a vast, diverse welter of 'little traditions' which differ markedly from the 'great tradition' as we move from locality to locality. It is also that the 'great tradition' is itself heterogeneous in character. To understand this, one would need to look at the multiplicity of gods and their manifestations, at the varied myths, sects and so

[2]A. Nandy, *At the Edge of Psychology* (Oxford University Press, Delhi, 1980), p. 56, and R. Kothari, *Politics in India: A Country Study* (Little Brown, Boston, 1970), pp. 25 and 48. I have discussed this further in chapter three of this book.

[3]See for example, S. N. Eisenstadt, 'Dissent, Heterodoxy and Civilizational Dynamics: Some Analytical and Comparative Implications', in S. N. Eisenstadt et al., (eds), *Orthodoxy, Heterodoxy and Dissent in India* (KNO, Berlin, 1984), pp. 1–10.

on and, crucially, at the fragmentation of Indian society into *jatis* (usually endogamous groups or 'sub-castes') which tend to possess somewhat distinctive cultural traditions and orientations. Religious movements within Hinduism tended not to reconstruct the cultural centre of this civilisation but instead 'concentrated on continually expanding the institutional scope and diversity' of the culture and the society.[4]

A society in which caste is a central element and in which ascription, hierarchy and compartmentalisation are therefore predominant features, cannot directly generate the kind of liberal outlook that is usually associated with the working of an electoral system based on universal suffrage. A general belief in the sanctity of individuals is unlikely to take hold where one has close bonds with members of one's own family and *jati*, but where one regards persons from other *jatis* as suspect and sometimes unclean.[5] Yet these traditional attitudes still flourish in most of rural India.

Most Indians are, even after nine general elections, still not 'liberals' in any meaningful sense. But to make a liberal political system work, it is no more necessary for them to be liberals than it is for them to be literates. This system is not anchored in a widespread commitment to liberal principles or rights (although such a commitment in certain quarters is important); or in a belief in a neutral state (although some adhere to that as well); or even in the force of law. It is mainly rooted in a proclivity on the part of many individuals and groups to forge and maintain accommodations. Lest this statement convey a misleadingly rosy impression, it is important to re-emphasise that political accommodations, bargains and compromises in the Nehru years occurred within a hierarchical social order. Prosperous landed groups exercised dominance in village life, often intimidating and exploiting their poorer neighbours. (Indeed, they continue to do so to this day in most parts of India.) Many of the political accommodations of that period served to sustain old

[4]See for example, ibid., p. 8.

[5]It is also true, however, that Hinduism encourages a deep concern for the self and its protected cultivation which may serve to promote a concern for the individual.

inequalities and to create new ones. This tended to legitimate the new, open politics in the eyes of dominant rural groups, but that kind of politics also offered poorer groups hope of a fairer share in such bargains once they became more politically aware and assertive. In the 1970s and 1980s, the process of accommodations has survived the emergence of those poorer groups in most regions of India.

Certain persistent habits of mind and patterns of behaviour have helped to produce this penchant for accommodation in India. One example emerges from the study of what might be called the 'judicial' process at the village level. Bernard Cohn has shown how, when disputes arose in rural areas, meetings of village elders in the presence of the village population were intended to apply collective pressure on disputing parties to resolve their differences. This exercise, unlike British judicial procedures, was based on the presumption that there was no contradiction between the interests of the disputants.[6] This can be read by those who contrast Hindu civilisation with western or Chinese civilisations as one of several examples of a general reluctance and tardiness in India to perceive certain kinds of contradictions,[7] and of a tendency to seek to overcome them. Other examples range from the trivial—the belief of a Bangalore astrophysicist in astrology—to the fundamentally important—Gandhi's presumption that there was no such thing as a contradiction between the interests of persons or groups, because they were united by their common humanity.

Another indirect contribution to the establishment of a liberal order arose from a combination of three things: the vibrance and resilience of India's indigenous cultural tradition; the strength of indigenous institutions which sustained that culture; and the massive size of the Indian population. India's British rulers were confronted with a complex and sophisticated society and civilisation, sustained by long-standing institutions: temples, mosques, schools

[6]B. S. Cohn, 'Some Notes on Law and Change ... in North India', *Economic Development and Cultural Change*, 8 (1959–60), pp. 79–93.
[7]The emphasis here should be on the reference to *'certain kinds* of contradictions'. Some other sorts of contradictions or, more accurately, social barriers—those between *jatis* or endogamous caste groups, for example—are seldom overcome.

or other agencies of cultural transmission anchored in sect, caste, extended kinship ties and family. This civilisation was also capable of generating 'modern' western-style schools and of educating their young people in schools created by the British without losing their own cultural ties in the process. These things, and a density of population that far exceeded that of British colonies elsewhere, meant that Indians were a more formidable and resilient subject people than were most of their counterparts in other parts of the empire.

This emerges clearly from a comparison of the experience of the indigenous population in the Madras Presidency (a major province of British India) with that of the Low Country Sinhalese in British Ceylon,[8] or with the subject peoples of the African colonies. The British in Madras (and in India generally) were compelled to be far more accommodating and restrained, respectful of indigenous sensibilities and customs, and willing to tolerate and even to ratify a wide dispersal of power, than they were elsewhere in the empire. So many concessions were made by the British that one historian has gone to the extent of describing their regime in nineteenth-century Madras as a 'Hindu raj'.[9]

That is putting it too strongly, but it is not a gross exaggeration. Those accommodations were reinforced in the twentieth century by three great sets of political reforms (discussed later) which the British felt forced to implement. Out of this array of accommodations, which were to a considerable degree the product of India's indigenous resources, emerged the liberal political order of the present day.

While it is an overstatement to say that India's culture and social structure compelled the British authorities to develop a liberal colonial regime, they certainly made it difficult for the British to avoid building a system which consisted in significant part of

---

[8]Compare D. A. Washbrook, *The Emergence of Provincial Politics: The Madras Presidency 1870–1920* (Cambridge University Press, Cambridge Press, 1976) with J. Manor, *The Expedient Utopian: Bandaranaike and Ceylon* (Cambridge University Press, Cambridge, 1989).

[9]This is based on numerous conversations with Robert Eric Frykenberg.

accommodative institutions that were in important ways restrained. When they began to extend their power across the subcontinent in the eighteenth century, the British encountered neither a pre-existing oriental despotism nor an effective Mughal imperial state. There existed 'a variety of claims to entitlement to land and shares in its product', and water was also 'controlled by a wide variety of agencies, from village communes through individual land holders, temples and regional kingdoms'. This 'provides a basis for political pluralism, not centralization'.[10] So did the patchwork of semi-autonomous little kingdoms, interspersed with and overlaid by somewhat larger regimes which the British found in south India in the eighteenth and early nineteenth centuries. None of these constituted an effective 'state' administration extending over wide areas until the exigencies of war with the East India Company drove military chieftains to create one to extract resources for the struggle.[11]

The British conquered different sections of India in largely separate operations. Since they tended to forge understandings with powerful groups and thereby to conform to pre-existing patterns of power in the areas that they took over and, since India was heterogeneous, the resulting British imperium was marked by considerable regional diversity. As communications improved and their modern colonial state acquired greater substance, some homogenisation occurred, but the Raj remained heterogeneous, accommodative and solicitous of local sensibilities and structures. It both 'aggregated diverse territorial, cultural and functional communities and was constrained by them'.

The British protected social pluralism. In India, society concep-tualised as diverse social groups possessed of particular laws and customs was taken to be prior to the state and independent of it. The obligation of rulers '... was not as in Europe's sovereignty seeking

---

[10]L. I. Rudolph, 'The Subcontinental Empire and the Regional Kingdom in Indian State Formation', unpublished typescript, pp. 7–8. He is drawing here on the work of Romila Thapar, Tapan Raychaudhuri, Burton Stein, Irfan Habib and others.

[11]B. Stein, *Peasant, State and Society in Medieval South India* (Oxford University Press, Delhi, 1980).

states to embody and articulate the values and interests of a civil society but to protect and uphold the respective customs and laws of self-regulating social orders'.[12] The British, like the Mughals, 'formed alliances that recognized and legitimated the ordered heterogeneity of Indian society'.[13] They did so, curiously, out of a mixture of pragmatism and 'racial arrogance' which reduced all Indians to mere 'natives, an inferior species distinguished by a wide variety of esoteric beliefs and practices'. With limited British manpower at their disposal, they had to avoid heavy-handed intrusions on traditional customs that might provoke unrest. Instead, they co-opted large numbers of Indians. As a result, the modern state in India developed along very different lines from those of Europe.

> States in Europe sought to become nations ... to 'solve' the state-society relationship by subordinating society to the nation and identifying the nation with the state. The aim was to substitute loyalty to pre-existing historic communities, whether territorial, linguistic, religious, functional or ethnic....[14]

In India, this did not occur until the rise of Indian nationalism after 1885 'and even then the claim that Indian nationalism precluded loyalty to regional (primarily linguistic) and religious communities was ambivalent and contingent'. Nationalists stressed a vision of an accommodative 'imperial state rather than a nation state, as the spread of popular consciousness in Gandhi's time nurtured the growth of regional identities and vernaculars parallel with the national'.[15]

The emergence of a liberal political system was also facilitated, both before and after independence, by the stability of the agrarian socio-economic order across most of the subcontinent. In most parts of India, the predominant mode of production was peasant proprietorship, small and medium-sized landholdings distributed among owner-cultivators who formed a substantial minority of

[12]Rudolph, 'The Subcontinental Empire and the Regional Kingdom in Indian State Formation', p. 10.

[13]Ibid., p. 16.

[14]Ibid., p. 12.

[15]Ibid., pp. 11 and 13.

the rural population. This ensured the existence of ubiquitous but less than extreme disparities between rich and poor. There were important exceptions to this pattern, but however important they were, they were exceptions nonetheless, and post-1947 reforms dealt with many of them by establishing peasant proprietorship there as well. It is therefore not surprising that most parts of India, where peasant proprietors predominated and in which grotesque inequalities were not a problem, provided infertile ground for political movements seeking drastic change.

The overall stability of the agrarian order cannot, however, be fully explained by the existence of peasant proprietorship. It is also intimately related to a central feature of Indian civilisation, the remarkable resilience of family, kinship and *jati* institutions in rural areas. They possess an extraordinary capacity to bend without breaking, to accommodate to change without discontinuity or collapse. They have more than held their own in the encounter with market forces over recent decades. These institutions also facilitated the survival of small and medium peasant proprietorship as the predominant mode of agricultural production, and as an impediment to agrarian radicalism. (Both peasant proprietorship and these institutions also owe a great deal to the accommodative character of British Indian law which—in dealing with matters such as caste, inheritance and landownership—mainly sought to reinforce kinship and *jati* structures.[16] However, *jati*'s contribution to the stability of the rural socio-economic order—before, during and since the British period—entails much more than just the reinforcement of peasant proprietorship.

By fragmenting rural society, by confining people within social compartments and by preoccupying those people with questions of superiority and inferiority, of purity and pollution when they think of other groups that stand near them in the social hierarchy, *jati* undermines efforts to persuade rural folk to make common cause.

---

[16]I am grateful to D. A. Washbrook for clarifying my understanding of this point. See his 'Law, State and Agrarian Society in Colonial India', *Modern Asian Studies* (February 1981), pp. 649–721.

There is clear evidence that those near the bottom of the rural status hierarchy are more fragmented by *jati* than others.[17]

All of these elements have combined to impede mass-based revolts over wide areas by the rural poor against the agrarian social order and political regimes. This is not to claim that India is devoid of a tradition of resistance from below,[18] but to say that such resistance has not generated mass revolts that reach well beyond the barriers of social compartments and extend over wide geographical areas. There is no Indian counterpart to China's tradition of broadly based agrarian revolt of the kind which brought down imperial dynasties and manifested itself in the Taiping rebellion. Neither the complex events of 1857, nor the overwhelmingly Muslim Moplah rebellion qualify. So it is no surprise that twentieth-century India should have generated a political movement that stopped well short of violent insurrection, the sort of movement which could ultimately produce a liberal, representative political system.

Encounter with Imperialism

A more direct set of contributions to the emergence of such a system arose out of the interplay of the British Raj and India's nationalist movement. One important element was the split personality of the colonial state. The British possessed formidable coercive powers which they were fully prepared to use to maintain order. So even if radical movements had developed, the regime would not have permitted them to gather much momentum before vigorously suppressing them. In the areas which they administered directly, the British possessed a sufficiently effective and comprehensive information-gathering system to learn of such movements at a very early stage. They could then come down hard with armed police

---

[17]I am grateful to Professor C. Parvathamma for information on this. For more detail, see J. Manor, 'Karnataka: Caste, Class, Dominance and Politics in a Cohesive Society', in F. Frankel and M. S. A. Rao (eds), *Dominance and State Power in India*, vol. 1 (Oxford University Press, Delhi, 1989).

[18]See volumes 1 and 3 in the *Subaltern Studies* series.

forces and, if necessary, army units to extinguish them. They were also able and willing to take repressive action in India's princely states. No violent insurrection had much chance within Britain's Indian empire.

There was, however, another side to the Raj. The British ruled India by means of compromise as well as coercion and, since the frequent use of coercive force was rightly seen as an inefficient way of maintaining a regime, compromise was almost always more important. Under the general heading of 'compromise' can be included: the wide array of accommodations that the British made with powerful indigenous groups in the years before 1820 or so, when they were consolidating their control; many of the actions which they took to substantiate their moralistic claim to have a 'civilising mission' in India; their introduction in the present century of increasingly liberal political reforms; and their willingness—most of the time—to allow Indian nationalists a large measure of freedom to develop a non-violent and usually lawful campaign for self-rule. Since each of these elements gave a liberal non-violent nationalist movement promising openings, since the Raj would have cracked down on any radical insurrection, and since India's rural social order was unlikely to generate mass-based revolt in any case, it is hardly surprising that Indian nationalists took the Gandhian path. Although Gandhi may not have fully intended it to do so, that path led towards a liberal, representative state structure once self-rule had been achieved.

How did the four elements mentioned above provide opportunities to liberal, non-violent nationalists? British accommodation with powerful Indians in intermediate and local power centres rendered them partially dependent upon the support or at least the acquiescence of key indigenous groups. If Indian nationalists could insinuate themselves between the Raj and these groups, they could seriously undermine the imperial enterprise. The British claim to have a 'civilising mission' to raise Indians from their supposedly benighted condition, carried the implication that once Indians had shown themselves to be 'civilised', the British mission would be fulfilled. One way for nationalists to show that Indians were not merely 'civilised' but more 'civilised' than their masters was to develop a movement which could appear morally edifying even as it drew the coercive side of the Raj out into the open, thereby exposing the moral pretensions which the British had unwisely advertised.

It is important that we note the connections between the claim to have a 'civilising' empire and the British political reforms in India. In British eyes, 'civilised' politics was liberal, representative politics. It was therefore not surprising that they enacted three sets of reforms in 1909, 1919 and 1935—each of which expanded opportunities for elected Indians to take part in government, although a philanthropic spirit and the liberal proclivities of the British authorities played a minor role in these reforms. Political pressure from nationalists for reform was much more important and it was decisively reinforced by economic compulsions which arose in part from the need to provide a semblance of 'civilising' rule. This needs to be explained.

The British Crown (and hence the British Parliament) was formally responsible for governing India after 1858. The opposition at Westminster was always eager to criticise, so the Secretary of State for India was under pressure to spend money in order to avoid criticism or to claim credit as a developer. To reduce the risk of embarrassing epidemics in the burgeoning cities of India, he had to oversee the creation of at least minimal sanitation systems and medical services. To pose convincingly as a master 'civiliser', he had to build Indian universities, and so it went on. The funds for these 'civilising' efforts and for the immensely expensive Indian army had to be generated within India. By 1900, it was apparent that to meet these costs, major new taxes would have to be imposed, even as nationalism was quickening. In 1909, India's rulers ceased to pay for certain services at the local level, using the money thus saved to fund their doings at higher levels in the political system and creating elected local councils with modest taxation powers to deal with local affairs. They thus forced elected Indians, including nationalists, to bear the odium for imposing the new taxes. Something like the same logic applied in 1919 when the British created elected councils at the district (sub-provincial) level and again in 1935 when they created Westminster-style legislatures at the provincial level, where elected politicians were to be allowed to form governments with control over a very wide range of departments.

In these three cases, the British were undertaking partial withdrawals from the local, then the district and the provincial level, so that by 1935 they were under normal circumstances in full command only at the national level.[19] In each instance, elected politicians did incur some resentment by imposing taxes, but they were also able to cultivate popular support by carefully managing the resources thereby accruing to them. In so doing, they developed a taste for the exercise of power within liberal, representative institutions.

Turning to the Indian National Congress: after Gandhi took over the leadership in 1920, Congress actually sought to force the British out of India. This needs emphasis because in many British colonies—for example, in Ceylon and much of Africa—nationalists did little except wait for the British to decamp as a result of external events. Given the nature of the Raj, a non-violent struggle would be most effective. This carried certain consequences. First, since the pressure which a non-violent movement could exert in any arena or at any level of the colonial state structure was bound to be less severe than that which an armed insurgency might generate, Congress had to be able to maximise its effectiveness at every level at which the colonial state had an administrative presence. It had to develop strong organisational units at the national, provincial, district and sub-district levels. Given the daunting heterogeneity of India, Congress was compelled to allow a reasonable amount of autonomy to people at each level, since only they could understand the particular logic in their own area. As a result, by the mid-1930s power within Congress was—except during civil disobedience campaigns—quite widely dispersed through the organisation. This marks Congress out as a far more impressive organisational instrument than was developed in other parts of British Asia and Africa in the pre-independence era.

The second thing which followed from the nature of the Congress struggle and of the Raj was the broadly inclusive character of Congress. One formidable south Indian freedom fighter confided

[19]B. R. Tomlinson, *The Indian National Congress and the Raj, 1929–1942: The Penultimate Phase* (Macmillan, London, 1976).

that when he thought about the Raj before 1947 and about the non-violent weapons which Congress had at its disposal, he always felt 'like an ant at the feet of a giant'.[20] It followed that the only way to overturn the Raj was to unite every possible section of Indian society in the struggle, so that Congress would become the sole authentic voice of India, an all-inclusive organisation. Gandhi shared this view, because it made good political sense, because he was inclined not to see the contradictions between the groups, and because the British always claimed that the nationalists were only an unrepresentative minority of Indians.

Congress never quite succeeded in making itself an all-inclusive body, but it still managed to include a remarkably broad array of interests. This, together with the need for an organisational presence at so many levels and arenas, made Congress use the principle of representation in managing its internal affairs. The only way that people from so many different social groups, levels in the system, regions and sub-regions could be expected to interpret candidly the peculiar political logic within their varied political subcultures to the wider movement, was to ensure that they were genuine representatives of their base areas. Therefore, although during civil disobedience campaigns Gandhi radically centralised power within Congress, internal democracy prevailed throughout most of the pre-independence period (and until 1972 when Indira Gandhi abandoned it). Congress therefore became, among other things, a training ground where people learned to cooperate and accept a liberal, representative system. It allowed, indeed encouraged, anyone to join it; it has never exercised any real check on those who signed on. To include so many diverse groups, Congress's ideology had to be kept vague and incomplete, so that there were few criteria against which to test members. It is hardly surprising, therefore, that the number of outright expulsions from Congress, before independence or since, has been tiny.

This is not to say, however, that Gandhi's Congress was unable to deal with people of faint heart or dubious motives. Gandhi actually welcomed such people into the movement because he believed

[20]Interview with B. N. Gupta, Bangalore, 1972.

that the means existed either to transform them into committed servants of the struggle or to embarrass them into withdrawal. The means was *satyagraha*, non-violent civil disobedience. Every time a mass agitation began, people who had joined Congress in quieter times because it was fashionable were faced with the prospect of confronting sometimes violent police and long jail sentences, often under the harsh terms. That not only meant an extended absence from family but also a loss of income and perhaps even the destruction of one's career. Lawyers, for example, might be disbarred for such 'crimes'. It is hardly surprising that many hesitated and agonised while a satyagraha built up ferocious pressures upon them. Many others quietly resigned.

The effect of courting and then suffering imprisonment was often—as Gandhi had anticipated—quite dramatic for a time. People who were locked up together for months or years had little to sustain them except mutual support and the ideals of the cause. Since their number usually included members of different castes and religious groups, the solidarity that developed among them burned away caste and sectarian barriers, which was precisely what Gandhi had in mind. The British were a target of *satyagraha*, but so were the Indians who undertook it. *Satyagraha* was crucially a device to overcome the daunting array of parochial divisions that fragmented the Indian people and rendered them politically impotent, a device to build nationalist solidarity. Many of those who came out of the jails threw off their former prejudices, at least for a few years,[21] and became good Gandhians. *Satyagraha* then, was a reasonably effective means for ridding Congress of timid or insincere members, or for changing them.

The encounter between Congress and the Raj developed in phases, alternating between periods of agitation (major *satyagrahas* every decade) and longer periods of compromise in which Congress

[21]I have dealt in detail with the example of S. Nijalingappa, who became president of the Indian National Congress, in J. Manor, 'The Lesser Leader amid Political Transformation: The Congress in Mysore in 1941 and 1951', in W. H. Morris-Jones (ed.), *The Making of Politicians* (Athlone Press, London, 1977), pp. 140–55.

operated within the laws of what it saw as an illegitimate colonial regime. It was during one of these quiet periods, between 1937 and 1939, that an episode unfolded which played a major role both in preparing the ground for liberal politics after independence and in rendering Congress capable of integrating state and society. The last great set of reforms that the British introduced in India—the Government of India Act of 1935—both angered Congress since it fell far short of self-rule, and enticed it by offering substantial powers to provincial assemblies consisting of elected Indians.

The assemblies could choose ministers to control most government departments and the principle of collective responsibility applied, allowing for party rule. But this was nonetheless a system of dyarchy in which colonial officials retained control of certain key departments and in which British provincial governors could suspend or dissolve the government and legislature at any time. Congress resolved to fight provincial elections of 1936, in which a much expanded electorate of 10–15 per cent of the population was being consulted, with two aims: to prove its popularity and to wreck the working of the provincial assemblies from within. It triumphed in the elections, winning outright control of eight of the eleven provinces and performing creditably in others. But this success created immense pressures within Congress to abandon its second goal. After many years of dour struggle and near-total refusal to partake of the powers that the colonial state offered, most Congressmen in provincial arenas were eager to enjoy a spell in office and to use the resources that became available to build support for the movement. After much soul-searching, they overcame the opposition of their national leaders and, in June 1937, Congress agreed to form governments in most provinces. They held power there until September 1939, when they resigned in protest against the Viceroy's declaration of war without consulting Indian opinion.

Once in office, most Congress ministers and legislators performed impressively in this new mode of politics. They shrewdly channelled patronage to powerful groups that had previously remained rather aloof from the struggle. The most important of these were the most formidable people in India, the landowning peasant cultivators that then dominated village society in most regions. For many years, Gandhi had been including representatives of these groups among his subcontractors in the provincial units of Congress. By 1937, enough of them were on hand to ensure the efficient distribution of resources derived from state control. As a result, many landowning peasants in rural areas began to see that if Congress took power in India, there would be tangible advantages for them. Many therefore began to offer active support for the struggle and since these groups had long been an essential part of the foundation on which British rule rested, the Raj was seriously weakened as a consequence.

Between 1937 and 1939, Congress began to assume the shape and the crucial role that it eventually took on after independence. It showed the first signs of becoming a partisan political machine, or rather a cluster of regional political machines—distributing goods, services and resources among a carefully selected array of interests. This enabled it to begin to integrate the institutions of state and the most powerful elements in the socio-economic order. Given the limited time that was available, and given the existence of dyarchy, this occurred imperfectly and incompletely, but the trend was clear.

Congress activists responded to this brief taste of power in different ways. Those fired by nationalist fervour and Gandhian idealism found the new transactional politics distastefully mundane after the heady days of sacrifice. But those who hankered after power, especially those from the dominant landed groups who saw how indispensable they were becoming, found it exhilarating. The number of people in the latter category increased steeply as new members flooded into Congress after 1936. So many joined that the old check and corrective, *satyagraha*, was now to prove rather ineffective. The next great civil disobedience campaign, the Quit India movement between 1942 and 1944, was regarded by many as perhaps their last chance to acquire credentials as sufferers for the cause. For them *satyagraha*, which until recently had been a counterweight to careerism, became a springboard to a future in politics. For this latter sort of Congress activist, the brief spell in power between 1937 and 1939 rendered liberal, representative politics acceptable. For many, it was not something that they thought much about, nor was it the result of a philosophical commitment to basic liberal values. It was more a case of liberal politics, which they had long used to manage the internal affairs of Congress, becoming the natural way to conduct public affairs in general. It was also, crucially, a kind of politics that did not threaten the interests of Congress and of their landowning peasant supporters but actually served the interests of both quite effectively. There seemed little reason to suppose that it would ever cease to do so.[22]

Even if all of this had not occurred, India would initially have adopted a liberal, representative model after independence. It is inconceivable that a ruling party led by Jawaharlal Nehru would have done anything else. But this wider acceptance of liberal politics was important in ensuring that that model was roughly adhered to in this vast, complex polity in the uncertain early years after independence when the great mass of Indians was participating in the system for the first time and—gradually and unevenly—comprehending and accepting it. That did not happen in many new Asian and African states.

One other thing that seldom happened elsewhere occurred in India between 1937 and 1939. The Congress organisation, which already possessed great sinew and reach as an instrument of non-violent resistance to British rule, began to develop new skills and acquire further substance as an instrument not of opposition but of government, an instrument capable of integrating state structures and the agrarian social order. Nationalists in other British colonies were often given experience in government before independence but seldom were they given so much power. Never did they take up that power with such aptitude and assisted by such a formidable organisation as the Congress at their disposal. Congress then developed fully into a shadow government with a solid corporate presence at every level of the political system. Congress operatives also learned that bureaucrats—who by then were predominantly Indian—were people with whom they could work in good faith

---

[22]These comments are based on a large number of interviews with people involved in these events in southern and western India. See also, on the importance of this two-year period, W. H. Morris-Jones, *The Government and Politics of India* (Hutchinson, London and New Delhi, 1971), pp. 62–71.

and the bureaucrats came to the same conclusion. As a result, post-Independence India was not afflicted with the kind of distrust and conflict between politicians and bureaucrats that proved so destructive in Burma[23] and elsewhere.

After Independence

In the critical first phase after independence, India managed to neutralise or overcome problems and forces that have often wrecked liberal regimes elsewhere. Civilian and military elites that had been associated with the colonial power were promptly assured of important roles in the new scheme of things, before they could feel disaffected. The global economy presented no severe problems. At home, the agrarian socio-economic order in most regions was quite stable, and in most of the places where it was not, moderate reforms—usually to break up large estates—reduced the kind of extreme inequalities that can generate serious violence. The peasant proprietor groups who dominated village society in the more stable regions, where land was more equitably distributed, had no reason to oppose the new political order. They were drawn into transactional relationships with regional Congress political machines which were themselves largely controlled by representatives of those groups.

The Congress organisation, which also attended to urban middle-class interests, developed into the most effective instrument of government to arise in the non-communist new nations. It became and long remained not only the dominant party in the multi-party system,[24] but also the nation's most important political institution and central integrating force. It soon gained substantial

[23]See L. W. Pye, *Politics, Personality and Nation-Building: Burma's Search for Identity* (Yale University Press, New Haven and London, 1962), especially chapters 7 and 15.

[24]The classic studies of this system are R. Kothari, 'The Congress "System" in India', *Asian Survey* (December 1974) pp. 1161–73 and W. H. Morris-Jones, 'Dominance and Dissent: Their Interrelations in the Indian Party System', *Government and Opposition* (August 1966), pp. 237–52. See also J. Manor, 'Parties and the Party System', in A. Kohli (ed.), *India's Democracy* (Princeton University Press, Princeton, 1988).

control over bureaucrats, especially those at and below the regional level where policy implementation actually occurred. This enabled it to arrange bargains and placate discontents that might eventually have festered into radical, parochial or secessionist movements. India, unlike Pakistan, did not suffer the early loss of its pre-eminent post-Independence leader. If it had, Congress would almost certainly have possessed the substance to cope with the problem as effectively as it did with the loss by 1950 of Gandhi and the main alternative to Nehru, Vallabhbhai Patel.

Given the strength of Congress—an informal institution—the formal institutions of state were not of decisive importance in the years under discussion here. But the structures that emerged from the constitution-making process were neither so weak as to invite instability nor so rigid and over-centralised that they smothered open, liberal politics. A prime concern for the Indian leaders who devised that framework was the question of how the need for change, which the freedom struggle seemed to promise, could be reconciled with the need for a stable civic order. In the event, their anxieties about disorder (which were understandable after the ghastly communal violence at Partition) caused them to give the need for order far more emphasis than it deserved. They accomplished this by retaining most of the structures of the colonial state, so that this was more a case of maintaining and adapting a settled order than of creating or imposing a markedly new one. Indeed, the Constitution that emerged in January 1950 bore an uncanny resemblance to the Government of India Act of 1935. Important modifications were made with the abandonment of dyarchy and the introduction of universal suffrage, fundamental rights, directive principles and institutions like the Supreme Court. But at the core of things stood the model of the 1935 Act, which in the 1930s had been described by Nehru as a 'charter of bondage'. The framers of the Constitution appear not to have seriously considered whether the strong emergency provisions that they wrote into (or left in) the document might someday threaten the liberal political system. It was unnecessary to bestow such powers on the state, but they failed to see this because they underestimated the strength of two sources of order which lay outside the formal institutions of state—the organisation of the Congress Party and the socio-economic order in most parts of rural India.

Nearly all of the people—both Indian and British—who had manned the bureaucracy before independence were welcome to stay on. Most of the former did so, including some who had been so loyal to the Crown that Congressmen jokingly claimed that their postal address was simply 'c/o the British Empire'. Their retention reassured members of the Indian establishment who had had dealings with the Raj and whose disaffection from the new regime might have compounded its troubles, although they lacked the power to wreck it. Members of India's military elite were similarly reassured. Their disinclination to attempt a seizure of power in subsequent years is partly attributable to civilian leaders' sympathetic attention to the needs of the armed forces and partly to the structure of command which prevents sustained contact among officers from the various services until they reach the very highest ranks, so that the coordination of a coup is extremely difficult. They have also had the wretched example of military regimes in Pakistan and elsewhere to warn them off attempts to govern a society of such complexity. But the decisive reason for the restraint of the Indian military has been the success of civilian institutions. In the period between independence and the late 1960s, that mainly meant the Congress Party.

After the transfer of power, nationalist leaders set about completing the transformation of Congress from an opposition movement into a ruling party. It had to become an instrument capable both of winning elections under a system of universal suffrage and of governing the country satisfactorily. Representatives of the landowning, cultivating groups who had long dominated life in the villages and who now had great influence in regional units of Congress, believed that both of these aims would be served by packing the organisation with people like themselves. This was not the opinion of Nehru or of many other reformists in the national leadership. Such views took hold where representatives of landed groups were strongest: in the states of the new federal system. It was at the state level and below that many crucial changes—usually of an informal character—took place. Right through the late 1940s and early 1950s, two overlapping categories of Congress activists—people from numerically or economically weak social groups and altruists who were unwilling or unable to wheel and deal—were eased out of key positions at state, district and sub-district levels of the organisation. At the same time, token posts were being found for members of certain disadvantaged groups: usually members of Scheduled Castes (SCs), religious minorities and numerically powerful lesser castes.

This did not begin to compensate for the rising power of landowning groups within the party, but it made it possible for Congress to respond sufficiently as new groups developed self-awareness and began to participate in the political process. If such groups became still more assertive, the regional Congress machines were usually able to detect the change and to react by moving from tokenism (usually the cooption of leaders) to a more generous bestowal of resources. By mediating demands on the political system, by defusing potentially destructive discontents, and by arranging bargains between different interests that might otherwise have come into serious conflict, the Congress organisation protected state institutions from potentially damaging stresses although, paradoxically, the growing importance of the party also stunted their growth somewhat.

These early years did not witness a major increase in private profiteering by Congress operatives. The old check on self-aggrandisement—civil disobedience was now no longer in use but the party possessed enough institutional substance to discourage such behaviour. This was less the result of formal disciplinary action, which was rare, than of self-discipline learned in the nationalist struggle and, more crucially, of a widespread belief among Congress activists that their personal interests were best served by advancing the collective interests of the party. There was a certain logic in recruiting new party personnel from the dominant landed groups (clusters of cultivating *jatis* or castes). Congress's reputation as the force that had won India her freedom might carry it through early elections. But to stay in power over the longer term, Congress needed the landowning groups' votes, since they usually constituted 15–40 per cent of the rural population. More importantly, it needed their influence over less prosperous villagers. During the 1950s and early 1960s, these landed groups received deference from many poorer neighbours in the villages where four out of five Indians lived. They had enough economic leverage to influence enough disadvantaged voters to ensure victory in rural constituencies where elections were won and lost. Between elections, the complex network of Congress connections to these powerful groups on the land operated as a political machine, distributing resources, cultivating support, collecting and transmitting information, managing conflict and overseeing the work of bureaucrats, which added up to an effective instrument of government capable of integrating state structures and society.

Nehru was intensely anxious in those early post-Independence years about the potential for violence between Hindus and Muslims and between India's many linguistic groups. The latter fear was most apparent in his reluctance during the early 1950s to give way to pleas for a revision of state boundaries along linguistic lines. It is in some ways remarkable that he held out against this, since Congress had been using linguistic regions as the basis for its regional organisational units for fully 30 years. As a result, Congressmen from linguistic groups that were rendered disadvantaged minorities by provincial borders inherited from British India, assumed that a revision of borders was only a matter of time and natural justice. By resisting this, Nehru seemed to be defending legacies of the old imperial order.[25] He agreed about the irrational nature of the old boundaries, but he was more concerned about unleashing a greater irrationality, linguistic chauvinism, by redrawing them. He found it difficult to imagine that this could produce anything other than a 'boiling cauldron of redistribution all over India'.[26] He said that in 1952, but four years later, under enormous pressure from groups in Congress, he agreed to a substantial revision of borders.

---

[25]This is based on numerous interviews between 1970 and 1973, with leaders of the Karnataka unification movement.

[26]J. Nehru, *Jawaharlal Nehru's Speeches*, vol. II (New Delhi, Government of India, 1954), p. 38. The speech was made on 7 July 1952.

Less than two years after that (by early 1958) his anxieties on this matter appear largely to have subsided. They did so for two main reasons. It quickly became apparent that 'States Reorganisation' had undermined and not intensified linguistic group assertiveness. Linguistic campaigners now had what they had been seeking and their constituents quickly realised that it did not solve very many of their problems. They began to discover that within each new linguistic state there were many conflicting interests: sub-regional groups, castes and caste clusters, sects, classes and other economic interests. Linguistic fervour waned. Given such heterogeneity within linguistic states, it would be impossible to generate the kind of state-level solidarity that was needed to develop secessionist movements. It was this central reality that Nehru and writers who had foretold the balkanisation of India had failed to see before 1956. Ill-informed commentators who continue, decades later, to predict the break-up of India have far less excuse for their misperceptions.

Nehru was also encouraged by the way in which States Reorganisation strengthened Congress in most regions. The party reaped the credit for the gains that accompanied this rational-isation of government. For example, most people now found that the language of administration and of law courts was (at least at subordinate levels) their own language and not that of a neighbouring region to which British rulers had attached them a century and a half earlier. What Nehru probably did not realise was that States Reorganisation also produced another sort of rationalisation that reinforced the power within Congress of locally dominant landowning groups. Each linguistic region in India tends to possess something like a single, distinct caste system. It is therefore possible—despite exceptional areas in some regions—to speak of a single caste system in the Kannada-speaking region, the Telugu-speaking region, and so on, and therefore of a distinct caste system in the post-1956 states of Andhra Pradesh, Tamil Nadu, and so on.

As a result, it was much easier after 1956 to integrate regional caste systems into the logic of state politics and into the operations of the Congress regional machines which were helping to aggregate the landed caste groups that dominated the village level into ruling coalitions in state-level politics. In general and over the medium term at least, States Reorganisation consolidated the hold of dominant landowning castes both in supra-local politics and in the villages. (For dramatic changes that came later, see chapter thirteen of this book.)

Their influence and the influence of Congress politicians at the state level and below had grown so much by the mid-1950s that it is possible to say that, by then, the decisive events in Indian politics were no longer occurring at the national level. This change has enormous importance for our understanding both of the survival of liberal politics and of Nehru's role in this phase of Indian history. At the level of policy-making, Nehru and other reform-minded Congress leaders usually got their way, but when it came to implementation it was a different story. All policies had to be implemented at or below the district level by relatively junior bureaucrats and by Congress activists overseeing networks of party link-men who delivered patronage and spoils to key social groups. In most Indian states in the Nehru years up to 1964, bureaucrats found it difficult to imagine that an opposition party might displace Congress as the ruling party in the foreseeable future. They were therefore under immense pressure to conform to the wishes of Congress politicians in district and sub-district arenas. Most conformed and those who did not were often transferred. Conforming meant two things: assisting in the distribution of resources for partisan purposes and thwarting the implementation of reformist policies that might ruffle the sensibilities of the landed groups who dominated both the surrounding rural areas and the Congress machine.

The failure of reform in the Nehru years can be illustrated by referring to attempts to impose land reform and to build 'socialism' by giving the state a role in the delivery of a wide range of goods and services. Most land reforms then enacted had only a minimal impact. This was partly the result of naivete on the part of Nehru and other genuine Congress progressives, who did not anticipate the formidable resistance that greeted their quite moderate programmes, which therefore had too few teeth. But a more serious impediment lay within the Congress itself. The same legislators who spoke and voted for land reform in the state assemblies returned to their constituencies to instruct bureaucrats and party activists to avoid implementation at all costs, lest they alienate the landed elements on whom they relied for re-election. They often did this with the knowledge and support of state Congress leaders but this also happened when such leaders actually sought reform because, by the late 1950s, state legislators had come to understand the logic of the system within which they were operating. They saw that state-level ministers and cabinets needed their backing to remain in power and they began to assert themselves: exacting patronage and concessions from ministers and paying greater heed to powerful constituents than to Nehruvian reforms. As a result, power became still more widely dispersed within both Congress and the political system, and Congress became less than ever an instrument of change.

These same Congress legislators and their conservative supporters welcomed the system of state controls over the distribution of goods and services since this enlarged the supply of what Indians call 'loaves and fishes' to be passed out in exchange for political support. Nehru extended the public sector in this way to promote a more equitable distribution of resources than the market could have accomplished. But since most of these resources found their way to prosperous elements in rural society, this sort of 'socialism' tended not to serve redistributive purposes. In the last years before his death in 1964, Nehru appears to have been aware of this. Young radicals in Congress who went to him to tell him of the failure of reforms found him well informed on the subject. He told them that, given time, the poorer rural groups who form a large majority of the population would come to understand the logic of the representative system and would assert themselves. They protested that this was just a naive hope and went away regarding him as a tragic figure,[27] and so he seemed for several years after his death. During the 1970s, however, evidence emerged from across much of India that poorer voters were indeed growing more aware and assertive. In some regions, politicians have responded by drawing them transactionally into more progressive coalitions that have often succeeded at the polls.

[27]This is based on interviews with the men in question in New Delhi, 1980 and 1982.

India's liberal, representative order has—slowly and imperfectly—become more democratic. This change—and the institutional decay that occurred alongside it—meant both that the liberal system had greater promise and that it was at greater risk.

It should be clear by now that there were good reasons for the emergence of liberal and representative politics in India between 1937 and the mid-1960s. Indigenous culture and social institutions played their part. More important was the complex encounter between Indians—especially Congress nationalists—and the British colonial state. After independence, the liberal order might have broken down had Nehru pressed aggressively for the substantial social reform with which he had great sympathy. He believed that it was too early for such an effort to succeed; that in his lifetime the poor were still too afflicted by caste divisions, localism, illiteracy and economic deprivation to mount a plausible challenge to more prosperous groups. He therefore concentrated on preserving the Congress Party as an instrument capable both of governing and of integrating the two main sources of order in India—the agrarian social order and the machinery of state.

Nehru might also have sought to centralise power radically in his own hands, at the expense of his party and of formal political institutions. He might have employed populist slogans, promises and programmes as a substitute—however inadequate and transient—for such institutions. Plenty of other leaders in Africa and Asia did so, and they and their countries often paid a heavy price for it. Nehru chose not to and, as a consequence, the liberal representative order took root and acquired enough substance to endure into the 1970s and 1980s—despite attempts by his daughter and other populists to undermine institutions in pursuit of personal dominance.

— three —

ANOMIE IN INDIAN POLITICS
Origins and Potential Wider Impact

This appeared in 1983, at a time when anomie—normless behaviour by Indian politicians—was a cause for widespread concern. It traces the origins of anomie to the decay of norms, practices and institutions which had prevailed in the Congress Party in the era when it had dominated the political system under Nehru. It argues that a political awakening, which had gradually acquired great momentum among ordinary people, offered an important counterweight to normlessness—not least because voters tended to reject leaders who indulged in it. Much has changed since 1983. The awakening has gained far greater force, and citizens' expectations and demands have increased, so that pressures on politicians from below to behave responsibly and responsively have mounted. Politics affects people at the grassroots more powerfully than it did then, and politicians have become more aware that normless actions alienate voters. Many politicians have therefore sought to deliver more effectively—in part by protecting government programmes from those who try to divert resources for profit or patronage distribution (see chapters thirteen and fourteen of this book). Most party organisations remain weak, but many political institutions underwent regeneration after 1989, when no single party could gain a parliamentary majority (see the next chapter of this book). And yet unbridled, normless actions by politicians remain a source of dismay.

T wo major changes have occurred in the Indian polity since the mid-1960s. Competition and conflict among interest groups have quickened and the Congress Party organisation—which had been the central political institution, the instrument for conflict management—has crumbled.

How great an impact have these political developments had upon Indian life in general? In many other developing countries (and in some industrialised nations too), similar or less severe political difficulties have produced more general crises. In India this has not happened and seems, at least at first glance, unlikely to happen soon. Is that an accurate impression?

A great deal of research needs to be done before we will be able to answer these questions with any adequacy. What follows is an attempt to set out a framework for discussion which will probably need amending. This chapter is divided into two parts. Part one sketches the growth of serious problems in Indian politics which have generated potent anomic (normless) forces. Part two discusses the degree to which anomic forces from the realm of politics[1] can penetrate into other spheres of Indian life. Until recent decades, Indian civilisation was better equipped than other great civilisations to absorb and contain political decay, crisis and anomie without suffering severe damage in other spheres. Has its ability to do so been eroded to the point where political crisis might cause a crisis of a more general character?

I

Two changes have occurred in Indian politics since the mid-1960s which, when they are set against the background of the preceding years, take on immense significance. The first of these is the gradual development of a certain political maturity among a great many members of the poorer groups which form a huge proportion of India's population. The 'weaker sections of society' have—however

[1]In this chapter, the term 'politics' refers not to the totality of power relations in Indian society but more narrowly, to things pertaining in some way to the state.

unevenly and imperfectly—tended to develop an awareness of their rights under law, and have begun to use their numerical strength to assert themselves, despite pressure from the groups that have long exercised dominance over them. As a result, competition and conflict have quickened, appetites for political spoils have grown among all sections of society, and India has become an increasingly lively polity and an increasingly difficult country to govern.

The second change is no less important than the first. Even if the first change had not occurred at this time, the second would easily have qualified as a monumental loss which would have been sufficient to generate a political crisis at the systemic level. This second change is the breakdown of the Congress Party's organisation which was India's central political institution, and its main instrument for conflict management during the first two decades or so after independence.

These two changes occurred gradually, so that it is impossible to speak of a calamitous moment, a sudden gross disruption in India's political history. (Not even the Emergency qualifies. Had the Emergency not occurred, this problem would have still been present.) But the joint (indeed, the related) occurrence of these two changes in the years since the mid-1960s certainly makes this a calamitous phase in which a very considerable disruption has occurred within the political order. Indeed, it poses a threat to the existing order, though it is by no means a perceived threat. One of the marks of the current troubles is the patent incomprehension of a great many political actors. For them, what has happened is unprecedented and impossible to understand.[2]

For Durkheim, 'anomie' implied an insufficiency or absence of norms, rules, standards for conduct and belief. It implied an inadequacy of forces—forces within the individual, and collective or institutional forces outside him or her—to regulate appetites, behaviour and social life, so that a person experienced disorientation

---

[2]The comments in the last two paragraphs are made in response to notes by Paul Brass, Veena Das, Ralph Nicholas, T. N. Madan, and V. S. Vyas, prior to a conference on South Asia Political Economy at Ahmedabad, December 1981.

and unease.[3] But 'Durkheim's notion of anomie ... can be understood only against the background of the 'normal' or 'natural' condition from which it is held to be a pathological deviation'.[4] It implied a departure from or decay of an overriding order which had carried with it, or at least reinforced, a set of norms.

This can help us to understand the changing behaviour of full-time and part-time politicians in India in recent years, particularly since about 1973 or 1974. The intervening years have witnessed a marked erosion of restraint, mounting disorientation and incomprehension, and increasingly aggressive, short-sighted and often brutish behaviour among politicians at all levels within the 'soft' parties in the broad centre of the right-left spectrum. Norms, values and constraints which had substantial influence in political life between 1947, and the mid-1960s have been increasingly abandoned, and—except in a few cases—new structures and reformulated norms have not been developed to take their place. It is important to stress at the outset that in our view the norms and values which have been abandoned were of a very mixed character. They consisted in part of what we might call the liberal Nehruvian virtues—commitments to secularism, open discussion, tolerance of diversity, probity, the need for reform to promote greater social justice, and so forth. But it is also our view that these notions were of far less importance than another, less inspiring set of norms. The most compelling set of constraints on the behaviour of politicans in that period were those generated in the corporate interest of the Congress Party which operated as a formidable but rather unedifying political 'machine' that was ultimately dependent upon the coercive power of dominant landowning groups.[5]

---

[3]E. Durkheim, *Suicide: A Study in Sociology* (Routledge and Kegan Paul, London, 1952), pp. 253–54, 258 and 382.

[4]S. Lukes, *Emile Durkheim: His Life and Work: A Historical and Critical Study* (Penguin, Harmondsworth, 1973), p. 173.

[5]For detailed argument in support of this view, see J. Manor, 'The Dynamics of Political Integration and Disintegration', in A. J. Wilson and D. Dalton (eds), *The States of South Asia: Problems of National Integration* (Hurst, London, 1983), pp. 89–110.

These comments may make more sense if we provide a little context in the form of a severely compressed and therefore necessarily sketchy survey of India's political history since the late 1930s. In the struggle against the British Raj, it was necessary to build an organisation that could plausibly claim to speak for all or nearly all Indians. As one formidable regional strategist in the nationalist struggle put it, he 'felt like an ant' standing in the shadow of the Raj, which 'seemed to fill the whole sky'.[6] To oppose that sort of an adversary, a national con-gress (a word which means 'coming together') was needed, a massive coalition including nearly all important interests. The pre-independence Congress therefore developed an organisation of great sophistication and complexity in which a wide range of important interests was at least tenuously represented, that eventually became an alternative government-in-waiting.

Within the broad Congress coalition, certain interests were more important than others. Most crucial of all were the urban middle classes and, more especially, the cultivating groups who held a position of dominance over the poorer majority of the population in rural areas across most of India, and whose representatives came increasingly into Congress after the mid-1930s. These landowning groups had provided the bedrock on which British rule had rested in most parts of the subcontinent since the days of the East India Company. They were not all active supporters of the Raj. Most had remained rather aloofly acquiescent, but that was all that the British needed. The key change which equipped Congress to win over substantial numbers of these people was the decision to enter the councils in numerous British Indian provinces in 1937. Control of certain ministries enabled Congressmen to distribute patronage in rural areas and, thereby, to demonstrate to members of these groups the advantages that could follow from Congress rule. The message got through to many and there emerged substantial support for the nationalist cause. This was a major and possibly a decisive setback for

---

[6]Interview with B. N. Gupta, Bangalore, 2 August 1972.

the British.[7] It also ensured that the landed peasant groups acquired an extremely powerful voice within most regional and sub-regional units of the Congress before and, increasingly, after independence.

After the transfer of power in 1947, Congress quickly became India's central political institution, more important than Parliament or the bureaucracy or any other formal institution of state. Legislatures at the national and regional levels were rubber stamps for the bills which resulted from bargaining and debate within Congress rather than arenas where statutes were shaped and refined. The party's operatives soon gained very substantial influence over the actions of civil servants, particularly at the district level and below, so that the formal machinery of state was largely subordinated to the needs and demands of the party. The crucial conflicts in Indian politics occurred not between Congress and the opposition, but *within* Congress. The party occupied most of the space on the political stage, extending itself beyond the broad centre to take in most of the left and right as well. Opposition parties were relegated to the fringes and operated as narrow pressure groups.[8] Congress maintained its dominance in the political system between 1947 and the mid-1960s by preserving a certain minimal harmony among many potentially contradictory interests. This was no easy task, but the party possessed the skills, the spoils and the clout to resolve or mitigate most conflicts that arose within it. In that period, interest groups in rural areas had in most cases not yet fully crystallised and those that had were usually not well-organised, so conflicts were neither too numerous nor too sharp to overcome.

Congress could succeed as India's central integrating institution and as an agency for conflict management because it was, fundamentally, a political 'machine'—or to be precise, a cluster of regional political machines operating in the various states. It was far larger and more loosely integrated than the machines of urban

[7]See for example, D. A. Low, 'Introduction', in D. A. Low (ed.), *Congress and the Raj: Facets of the Indian Struggle* (Heinemann, London, 1976), pp. 1–46.

[8]R. Kothari, 'The Congress "System" in India', *Asian Survey* (December, 1964), pp. 161–73.

America, but it functioned on the same basic principles. It passed out spoils which were derived from its control of state power and, in exchange, it obtained the support of people of influence in local and intermediate level arenas all across the subcontinent. Its huge, complex network of transactional alliances made it the largest and most formidable agency for the distribution of patronage and the extraction of loyalty that the world has ever seen or is ever likely to see.

The Congress machine performed at least three crucial roles in the political system. First, it integrated the different levels of the system, linking New Delhi with state, district, sub-district and local levels. Conditions at each level differed, often strikingly, from those at higher and lower levels and, as a result, the logic of politics at any one level differed significantly from that above and below it. Congress knit these levels together by arranging bargains and an acceptable division of authority between people of influence at each. By promoting mobility for individuals between levels, it developed a huge cohort of people who understood the logic of politics at two or more levels. Second, and by the same process, the party machine integrated India's astonishingly diverse states into a common fabric. As in America,[9] party organisation provided the essential glue which held the political system together, but in India it was a single party which performed this task and it did so with far less reinforcement from the formal institutions of state than was the case in the US. Finally, as we have noted, the party machine used enticement and (less often) intimidation to manage conflict between interests within its broad coalition.

This and its close alliance with the dominant landowning groups gave Congress loose control over Indian society. The landed elite which managed to influence or control the votes of the poorer majority by virtue of their coercive power and of the deference that they enjoyed, therefore provided the foundation upon which Congress rule rested, much as it had in the British era despite obvious differences in the rules of politics. This meant that elections,

[9] C. Rossiter, *Parties and Politics in America* (Cornell University Press, Ithaca, 1960), pp. 38–65.

within both the Congress organisation and the nation at large, were less than fully democratic since they gave an inadequate voice to the disadvantaged majority. But elections within the Congress Party did at least take place and this reliance upon the principle of representation was very important. It allowed information, pressure and people to pass up through the ranks and levels of the party organisation and promoted renewal and changes of tactics which were decidedly rational in character.

Both at the level of ideas and at the level of action and transaction, the old Congress organisation crumbled during the 1970s. At the level of ideas, the cynical misuse of ideology destroyed the rather vague and inconstant but nonetheless important commitment to ideals which lent coherence to the upper levels of the party organisation. It contributed to a near total devaluation of language which is an essential medium for political bargaining and is crucial to the development of collective commitment to ideals and to organisations.

At the level of action, the Congress machine by the early 1970s suffered from mounting complacency and corruption and from the loss of skilled operatives as old men grew weary, retired or died. Efforts to centralise power at the apex of the party led to the abandonment of the principle of representation for the selection of personnel at every level of the organisation. After 1972 Congress committees and party offices, both great and small, were filled by appointment from above rather than by election.[10] This severely impeded the flow of information and diverse opinion up through the organisation to decision-makers who were increasingly concentrated at the top. The distribution of patronage which had been the lifeblood of the old machine was rendered unreliable. Many of the party's skilled operatives were cast aside in favour of people of dubious competence as political managers who were selected for their protestations of personal loyalty.

From 1975 onward, the party experienced not only the centralisation of power within it but the establishment of personal rule over it. Given the personalities involved, this quickly led to

[10]I am grateful to Myron Weiner for calling this to my attention.

increasingly inconsistent, purblind and capricious conduct of party business from the apex of the structure. Congress leaders in some states were allowed to proceed with little guidance and interference from above, but in other states leaders were inserted with orders to destroy the existing organisation of the party because this was seen as a threat to the national leadership. And yet when such structures were wrecked, little of substance was put in their place. The bizarre character of initiatives from above caused even those state-level leaders who were smiled upon to insulate themselves as much as possible from interference from above—by, *inter alia*, the concealment and falsification of information.

By centralising power, the national leaders had intended to make their influence penetrate more effectively, but it was actually producing the opposite result. That they were unaware of this is another measure of their problems. India's rulers since 1820 (and most especially those who had led the Congress over the first two decades after independence) had understood that in such a huge, complex society in which power has been so widely dispersed, influence penetrated down from the top most effectively by means of bargaining, compromise. The abandonment of that principle caused serious problems. As a result of inconsistent handling of the various states, and state leaders' consequent insulation of their bailiwicks from external intrusions, the natural heterogeneity of the regions began to assert itself. By 1977, units of the Congress Party in many states had diverged to the point where they resembled regional parties more than extensions of a national organisation.[11] The party had become incapable of serving as the polity's central integrating institution. It no longer maintained a steady flow of patronage, information and pressure between levels in the system. It no longer cultivated and promoted personnel with subtle knowledge of the political logic at more than one level. It was no longer capable of generating rational changes of tactics. Its transactional links to many key groups at the grassroots were severed. If the central institution

---

[11]See J. Manor, 'Where Congress Survived: Five States in the Indian General Election of 1977', *Asian Survey* (August, 1978), pp. 785–803. For a more recent example, see chapter five in this book.

of a polity is allowed to decline in this way and nothing is put in its place, serious consequences are bound to follow.

The Janata coalition was too heterogeneous, factious and plagued by personal rivalries to provide, a reintegrating structure. Political decay continued in many respects during its time in office. Since its defeat, most of the trends outlined above have reasserted themselves, often in a more extreme manner.

It is important to remember that all of this has occurred against a background of the increasing political maturity of the Indian electorate. It has been clear since the late 1960s, from survey data and from studies of small political arenas, that disadvantaged people have become increasingly aware of their rights under law and increasingly assertive. At recent elections, poor villagers have tended to decide for themselves how they will vote—collectively, more than as individuals, but for themselves nonetheless. In most areas the *diktat* of landowning groups no longer carries decisive weight.[12] It is not only the poor who have become politicised. Interests within every section of Indian society are far more self-aware than in Nehru's lifetime and their links with similar interests beyond the local arena are far more numerous and substantial. Competition between interests has quickened enormously over the last seventeen years, people's appetites for patronage and preferment have grown. Conflict has naturally increased as a result, but it has done so at a time when decay prevents the Congress organisation from defusing or managing conflict as it once did. (For later developments, see chapters six, eight and nine in this book). This has led to exasperation among competing interests and—more frequently of late—to outbursts of violence, few of which can be interpreted as in any way constructive.

[12]These comments are based upon the author's studies of the 1971, 1977 and 1980 elections in India and upon conversations with Bashiruddin Ahmed, D. L. Sheth, Ramashray Roy and G. K. Karanth. See also, J. Manor 'The Electoral Process amid Awakening and Decay: Reflections on the Indian General Election of 1980', in P. Lyon and J. Manor (eds), *Transfer and Transformation: Political Institutions in the New Commonwealth* (Leicester University Press, Leicester 1983), and D. L. Sheth (ed.), *Citizens and Parties: Aspects of Competitive Politics in India* (Bombay, 1975).

These events have further unnerved politicians who were already seriously disoriented. Leaders sitting atop state and national political systems often pull the levers of party and government which in former times produced positive results, only to find either that nothing happens or that unanticipated results emerge which only compound their difficulties. (After this chapter was published, Prime Minister Rajiv Gandhi, drawing on his days as a pilot, noted that there was a lot of 'free play in the controls'.) India's political system has increasingly become a *terra incognita* to many professional politicians.[13] In their search for ways to make politics respond to their initiatives as it once did, they have often turned to four highly dubious 'solutions'.[14] The first of these has already been mentioned, the centralisation of power at the apex of the system. It was always likely, in whatever way it was attempted, to be counter-productive, but it has been applied so inconsistently and capriciously that it has had almost no constructive impact.

The second is what might politely be described as 'fund-raising'. This is the process by which leaders in the regions have been required to deliver extremely large sums to the national level. It has had several results, all of which have damaged the coherence and effective working of the party organisation. It has led some top leaders to think that the mere *possession* of massive funds renders them powerful, a notion that has restrained them from the careful and constant distribution of largesse which might have strengthened their hands. More seriously, it has actually *reduced* the influence of national leaders by making them dependent upon leaders in state capitals for tributary payments. Regional leaders have themselves begun to use the disbursement of very substantial sums to cultivate networks of supporters and this, plus the often robust methods

[13]This is akin to a struggle among urban Sri Lankans to comprehend rapid change. See G. Obeyesekere, 'Social Change and the Deities', *Man* (1977), pp. 377–96. See also, the discussion of it in the context of Sri Lanka politics in J. Manor, 'The Failure of Political Integration in Sri Lanka', *Journal of Commonwealth and Comparative Politics* (March, 1979), pp. 21–46.

[14]These (and much of the argument set out thus far in the text) are discussed at greater length in J. Manor, 'Party Decay and Political Crisis in India', *The Washington Quarterly* (summer, 1981), pp. 25–40.

used to raise funds, has severely eroded the old tendency to put the party's corporate interests before private enrichment. That and other factors have also contributed to pervasive and often very caustic intra-party factional conflicts.

The third solution is the resort to menace, violence or the threat thereof which is one of the reasons why factional conflict has been so caustic. The fourth is the increasing reliance by professional politicians upon sundry soothsayers and sorcerers, and upon the propitiatory remedies that they propose. The use or threat of violence has severely damaged the complex web of transactional ties which bound important persons and interests to the party organisation of old. The reliance on sorcery has functioned as a serious distraction from the delicate, painstaking tasks of political bargaining, organisation-building and conflict management. These four 'solutions' are the most important immediate causes of the anomie which is our main concern in this discussion. They have helped to create a situation similar to that described in another context by Durkheim:

> The scale (regulating needs) is upset; but a new scale cannot be improvised. ... One no longer knows what is possible and what is *not*, what is just and what is unjust, which claims and expectations are legitimate and which are immoderate. As a result, there is no limit to men's aspirations ... appetites ... (they) no longer know where to stop.[15]

★ ★ ★

Thus far, this chapter has dealt with the problem of anomie in the political sphere, but politics does not exist in a vacuum. A full discussion of this subject would need to include consideration of the extent to which political decay is the product of events elsewhere, of social, cultural or economic change.[16] The remainder of this essay is,

---

[15]Quoted by Lukes, *Emile Durckheim*, p. 210. Another development of the period was the emergence of what I have called 'pragmatic progressives' (see chapter eleven in this book). Political decay and anomie threaten their future prospects, but a discussion of that must wait for another occasion.

[16]I am inclined to the view that politics has been the principal (though by no means the only), source of anomie in India in recent years, that in

however, devoted to a discussion of the other side of that coin, the impact of politics on other spheres.

How great an impact have these political troubles had upon Indian life in general? How great an impact can any essentially *political* crisis have in a society which in many ways is better equipped than other civilisations to withstand decay and disruption from the realm of politics? In many other developing countries (and in some industrialised nations too), similar or less severe political difficulties have produced more general crises. In India this has not happened and seems, at least at first glance, unlikely to happen soon. Is that an accurate impression? What follows is an attempt to set out a framework for discussion which will probably need amending after further research.

It is important to stress that the comments in part one of this chapter referred to a rather small slice of society. We do not mean to imply that anomie, normlessness is overtaking the whole of Indian society. Institutions such as the family, *jati*, lineage, kinship network and so on may be under greater stress than they were twenty years ago, but there is little evidence to suggest that they are often in crisis. Relations between *jatis*, factions, religious groups, between patrons and clients or between classes present more complications, which we must consider in due course. But the growing normlessness of which we speak has originated mainly among people who spend all or much of their time in politics, that is, among professional or semi-professional politicians in the organisationally and ideologically 'soft' parties. (Those in the 'hard' parties of the Marxist left and the parochially chauvinist right present different problems and are therefore excluded from this discussion.)

How serious a threat does the increasing normlessness among politicians pose to the general well-being? Certain aspects of India's political culture insulate society from this threat. Ashis Nandy has described '... the traditional concept of politics as an amoral, ruthless statecraft or a dispassionate pursuit of self-interest to which many of

---

this matter at least politics enjoys a certain primacy. But a full discussion of that must wait for another occasion.

the norms of the non-political sphere do not apply'. He has written
of the

> ... image of politics as far removed from day-to-day life ... Indian
> society is organised more around its culture than around its politics.
> It accepts political changes without feeling that its very existence is
> being challenged, and with the confidence—often unjustified—that
> politics touches only its less important self.

He adds,

> ... it is taken for granted that the values governing politics would
> be largely inconsistent with those governing other areas of life. At
> critical moments, therefore, the anomic forces released by political
> changes do not easily percolate into other areas.[17]

Ordinary people have tended to regard public affairs with 'distrust
and cynicism'. His ethical criteria have mainly been applied to
'primordial interpersonal settings—in face-to-face situations, in
families and small systems'.[18] Given the highly localised focus of
social organisation in much of the subcontinent, it is particularly
difficult for supra-local influences to break this down.

Rajni Kothari has told us,

> ... the unity of India owed itself not to the authority of a given political
> system but to the wide diffusion of the cultural symbols, the spiritual
> values and the structure of roles and functions characteristic of a
> continuous civilisation.

Indians lacked 'a strong identification with a given political order' and
they tended to 'de-emphasize the importance of secular changes'.
This helped to insulate them from some of the traumas which
originated as political crises and were felt by other civilisations,
notably China. 'In historical societies with a more continuous secular
tradition and in which the dominant identity was with the political
order, such (secular, often political) changes have given rise to both

---

[17]A. Nandy, *At the Edge of Psychology* (Oxford University Press, Delhi,
1980), pp. 48–49.
  [18]Ibid., p. 56.

prolonged resistance and a considerable sense of humiliation and futility when they eventually did come about'.[19]

Indian society and civilisation, then, are better insulated than others by habits of mind against disruptive influences from the realm of politics. Kothari develops this further by referring to,

> ... Indians' predilection for the autonomy of social and primordial institutions, the legitimacy of intermediate structures between state and society, the freedom to retain local identities, and the tolerance of cultural and religious diversities.[20]

The things mentioned here developed within a power structure and a society which were highly segmented. Recent research has shown, for example, that on the eve of the British conquest, power in most of India was widely distributed among relatively small political arenas marked 'dispersed and disputed sovereignty'.[21] We have long known this to be the case for much of south India,[22] but it now appears to have been a more general phenomenon. Power within the British system was still quite widely dispersed. Power holders at the provincial and district levels—either by design or by inaction— did not intrude unduly upon the prerogatives of powerful people and groups at the local level, unless disorder developed from below.

When the Congress Party moved into the structures bequeathed by the Raj and controlled them through regional political machines, it did not change things very radically. The nation's Constitution and the logic of the spoils system gave regional leaders very considerable autonomy over their own affairs. They used political patronage to develop transactional alliances with influential groups at intermediate levels and the grassroots—alliances which left

[19]R. Kothari, *Politics in India: A Country Study* (Orient BlackSwan, New Delhi, 1970), pp. 25–53.

[20]Ibid., p. 48.

[21]Remarks to the author by J. C. Heesterman, London, 9 July, 1981.

[22]B. Stein, 'Integration of the Agrarian System of South India', in R. E. Frykenberg (ed.), *Land Control and Social Structure in Indian History* (University of Wisconsin Press, Madison, 1969), pp. 175–216. See also his recent volume, *Peasant and Society in Medieval South India* (Oxford University Press, Delhi, 1980).

intermediate and local-level elites with quite substantial autonomy. So in its heyday, the Congress organisation of old—despite many obvious innovations—broadly conformed to the logic of power relations which had prevailed in the British period. Power remained widely dispersed at various levels down through a complex system of compromises with influential people and groups in intermediate and local power centres. So for these and other reasons, Kothari was correct in describing the result, during the period up to the early 1970s, as 'a secular order which is highly differentiated and segmental, and respectful of the autonomy of various subsystems'.[23]

Despite all of this, however, important changes have occurred in recent decades which have at least begun to cut away at the insulation between politics and other spheres of life. Nandy has remarked on the way in which Gandhi's saintliness 'negated the older idea of politics as amoral'. That idea was further eroded in the post-Independence period by the reformist, moralistic rhetoric of politicians and because politics has tended to operate (somewhat imperfectly) 'as the society's major means of self-correction'.[24] Nandy has also noted that after undermining the old status system and social leadership, politics and politicians have moved in at 'the apex of a new hierarchy ...', so that 'any activity which is outside the sphere of power politics is by definition low status'.[25] Partly as a result,

> ... there has grown a close link between politics and the other subsystems of the society. Today in India not only is politics spilling over its boundaries, it is paying for its primacy by carrying an enormous load of expectations ... many problems which were once non-political have now become the responsibility of politics.[26]

In the years since 1947, local arenas have been knitted gradually but very substantially into the national and regional political systems. Villages have felt the impact of supra-local politics as a result of the electoral process, various development programmes and (above all)

[23]Kothari, *Politics in India*, p. 255.
[24]Nandy, *At the Edge of Psychology*, pp. 50 and 62.
[25]Ibid., p. 55.
[26]Ibid., p. 63.

the growth of patronage politics under the old Congress machine. People in villages and in sub-district towns have come increasingly to understand the logic and rules of competitive politics and they are far more concerned with specific issues than they were during the 1950s.[27]

This has led to a curious reversal of an old pattern. In the early 1960s, Paul Brass found that ideological concerns tended to be reasonably prominent in the minds of politicians at the national and state levels, but when one moved down to the district level, ideology and issues paled into insignificance alongside factional disputes and the pursuit of narrow advantage. This trend continued as one moved further downward from the district level towards the grassroots.[28] Today, the opposite is true. Issue-oriented (more than ideological) conflict is welling up from below, from the village and the sub-district levels, as competition over the allocation of government resources intensifies, while politics at higher levels has grown increasingly issue-less.[29]

This brings us back to an important point in the discussion of anomie in political life. People at the grassroots who are more politically mature, more conscious of issues, aware of their rights, and more inclined to make common cause in their own interests are *not* tending towards greater normlessness. They are conducting themselves according to new norms which tend to contradict those that prevailed when the principle of hierarchy was relatively unchallenged and dominant landed groups held sway over village life. (For more detail, see chapter fifteen of this book.) So it is mainly among professional and semi-professional politicians that anomic forces are being generated.

[27]See, for example, M. F. Franda, *India's Rural Development: An Assessment of Alternatives* (Indian University Press, Bloomington and London, 1979), p. 120.

[28]P. R. Brass, *Factional Politics in an Indian State: The Congress Party in Uttar Pradesh* (University of California Press, Berkeley, 1965), p. 233.

[29]Compare the emphasis on issues in Indira Gandhi's 1971 election campaign with that of 1979–80.

This last statement might sound dubious to a reader who is aware of the growth over recent years of criminal violence and of clashes between caste groups, between religious groups, and between various sections of the population and the police. A great deal of research needs to be done on these trends, but it is the strong suspicion of this writer that to a considerable extent they are the result of growing political awareness, appetites and assertiveness among all groups at the grassroots, together with the decline of the old Congress regional machines—those once-formidable instruments for arranging bargains, distributing loaves and fishes, and defusing or limiting conflict. Groups from local arenas apply pressure in the political sphere and become frustrated when they find that sufficient largesse is not forthcoming because spoils have been diverted for private gain or because parties in power are no longer capable of conveying their appeals up through the system and patronage back down to them. When they get frustrated, their inclination for healthy conflict within the rules of the political system can easily escalate into conflict of a destructive, often violent sort which usually has a blind, anomic quality to it. But the main source of this seems *not* to be the perversity of ordinary folk, but the incapacities of politicians and political organisations to respond constructively or merely adequately to pressure from below.

There are, however, reasons for believing that the anomic influence of political decay may not prove as catastrophic in India as it might (and in some cases has) in European or African societies. We have seen that politics has become well nigh pervasive in the sense that it has penetrated down through all the levels of the political system, even to the villages. But that is only part of the story. We need to distinguish between *levels* in the political system and segments in the society and in the lives of individuals. Kothari and others have attributed Indian society's remarkable absorptive capacity to its genius for 'differential and segmented change'.[30] There is no doubt that since 1947, politics and the values (and sometimes the perverse ideas) that it bears have penetrated anew into many segments of life. This has certainly resulted in *some* erosion of society's capacity

[30]Kothari, *Politics in India*, p. 252.

to protect itself from anomic forces which are generated within the realm of politics. The question is: how much erosion has occurred?

At present, any answer to this question must be tentative. But it seems to this writer at least that, however great the problems within the political sphere, this society is far from being crippled in its capacity to absorb them. There is no doubt that anomie in the political sphere has generated a sense of futility among well-intentioned people in voluntary associations across the country.[31] It is also true that politics and self-aggrandising politicians have developed considerable (and lately, distinctly anomic) influence over key institutions which are less overtly 'political' than voluntary associations of farmers, labourers, etc. Note, for example, their power on the boards of temples, and the hostels and schools of castes or religious groups. The importance of these institutions is not to be underestimated. This becomes clear, from a comparison of the flaccid response of Sinhalese society in Sri Lanka to British cultural imperialism and the formidable response in most regions of India in which such institutions provided crucial infrastructure.[32] But in India, even this increasing influence of politics does not necessarily imply that serious erosion is taking place at the level of ideas, values and identities.

This seems true for at least three reasons. First, the intrusions which these institutions have suffered from politicians or their nominees have little or no ideational content. The people who come onto (for example) a temple board when a new state government packs such bodies with its supporters have been put there partly to reward them and partly to ensure that the wealth and power at the board's disposal are used to support the party in power. But however vigorously they pursue this, they bring very little with them in the way of a new political philosophy. They may indulge in illicit 'fund-raising', they may deploy muscle, but they tend to be the furthest

[31]This comment is based on a large number of interviews with analysts of such associations in Bihar, Gujarat and Maharashtra and with activists in such associations in Karnataka.

[32]See chapter four of J. Manor, *The Expedient Utopian: Bandaranaike and Ceylon* (Cambridge University Press, Cambridge, 1989).

extensions of patronage networks, owing their loyalties to *persons* and not to ideas (and in many cases, not even to parties). Their patrons, at whatever higher level, tend to be as bereft of ideas as they are. They may generate exasperation or despair, but they are unlikely to generate new, overriding identities which can intrude upon the integrity of existing values or ideas within these institutions. (The lack of penetrative strength of the BJP's organisation, examined in chapter seven of this book, is relevant here.)

Second, the impact of such intrusions from the realm of politics is bound to be weakened by the oft-proven incompetence of most of the supra-local politicians directing the effort, and by the inappropriate nature of their strategy. The central element in it is the idea that power can and should be centralised, not only within regional political systems but within the national system as a whole. This is a mistaken notion. It runs counter to the basic principle by which India has been governed under the Company, the Crown and Nehru's Congress: that the influence of those at the apex of the system penetrates most effectively by way of *bargaining* and *compromise* with people of influence in intermediate and local power centres (see chapter five of this book). An attempt to centralise power mainly through coercive means is almost certain to fail. Those at lower levels retain too many resources for concealment and subtle resistance, so that people at the apex become cut off from lower levels without realising it. As a result, the natural heterogeneity of regional and sub-regional arenas tends to intensify which, as we have seen, is the opposite result to that intended.[33]

It is even possible that this decline in the penetration of supra-local influence is leading to a re-emergence of certain features of the traditional relationship between the political and other spheres. The 'aggregative demands on parochial identities' which traditionally 'were minimal' may now be on the wane. The character of the intrusion from the political sphere tends, in new ways and for new reasons, to reinforce '... a low level of commitment to political tasks, lack of any marked compulsion to provide active support to political elites, and in general an absence of predominant collective

---

[33]For more on this, see chapter five in this book.

attachments beyond the primordial and local levels'. There is also, increasingly, 'a certain sense of distrust and insecurity' in dealing with large political collectivities.[34]

The third reason for doubting the threat posed by anomic political forces is perhaps the most telling. It is simply that in India most such institutions are not very susceptible to political intrusions. The governing boards of temples and parochial schools can be captured. But it is an altogether different task to penetrate a *jati*, clan, lineage or sect—to penetrate the thing itself, as distinct from a voluntary association which exists to represent the interests of a large collectivity (such as a caste association that represents a cluster of *jatis*). A further set of smaller institutions—families, marriage networks, etc.—are even less easy to penetrate.

[34]Kothari, *Politics in India*, p. 256.

— four —

POLITICAL REGENERATION IN INDIA

Curbs on the normless behaviour of politicians, discussed in chapter three, emerged between 1989 and 2014 when no single party could obtain a parliamentary majority. Power rapidly ebbed away from the once dominant Prime Minister's Office to other institutions at the national and state levels. Those institutions, which had been weakened before 1989, regenerated and checked abuses of power from the apex of the system and at lower levels (see, however, chapter fourteen of this book). As a result, India between 1989 and 2014 witnessed fewer abuses by prime ministers than the United Kingdom saw under either Margaret Thatcher or Tony Blair. This paper appeared in 1994 and called attention to that regenerative process at a time when it was only beginning to become apparent.

This chapter discusses important trends in India's politics since the early 1970s. One trend has been political decay.[1] It has undermined political institutions—both formal institutions of state and informal institutions, especially political parties. Their corporate substance; their organisational complexity,

[1]This term was coined by Samuel P. Huntington in 'Political Development and Political Decay', *World Politics* (April. 1965).

flexibility and strength; and their capacity to respond creatively or even minimally to the needs of and pressure from social groups, have all been eroded. The process of decay is explained in part by systemic factors: the tendency of all human institutions to ossify and succumb to complacency and malfeasance. But it has also been the result of conscious attempts by political leaders to weaken and even to destroy institutions, in the often mistaken belief that this will strengthen their hands.

Decay has also entailed degeneration in the behaviour of individuals and groups. Corrupt, unconstitutional and wilfully destructive acts have become more common among actors within political institutions. At times, a kind of galloping normlessness (anomie—see chapter three in this book) has appeared to take over the politics of particular Indian states and at the national level. This has bred exasperation among social groups which seek responses from political actors and institutions. Members of such groups come to regard politicians as unhelpful at best, and often as malevolent and unclean. In these circumstances, social groups have tended to turn inward, to regard politics and other social groups with suspicion. With political institutions no longer able to arrange accommodations between such groups, destructive social conflict often ensues.

It is not necessary to elaborate on this tendency towards decay. It is depressingly familiar to analysts of Indian politics and to the people of India. It has been extensively discussed in academic writings—not least in those of this writer.[2] It is clearly the predominant trend in India's recent political history.

It is, however, not the *only* trend. Certain countervailing processes exist, the most important of which is the main concern

[2]See chapter three in this book and J. Manor, 'Indira and After: The Decay of Party Organisation in India', *The Round Table* (October, 1978); 'Party Decay and Political Crisis in India', *The Washington Quarterly* (Summer, 1981); 'The Electoral Process amid Awakening and Decay: Reflections on the Indian General Election of 1980, in P. Lyon and J. Manor (eds), *Transfer and Transformation: Political Institutions in the New Commonwealth* (Leicester University Press, Leicester, 1983), pp. 87–116.

of this chapter: the tendency towards political regeneration. What does this phrase mean? It is the reverse of political decay. It means the restoration of the capacity of state institutions and political parties to respond minimally or even creatively to the needs and desires of social groups.[3] It also entails changes in the behaviour of individuals, so that they are less inclined towards corruption, illegality, destruction and normlessness, and more inclined towards accommodation, responsiveness, accountability, restraint and the observance of agreed norms and procedures. Political regeneration tends to improve relations between political institutions and social groups, between state and society. It often facilitates accommodations between social groups.

Much less has been heard about political regeneration than about political decay in academic or other analyses of Indian politics. That is not surprising, since more decay has occurred in recent times than regeneration. But regeneration has often occurred—for brief and not-so-brief periods—in many diverse and widely scattered political arenas, at many different levels of India's political system and in many different forms. So while it is not the main theme in recent history, it is not insignificant.

Indeed, this enduring capacity for regeneration in India is remarkable. This becomes apparent if we consider the Indian case alongside some other political systems in Asia and Africa where this capacity is less (often much less) evident. This quickly becomes clear to any India specialist who spends time talking with academics who study politics in most African countries. Until very recently, visits to centres for African studies took one into a world bordering

---

[3]Other words might be used instead of 'regeneration'. 'Reinstitutionalisation' would do just as well. Huntington would use 'political development', but I avoid this because it has become entangled with an approach to the study of the politics of less developed nations that has encountered very serious difficulties. (The term 'political decay' is not so encumbered with difficulties, so it remains quite useful.) I have explained my disenchantment with the 'political development' paradigm in the introduction to J. Manor (ed.), *Rethinking Third World Politics* (London, 1991). That entire volume is intended as a departure from both the 'political development' and the 'dependency' schools.

on despair. A few promising changes of late—moves towards multiparty politics in a few cases and democratic decentralisation in a few others—have eased the gloom a little, but only a little. Many analysts suspect that these trends will not endure. The best recent studies of African politics offer little cause for optimism, as the intentionally coarse subtitle of one of them—'The Politics of the Belly'—indicates.[4]

When political decay occurs in these countries, it is difficult to reverse the trend, and it is well-nigh impossible to sustain such a reversal for any length of time or to extend whatever rebuilding is possible from one limited sector of the polity to others. Despite the fact that it has received little attention, the proven ability of Indians to rebuild decayed institutions, and to adapt or create others to take their place, means that it is far from certain that the political drama now being played out there will end in a colossal tragedy.

Any full discussion of political regeneration, in India or anywhere else, would need to pay close attention to the socio-economic conditions which impede or facilitate it. In a chapter of this length, it is impossible to do that. But it is obvious that it is harder to rebuild political institutions in places like Bihar, where social and economic disparities are marked and where social conflicts are bitter and extreme, than in most parts of Maharashtra or Karnataka where conditions are quite different. This is not to say, however, that socio-economic conditions or forces *determine* the political trends discussed here. Politics has considerable autonomy in shaping trends, and it sometimes—not always, but sometimes—enjoys primacy in influencing events.

Let us now look in more detail at what the term 'political regeneration' signifies. We have noted that it was the process by which political institutions (formal and informal) become more

---

[4]This is from J. F. Bayart, *The State in Africa: The Politics of the Belly* (Hurst, London, 1991). See also P. Chabal (ed.), *Political Domination in Africa: Reflections on the Limits of Power* (Cambridge University Press, Cambridge, 1986) and D. B. Cruise O Brien, J. Dunn and R. Rathbone (eds), *The Contemporary West African State* (Cambridge University Press, Cambridge, 1990).

capable of responding to pressures from and to the needs of social groups. But several different processes have served this purpose in India in recent years. We need to take note of at least six types of political regeneration:

(a) the rebuilding and/or the revival of decayed institutions;
(b) the creation of new institutions;
(c) the creation of new government programmes which enhance the capacity of the state to respond constructively to society;
(d) the reassertion of political and/or legal and/or constitutional norms when they are in doubt;
(e) processes by which an existing institution steps in to perform tasks that are supposed to be performed and may once have been performed by another decayed or incapable institution; and
(f) processes by which an existing institution is strengthened so that it can perform tasks that no other institution has previously performed.

This list will make more sense if we say more about each type and provide some examples.

Type 'a' covers a multitude of things. The rebuilding of decayed institutions can occur piecemeal, when a single government department is given new life under a new minister or senior official with a commitment to institution-building. Or it can occur more generally, when an entire government or a chief minister or prime minister changes. The rebuilding of party organisations should also be included here. So should processes whereby parastatal institutions or supposedly semi-autonomous institutions are rebuilt, revived or provided with greater autonomy or opportunities to play constructive roles. There are numerous examples, but for striking illustrations, consider the changes wrought in the formal organs of government and in the ruling party's organisation when Sharad Pawar became chief minister of Maharashtra in 1988 after a long spell in which the excessively bureaucratic S. B. Chavan, the incapable Babasaheb Bhosale, and the normless A. R. Antulay had held office.

Type 'b', the creation of new institutions, happens more rarely, but some important advances have occurred here. Everything from the establishment of ombudsmen in various arenas to the creation of some of the new technology missions might qualify for inclusion. One impressive set of examples are the experiments with democratic decentralisation in West Bengal since 1977 and Karnataka since 1987. These bodies constitute something approaching devolved governments under democratic control which have enhanced both the responsiveness and the effectiveness of the state. They also enhance the strength and democratic character of party organisations. So they are not only creative in themselves, but they assist in reversing the process of decay in certain other institutions.

Type 'c' refers not to every conceivable new programme that might be created by state or national governments, but only to those that bolster the capacity of institutions to respond to social groups. We need to exclude programmes which entail hugely expensive populist giveaways that may make the government appear more availing in the short run, but which drain the exchequer and undermine other programmes that have useful developmental impacts. N. T. Rama Rao's rice subsidy is one example, which contributed to political decay by diverting massive resources from other existing and potential programmes. But it is not just poorly or unwisely *designed* programmes that should be excluded. We also need to leave out poorly *implemented* programmes—however well designed—including those whose main purpose is to provide politicians and their friends with opportunities to enrich themselves. Rajiv Gandhi called attention to this sort of thing when he complained during the 1989 election campaign that 83 per cent of the funds for development programmes were being stolen before they reached the intended beneficiaries—although, strangely, he was referring to his own government.[5]

---

[5] This writer heard him make this claim at an election rally in New Delhi in mid-November, 1989. Subsequent discussions with journalists, civil servants and politicians in numerous Indian states indicate that he was certainly overstating the scale of the malfeasance then occurring, but this was and is nevertheless a serious problem.

But even after we make these exclusions, we are still left with a significant number of programmes that succeed in enhancing the state's capacity to respond to society. Governments run by a broad array of political parties provide examples. The *antyodaya* programme developed by the Shekhawat government (BJP) in Rajasthan qualifies. So do a great many of the programmes of the Communist government in West Bengal since 1977. And in some states, the Congress's *Jawahar Rozgar Yojana* programme has had a largely constructive impact, thanks in certain cases to non-Congress state governments.

Type 'd' refers to occasions when either the actions or the statements of individuals or groups serve to reassert political, constitutional or legal norms that are at risk. These reassertions may succeed completely or only partially, but if they have an impact, they qualify for inclusion here. The refusal in 1988 of the Allahabad district magistrate to accede to a request from certain politicians that he rig the result of a parliamentary by-election against V. P. Singh provides an example of a regenerative action. President Venkataraman's Independence Day address a few weeks thereafter, cautioning all parties against attempts to subvert the electoral process, is an example of a statement that served the same purpose.

The processes that can be included in type 'e' occur only infrequently and tend to have a rather limited impact, but they are worth noting. One example illustrates both the phenomenon and its limitations. It has been apparent for at least 20 years that it is exceedingly difficult to succeed in criminal prosecutions of politicians who enrich themselves through the improper use of their positions, even when they misbehave blatantly and on a vast scale. Indeed, such criminal cases are seldom even initiated. However, since the late 1970s, the Indian press has often moved into the vacuum left by the courts. Investigative journalists and their editors know that politicians rarely sue for libel, and if they do so, the courts' sluggish ways tend to favour the defendants. Newspapers have therefore made a practice of publishing detailed exposes of politicians' corrupt doings, daring them to sue. The politicians seldom respond publicly at all. As a result, numerous prominent leaders have, in effect, been prosecuted and convicted of high crimes. This is of course an imperfect substitute for effective court action, since the 'convicts' often escape any punishment other than popular disapproval. But despite these limitations, this is an example of one set of institutions stepping in to perform (after a fashion) tasks which other institutions are supposed to tackle.

An example of type 'f'—processes whereby an institution is strengthened to enable it to perform tasks that were not performed previously—is the enhancement of the role and powers of pre-existing *panchayats* in West Bengal after 1977. The recent growth of *panchayati raj* in that state is often linked to the same process in Karnataka, but there is a key difference. Karnataka's institutions were created *anew* by the Hegde government, but West Bengal's communists inherited their institutions from their Congress predecessors and then breathed life into them, so that they now perform a number of crucially important roles—some of which had never been performed before.

★ ★ ★

Let us now consider the various kinds of changes that can trigger regenerative processes. Several come to mind. The first and most obvious is a change of government at the state or national level as a result of an election. For example, when the Ramakrishna Hegde government succeeded Gundu Rao's harebrained regime in Karnataka in 1983, political regeneration occurred on a number of fronts.[6]

It is not always necessary to change ruling parties, however. Regeneration can begin as the result of a change of leadership within a ruling party. Such changes are rarities at the national level, but they often happen in the states. For example, political journalists in Jaipur

[6]For detailed discussions of this, see J. Manor. 'Blurring the Lines between Parties and Social Bases: Gundu Rao and the Emergence of a Janata Government in Karnataka', in J. R. Wood (ed.), *State Politics in Contemporary India: Crisis or Continuity* (Westview, Boulder and London, 1984); and E. Raghavan and J. Manor, *Broadening and Deepening Democracy: Political Innovation in Karnataka* (Routledge, New Delhi and London, 2009), parts two and three.

are unanimous in the view that when Harideo Joshi succeeded S. C. Mathur as Congress chief minister of Rajasthan in 1989, institutional rebuilding began apace.

Regeneration can also be triggered by a change of leadership within a single state-level or national-level ministry. When Ashoke Sen was made the union law minister after the election of 1984, he announced that he intended to end the invidious practice of punitive transfers of judges who rendered decisions that were not to the government's liking. He was doing so, he said, partly because he wanted to restore the autonomy of the judiciary and partly to attract to the bench talented lawyers who had been put off by the prospect of transfers. This initiative, like many others during Rajiv Gandhi's years as prime minister, eventually ran into the sand. But for a time, it began to have the desired effect.

Changes within political parties—whether they are in power or in opposition—can also initiate regenerative processes. Such changes can take many forms. Personnel changes among party office-bearers, factional realignments within a party, and intra-party elections (rare though they may be) can all have this effect. This writer has been a regular visitor to the offices of the Karnataka Pradesh Congress Committee (KPCC) over the years. For a time in the early 1980s, very little effective activity occurred there. The offices were equipped with a single telephone, a single typewriter of dubious reliability and no filing cabinets. Then a forceful organiser, K. H. Patil, was made the party president and in a matter of weeks the situation was transformed. He was eventually succeeded by less assiduous leaders and for a time the headquarters became moribund. Incoming mail was routinely incinerated—unopened. But then after some time, Veerendra Patil was made party chief, and things revived impressively. Similar stories could be told about other offices of the Congress and several other parties.

* * *

Readers will have noticed that several of the examples of political regeneration discussed above came to grief. It is also true that some of the people who were involved in the processes of regeneration mentioned have also contributed to political decay in other ways.

That is not surprising, since politicians and the political process are highly complex and ambiguous. But despite the fact that regeneration has usually proceeded in fits and starts, and that it is often dwarfed or snuffed out by decay, it is *happening*. It is happening in many different places and at different levels of the political system. It is the result of actions by people who belong to many different political parties and to no party at all. And it is not always overshadowed or wrecked by the countervailing tendency towards decay. Political regeneration is an important trend. It is not entirely unimaginable that it might become the predominant tendency given the electorate's habit of throwing out governments that perform poorly.

It should be apparent from this brief survey that political leaders in high positions usually play important roles in initiating regenerative processes, and that political activists who are subordinate to those leaders then almost always play crucial roles in building up and sustaining those processes. There are two things to say about this.

First, as the key roles played by political actors in the examples here suggests, politics usually counts for more than socio-economic forces or conditions in all of this—although, as we have noted, the latter can be very important in facilitating or impeding these processes. In this sphere at least, politics usually enjoys considerable autonomy from socio-economic forces and occasional primacy over them.

Second, the regenerative processes that we are describing cannot make much headway unless they are supported by the efforts of substantial numbers of political actors who are subordinate to the senior figures who usually initiate things. Since they often succeed at least for awhile in making headway, it would appear that there are significant numbers of people with the inclination and the skills to assist in making political regeneration happen—in most of India's regions and political parties, and at all levels of the political system. In many years of studying politics in various Indian states, this writer has continually encountered large numbers of people (prominent and obscure) who are impressively skilled in political management, bargaining, coalition-building, etc., and who are eager to turn their skills to creative purpose. If we compare India with other countries that find political regeneration more difficult, striking contrasts arise.

The others tend to lack this crucial resource—people in numbers with skills and inclinations that are congenial to the rebuilding of institutions on which open, democratic politics depends.[7]

None of these comments should be construed as an effort to belittle the efforts of those at and near the grassroots in India who are active in what Rajni Kothari has called the 'non-party political process'. On the contrary, these same skills and inclinations are evident there too. And there is some evidence—from the workings of Karnataka's experiment in decentralisation, for example—to suggest that it may be possible to link regenerative doings within political institutions with the creative work of people and groups at the grassroots.[8]

This discussion does not imply that political decay has ceased to be the predominant trend in Indian politics. But the capacity for regeneration, and the fact that in most parts of the country it can happen when it is given quite modest opportunities, both serve as important counterweights to decay. If we want to understand Indian politics fully, we need to pay attention to the interplay between decay on the one hand and regeneration on the other.

[7]For an important example, see the discussion of small-time political 'fixers' (or what Anirudh Krishna calls *naya netas*) in chapter ten of this book. It was published several years after the present chapter appeared.

[8]See another study published several years after this chapter appeared: R. C. Crook and J. Manor, *Democracy and Decentralisation in South Asia and West Africa: Participation, Accountability and Performance* (Cambridge University Press, Cambridge, 1998), chapter two.

— *five* —

WHERE THE GANDHI WRIT DOESN'T RUN

This paper was published in The Economist *on 15 May 1982—anonymously, as all contributions to that publication were and still are. It explains how Indira Gandhi centralised power so radically that, ironically, she weakened herself—by cutting herself off from reliable information from below. She so thoroughly deprived her once formidable party organisation of power that it could no longer do much to serve her interests. She failed to understand that leaders atop this immensely complex political system (or atop highly complex systems in India's states) make their influence penetrate downward most effectively by means of bargaining and accommodation rather than by* diktat.

Mrs Indira Gandhi is regarded by most people, including herself, as a strong centralising leader. She holds so many portfolios and by-passes ministers so often that the cabinet system in India has given way to prime ministerial government. Chief ministers of states ruled by her Congress Party openly acknowledge that they are merely her creatures, holding power entirely at her pleasure. Yet, the control Mrs Gandhi exercises over her state governments is far more tenuous than it seems.

Since her return to power in January, 1980, state governments run by her Congress Party have diverged, often radically, from one another. A few years ago, when the party was a strong corporate institution and not so much the leader's personal fief, the states of Haryana in north India and Karnataka in the south were run in similar ways. Congress politicians enjoyed great influence over bureaucrats at all levels, from the state capital down to the grassroots. This influence was a marketable commodity that enabled politicians to make some money on the quiet. But in both states, the system made political sense, since it ensured that civil servants were responsive to pressure from organised interests. The Congress Party restrained politicians from excessive demands on bureaucrats because a semi-independent and therefore semi-contented civil service was in the party's interests.

In recent years these two states have both changed—in opposite directions. In Haryana, the present Congress government defected *en masse* to Mrs Gandhi from the Janata Party in the wake of her 1980 election triumph. Chief Minister, Bhajan Lal, rightly feared an early sacking since he had called Mrs Gandhi a prostitute at a political rally only a few weeks before. His method of securing local support has had highly unfortunate consequences.

He created a large number of boards to supervise state enterprises, and packed them with politicians. Some of these people have proceeded to use their positions for personal gain. Private firms—foreign and domestic—have been awarded state contracts in exchange for huge kickbacks. One car company provided a large number of legislators with new cars and a generous monthly stipend cover 'running costs'.

Such legislators soon abandoned all restraint in their dealing with civil servants, since this was a further source of profit. The result, nearly two years later, is a completely powerless, demoralised bureaucracy. To avoid transfers and other indignities, civil servants have had to meet increasingly extortionate demands from politicians. Some bureaucrats have, in turn, levied even higher imposts on the state's citizens.

In Karnataka, Chief Minister Gundu Rao followed Mrs Gandhi's example by retaining a large number of portfolios in his own hands.

He personally oversees departments that account for roughly 70 per cent of government spending, which means that over 400 files cross his desk every day. This would tax even the finest of ministerial minds, yet Gundu Rao is described by a leading bureaucrat as 'barely educated and not very bright'. Happily for the civil servants, the chief minister has largely abandoned efforts to cope with this workload. He allows them to run the state while he concentrates on forays by helicopter to meet the people.

The result is a return of civil servant raj, on a scale practically unknown since the British period. Bureaucrats, largely freed of pressure from organised interests, have been less than ardent in promoting programmes dear to politicians' hearts. Some £30 million appropriated by the Karnataka legislature for welfare and development schemes in the financial year 1980–81 went unspent.

Such is Mr Rao's faith in civil servants that he has largely sealed them off from pressure by legislators. As a result, bureaucratic morale has soared and legislators are climbing the walls. With little influence to peddle, they are badly out of pocket. Legislators who drank nothing but imported whiskey two years ago now confine themselves to the local firewater.

Haryana, where the politicians rule unfettered, and Karnataka, where the civil servants do, are not isolated examples. Nor do they represent different regional patterns. Congress rule in Haryana's neighbouring state, Punjab, resembles that in Karnataka; Karnataka's neighbour, Maharashtra, bears an uncanny likeness to Haryana. Other Congress states present other eccentric patterns. If Mrs Gandhi's influence penetrated effectively into the states where her party rules, this would not be happening.

When a chief minister creates conditions in which legislators can get rich quick, he makes them loyal to himself and insulates himself from New Delhi's intrusions. The recently deposed chief minister of Maharashtra, A. R. Antulay, did this so well that he retained a grip over the legislature even after he was convicted of illegal money-making and dismissed by Mrs Gandhi. When chief ministers abdicate power to civil servants, the party—and its members and Mrs Gandhi—all lose influence.

Mrs Gandhi's close advisors concede that she is only vaguely aware of the problem. 'It's best we don't trouble madam with these things.' Stouter hearts who have raised such exasperating matters in the past have often paid a price for their candour. In her zeal to centralise power, Mrs Gandhi has ended up cutting herself off from the main means of taking her power to the people.

— *s i x* —

THE CONGRESS PARTY SINCE 1990

This paper, which appeared in 2011, just as the ruling United Progressive Alliance (UPA) led by the Congress Party was entering rough waters that led to its defeat in 2014. It offers a detailed analysis of the response of Congress to three new challenges that emerged in 1990: the 'backward castes' issue, assertive Hindu nationalism, and regional parties. It examines the party's severe organisational weakness, failed attempts to rebuild it, and efforts to stress economic liberalisation as a response to that weakness and to those three challenges. It also explains the party's need for the dynasty which has led it—a need born of organisational frailty and disorder. Today, with Congress in disarray after the crushing result of the 2014 national election, readers may find some of the arguments here valid and others debatable.

Since 1990, the Congress Party has faced challenges posed by three important changes in Indian politics. These are:

- an increased focus on the interests of the 'backward castes'— triggered by the 1990 pledge by V. P. Singh's Janata government to implement the recommendations of the Mandal Commission;

- the aggressive pursuit of Hindu nationalism—following a 1990 decision by the Bharatiya Janata Party (BJP) in reaction to Singh's announcement; and
- the growing importance of regional parties (which had already gathered momentum before 1990).

These changes have evoked mass responses, to varying degrees across India's regions and over time. More recently, we have also seen the emergence of the Bahujan Samaj Party (BSP) which draws much of its support from *Dalits* (ex-untouchables). These four trends add up to an overall popular political mobilisation—although all four also cut across one another. This chapter assesses the condition of the Congress Party, the impact of these changes upon it, and its responses.

From independence in 1947 until the late 1960s, Congress was the dominant party at the national level and in nearly all states within India's federal system. Opposition parties were disunited and relegated to the margins by Congress which occupied the centre ground, and much of the left and right as well. Congress then practised intra-party democracy. It had a formidable organisation consisting of quite effective state-level political 'machines' which distributed patronage (goods, services and funds) in exchange for electoral support mainly from prosperous landed groups. Most important debates occurred not between Congress and the opposition, but within Congress. Most key decisions occurred within it.

When other parties mounted serious challenges to Congress in the late 1960s, its leader Indira Gandhi split the party, abandoned democracy within it, and won a huge election victory in 1971 on a promise to reduce poverty—appearing to restore Congress dominance. But her promise went largely unfulfilled, and she set about undermining both the party's organisation and formal state institutions, in pursuit of personal rule. This led eventually to the Emergency (1975–77)—after which voters rejected her in 1977.

By 1983, despite an electoral comeback by Mrs Gandhi at the national level three years earlier, every major state had had at least one spell of non-Congress government. Competitive politics had replaced Congress dominance. Indira Gandhi's son Rajiv won a landslide victory in late 1984 amid an emotional upheaval following her assassination, but he governed ineptly, reversing himself on many major policy initiatives. In 1989, he lost a national election—and in the seven general elections beginning in that year, no single party has obtained a parliamentary majority. As a result, power has flowed away from the once dominant Prime Minister's Office (PMO)—to other formal institutions, to a diversity of parties, and to the state level. Congress still contends for power in most states, but it has been reduced to a minor role in several large ones.

This chapter opens with a discussion of the liberalisation of the economy by a Congress government after 1991. It went further than the immediate financial crisis required, partly to address the threats implied by the first three changes listed above. Those threats (and their limitations) are then examined in turn. The problems that afflict the Congress organisation are then analysed, as is the damage done by—and the party's systemic need for—dynastic dominance. The chapter concludes with a discussion of Congress today, as it heads the ruling coalition of parties in New Delhi—focusing on its troubled organisation, its imaginative new strategy, and its ambiguous prospects.

Narasimha Rao, Economic Liberalisation and Congress

When the Congress Party formed a minority government under P. V. Narasimha Rao in 1991, it faced a financial crisis which might have led to India's first default on its international debts. He and Finance Minister Manmohan Singh responded by beginning to liberalise the economy. Their reforms were cautious and limited by international standards, but by Indian standards quite startling. Their cumulative impact eventually produced a substantial revision of relations between the state and market forces.

Narasimha Rao's Aims in Liberalising

The political dilemmas faced by Congress played a significant role in persuading Narasimha Rao to go well beyond a minimal response

to the financial crisis.[1] Two beliefs about the party loomed large
as he devised his new economic strategy. First, he recognised that
the Congress organisation was plagued by serious factional conflict
at all levels and in all regions, and shot through with incapable or
destructive people. He said that it was 'like a railway platform ...
anyone can come and go as he likes, and can push others aside to place
himself in a better position'. He planned to attempt organisational
reform, but he knew that this would be difficult and that he might
fail. Second, he saw aggressive Hindu nationalism, the 'backward
castes' issue, and regional parties as serious threats.

His economic policy was intended to tackle these problems.
He liberalised in order to induce economic growth which would
yield increased revenues, so that governments would have greater
financial resources with which to meet important needs that the
private sector would not address. If more adequately resourced
official agencies could become more effective, this would reduce the
role which his party would need to play. The ghastly condition of
Congress influenced his decision to liberalise.

His economic policy was also intended to re-focus political
debates and popular preoccupations on economic issues—on
growth, but more crucially on development. This posed risks. Higher
growth rates and thus greater state revenues might not materialise
quickly enough to earn his party electoral benefits, but he saw no
promising alternative.

He knew that the issues of growth and development were
more mundane and less emotive than caste, religious or regional
issues. But he welcomed this because another of his basic aims
was to de-dramatise politics, which in his view had become too
inflamed for the good of the country and of his party. The more
heated politics became, the less able a centrist party like Congress
would be to compete with parties to its left (stressing preferment
for disadvantaged castes) and its right (stressing Hindu nationalism).
He knew that he was uninspiring on public platforms, but he

---

[1]This section, and much of what follows on Narasimha Rao's period
in power (1991–96), is based on extensive discussions with him during early
February 1992, when he was prime minister.

intentionally cultivated a low-key approach in order to damp down both popular excitement and expectations of the government and the ruling party. He sought to turn his inability to excite into a virtue.

Avoiding Confrontation

To cool politics down, Narasimha Rao sought systematically to avoid confrontation and conflict with other parties and important interests. This was apparent in his approach to every important issue, including liberalisation.

After an initial flurry of liberalising measures to reassure external actors, he carefully proceeded at a deliberate pace, allowing breathing space after each change, to permit tempers to cool before the next step was taken. He picked off diverse interests who were losers in this process, one at a time. After introducing a change which caused pain to one group, he would leave them alone for awhile before going further. He then took another modest step that affected another interest group, and then another. And so it went on, incrementally and cautiously—to prevent diverse interests from uniting in opposition to liberalisation—but relentlessly.

This frustrated neo-liberals. They complained about the excruciatingly slow pace of the process. They wanted dramatic action to achieve macro-systemic change. Narasimha Rao refused to comply—because he sought to avoid confrontation, but also because he was *no neo-liberal*.

As he stated flatly, 'my model is not Margaret Thatcher, but Willy Brandt.... I do not believe in trickle-down economics'.[2] He sought not to give market forces an unfettered role, but to enable them to operate within limits set by the state—so that they would generate wealth which would yield greater government revenues. State agencies would be cautiously withdrawn from areas in which they were unable to perform to society's advantage. But the enhanced revenues which he anticipated would prove *enabling* to the state—as they had done in countries led by social democrats like Brandt. Government would become more capable of playing

[2]Interview, New Delhi, 11 February 1992.

a redistributive role, and of doing more in areas where the private sector was disinclined to operate—in many development sectors and in poverty reduction. These ideas were anathema to Thatcher. Narasimha Rao was a social democrat—a liberaliser who stood on the centre-*left*.

There were also things that he did *not* do. He avoided cuts in the huge government subsidies on many goods. He knew that many subsidies which were said to help the poor disproportionately benefited prosperous groups (something that the Left parties refuse to acknowledge). If they had been cut, funds could have been liberated for genuine poverty programmes. But he took no action—to avoid politically unwise confrontations with prosperous interests. Second, he took little action to promote the closure of loss making public enterprises, and none to make it easier to dismiss workers—because 'I do not have the right to deprive people of their jobs'. He stated this, unusually, with palpable heat—he firmly believed it. This was the first time in a generation that a national leader of Congress had spoken of *moral* constraints on his right to take action.[3] Times had changed.

Two quite different ideas inspired inaction on these two fronts. On the first, he held back because it was politically risky, and on the second out of conviction. His management of liberalisation was guided by a mixture of Machiavellian calculations and moral judgements.[4]

Neither Narasimha Rao nor Manmohan Singh was/is a neo-liberal—contrary to the views of many today. The only genuine neo-liberal to hold high office in India since 1991 is P. Chidambaram. But he has been held tightly in check by the prime ministers throughout this period—except for a few weeks in early 1997 when he was

---

[3]Manmohan Singh then echoed and still echoes that sentiment.

[4]It is worth adding that at no time during several long and complex discussions, did the prime minister offer a single remark that was inconsistent with a highly sophisticated view of what his approach to the economy (and everything else) should be. This writer has interviewed hundreds of politicians in South Asia, but he has never encountered an intellectual *tour de force* of the kind offered by Narasimha Rao.

allowed to introduce numerous market-friendly measures. In that short spell, he arguably liberalised more than BJP-led governments did in six years between 1998 and 2004. But note that he was set loose by a *non*-Congress Prime Minister, H. D. Deve Gowda. (That episode, like Narasimha Rao's liberalising, demonstrates that politicians who make economic policy often operate with greater autonomy from social forces than some analysts believe.)

Narasimha Rao's strong determination to avoid confrontation in this and other spheres, in order to de-dramatise politics, was intended to serve the party's interests. He sought to sustain the capacity of the Congress to cultivate support from a broad array of interests—something that was threatened by strident Hindu nationalism, regional parties and the 'backward castes' issue. But he also sought to revive the social democratic strand of the Congress tradition. The party might cultivate support from prosperous, high status groups, but it also needed to respond to disadvantaged groups. In his view, it had to do so for both Machiavellian and moralistic reasons—because non-elite groups had more votes, and because this was the just approach.

He largely declined to explain his liberalising actions, lest that touch off avoidable controversy. He refused to explain himself even to his own party. During visits to Maharashtra and Karnataka in early 1992, this writer found that no state-level cabinet minister in the Congress in either state understood the prime minister's economic liberalisation project—except one junior minister in Karnataka who had studied economics at Cambridge. Next to no one outside major corporations and banks, and academic circles in both states, understood the aims or implications of the changes.[5]

So, did the Congress Party somehow cause economic liberalisation to occur after 1991? The answer is complicated. The party, as a collective entity, did not decide to liberalise. That was done by Narasimha Rao with crucial advice from Manmohan Singh. But in another sense, Congress can be said to have 'contributed' to the

---

[5]The main exceptions were a handful of learned journalists whose writings on the subject were largely ignored, and certain figures in the Left parties which were insignificant in both states.

decision. The dire condition of its organisation—which undermined its capacity to respond effectively to emergent threats—helped persuade Narasimha Rao to liberalise, in order to shift popular attention to other issues which might prove more advantageous to Congress.

The bewilderment within the Congress Party about liberalisation suited Narasimha Rao. He reckoned—shrewdly—that he would get further with it if public debate was limited and confused. He was pursuing what Rob Jenkins later called 'reform by stealth'.[6] He believed that the minimisation of confrontation best served the interests not just of liberalisation, but also of his government and party.

Let us consider the threats to Congress posed by appeals to the 'backward castes', aggressive Hindu nationalism, and regional parties. On close examination, the first two (but not the third) turn out to be less dangerous to Congress than we might expect.

Congress and the 'Backward Castes' Issue

The dangers posed by the 'backward castes' issue have been somewhat exaggerated, for five reasons.

The issue lacks evocative power in many states because those groups' interests were addressed before 1990, and/or because other issues have predominated. One or both of these things is/are true in the following states: all of South India, Goa, Maharashtra, Gujarat, Madhya Pradesh, Chhattisgarh, Rajasthan, Orissa, West Bengal, Jammu and Kashmir—plus much of Uttaranchal and most of the Northeast. Those states contain over 60 per cent of India's population. So in all-India terms, the potency of this issue has been overstated.

Before 1990, while in some states opposition parties mobilised the 'backward castes', in others it was Congress itself which

---

[6]R. Jenkins, *Democratic Politics and Economic Reform in India* (Cambridge University Press, Cambridge and New York, 1999).

did so.[7] So the issue is not an unmitigated threat to Congress, although it has had greater difficulty attracting 'backward caste' support since the issue became salient in 1990.

No long-standing Congress principle restrains it from embracing the 'backward castes'. That issue differs from Hindu chauvinism. To flirt with the latter is to defy party traditions.

The issue of *reservations* for 'backward castes' has, at times, proved to be narrow and thus politically counter-productive. In 1990, it dramatically signalled the progressive intentions of V. P. Singh's government. But especially when disputes arose among different 'backward' groups over benefits, the issue became a distraction from the more fundamental need for redistribution and poverty reduction. When Congress has taken significant steps to address those broader issues—as it did after assuming power in New Delhi in 2004—the evocative power of reservations has diminished.

The use of the 'backward castes' category has not consistently yielded electoral benefits to parties that champion those groups' interests. The 'backward castes' have often failed to remain a solid vote bank—they have fallen out with one another and with other disadvantaged groups whose votes are also needed to win elections—*Dalits*, *Adivasis* and (to a degree) Muslims.

Thus, the political utility of the 'backward castes' issue is more limited than many believe. So is the threat that it poses to Congress. As we see in section 4, regional parties have forced Congress to govern at the national level in a far less domineering manner than before 1990. Among them are parties stressing the 'backward caste' issue—but in only three of India's states.[8]

---

[7]This was true, for example, in Maharashtra and Karnataka. The latter story is told in great detail in E. Raghavan and J. Manor, *Broadening and Deepening Democracy: Political Innovation in Karnataka* (Routledge, New Delhi and London, 2009).

[8]See the list of regional parties in Part 4. The three states are Bihar, Tamil Nadu and Uttar Pradesh.

Congress and Assertive Hindu Nationalism

The threat to Congress from assertive Hindu nationalism is somewhat greater—but *only* somewhat. Two topics arise here: accusations that Congress leaders have unwisely resorted to 'soft *Hindutva*', and a problem that afflicts the Hindu right.

At times, Congress leaders have responded to Hindu nationalism *either* by giving ground to it[9] *or* with actions (or inaction) which underplay their opposition to it. In recent times, Congress timidity in opposing Hindu chauvinism was evident in the 2007 Gujarat state election when its leaders offered few challenges to the anti-Muslim extremism of the BJP government there, and in the decision of the Maharashtra government which Congress led to ignore the findings of the Srikrishna report into violence against Muslims.

So there is substance in the accusations that Congress has been 'soft' on *Hindutva*, but they have also been exaggerated. Consider two examples. Some argue that Prime Minister Narasimha Rao played too passive a role in the run-up to the destruction of the Babri Masjid at Ayodhya in 1992 because he secretly sympathised with the vandals who were responsible—in a state ruled by the BJP. In this writer's discussions with Narasimha Rao, before and after Ayodhya, his deep distaste for Hindu chauvinism was vividly apparent.

There is a better explanation for his passivity in 1992. He sought to avoid confrontation not just on economic liberalisation, but also in dealing with Hindu nationalists. On three occasions in early 1992, this writer asked him, 'is it not possible that a time will come when actions by Hindu militants will compel you to draw the line and confront them?' Narasimha Rao consistently refused to accept this. 'Confrontation', he said, 'leaves too much bitterness behind'. He was intensely—indeed, excessively—preoccupied with that idea.

His dismay over the confrontational habits of his Congress predecessors was unstated but obvious. Both his temperament and his position atop a minority government inspired an inordinate

---

[9]See Niraja Gopal Jayal's comments on pp. 23–25 of A. Ayres and P. Oldenburg (eds), *India Briefing: Takeoff at Last?* (New York: Asia Society/ M.E. Sharpe, 2005).

commitment to accommodation.[10] His tentative approach to the Ayodhya issue was explained by naivete—not covert sympathy with Hindu extremism.

The second exaggeration is the allegation that Digvijay Singh empathised with *Hindutva* when he was Congress chief minister of Madhya Pradesh. But instead of appeasing Hindu nationalists, he was seeking to out-manoeuvre them. He wrote to BJP Prime Minister Vajpayee complaining that the Central government was doing too little to address cow protection. This was a ploy. He wanted to be able to refer to this protest on public platforms (as he subsequently did) to prevent the BJP from using Hindu nationalist themes against him. We wanted to force them to attack him on development issues—*his* ground—and he succeeded.[11]

His firm opposition to Hindu chauvinism became obvious from his response to an attempt by a fire-breathing Hindu bigot who entered Madhya Pradesh to foment anti-Muslim sentiment. Singh promptly had the man jailed in a district town. The extremist professed delight at this, since he expected large crowds to gather to demand his release. None did so. After a few days of waiting, the would-be agitator meekly yielded and left the state. Digvijay Singh's hard line in this instance was not the action of a timid appeaser of extremism.

At times, Congress leaders have actually pursued 'soft' *Hindutva*, but we must also recognise that some accusations levelled against them are inaccurate. Let us now turn to a problem which besets the Hindu right, which undermines the threat that it poses to Congress.

First, to capture and retain power in New Delhi after 1998, it had to shelve virtually its entire Hindu nationalist agenda—because all

[10]These comments are based on interviews with Narasimha Rao in early February, 1992.

[11]At the December 2003 state election, that was the ground on which the BJP was forced to campaign. He lost not because he had a poor record on development, and not because of his alleged 'soft *Hindutva*', but for other reasons. J. Manor, 'The Congress Defeat in Madhya Pradesh', *Seminar*, February 2004.

but one of the twenty-three parties in its coalition opposed it. This exasperated Hindu extremists. One claimed that it was imposing a Muslim theocratic state! The BJP has nudged the political centre slightly towards the religious right. But thus far, Hindu chauvinism has had little appeal in national—or, except in Gujarat, at state—elections. Indeed, it is *dis*advantageous. The BJP de-emphasised Hindu extremism during state election campaigns in Madhya Pradesh (2003 and 2008), Uttar Pradesh (2007) and Karnataka (2008) and at the 2009 parliamentary election—to avoid damage.

Except in Gujarat, Congress has not been seriously menaced by aggressive Hindu nationalism. Elsewhere, the BJP has defeated Congress only when it has adopted moderate postures. Hindu extremism is no unstoppable force.

Congress and Regional Parties

Congress has suffered more at the hands of regional parties which have gained ground in many states over the last 20 years than from the 'backward caste' issue or aggressive Hindu nationalism. The term 'regional parties' here includes both explicitly and *de facto* regional parties. Until those latter parties—which claim to be national in character—can attract strong support across many states, it is appropriate to treat them as 'regional'.

If we consider regional parties of significance, some—but only six of sixteen—have stressed 'backward caste' issues, and only one (the Shiv Sena in Maharashtra) has pursued Hindu chauvinism. Most have pursued neither. (The parties in the list marked with asterisks have at times developed cooperative relations with Congress.)[12]

---

[12]Very small states, including all northeastern states—except Assam because of its greater size—have been excluded.

Stressing 'backward caste' Interests	Not Stressing Them
*Rashtriya Janata Dal (Bihar)	*Nat'list Congress Party
*Dravida Munnetra Kazhagam	(Maharashtra)
(Tamil Nadu)	Shiv Sena (Maharashtra)
*AIADMK (Tamil Nadu)	Biju Janata Dal (Orissa)
*Samajwadi Party	Telugu Desam Party
(Uttar Pradesh)	(Andhra Pradesh)
*Janata Dal-S (Bihar but not	*CPI-M (Kerala)
Karnataka)	*CPI-M (Tripura)
Janata Dal-U (Bihar but not	*CPI-M (West Bengal)
Karnataka)	*Trinamool Congress
	(West Bengal)
	*Asom Gana Parishad (Assam)
	*Lok Janshakti Party (Bihar)
	Bahujan Samaj Party
	(Uttar Pradesh)
	*Akali Dal (Punjab)
	Indian National Lok Dal
	(Haryana)
	*National Conference (J&K)
	*J&K People's Democratic
	Party (J&K)

Most of the parties listed above have weakened Congress as an all-India party. Congress has struggled to regain ground from most. They therefore represent a greater threat to it than the 'backward caste' issue or aggressive Hindu nationalism.

When Congress is confronted by a strong regional party in an individual state, it often begins to resemble its main adversary. There are a few exceptions to this generalisation. The most vivid is in West Bengal where, when it was confronted by the supremely well organised Communist Party of India-Marxist (CPI-M), it degenerated into an embarrassing rabble.[13] But when it faced the

---

[13]Other exceptions include three states where Congress has been marginalised: Bihar, Tamil Nadu and Uttar Pradesh. Still another is Maharashtra where Congress does not seek to plunder the exchequer and

same party in Kerala, Congress developed a solid organisation like the CPI-M's which has kept it competitive in a bi-polar system.

In Andhra Pradesh—where its main opponent has, since 1983, been the Telugu Desam Party (TDP) which has always been dominated by a single figure—Congress Chief Minister Y. S. Rajashekhara Reddy after 2004 assumed similar overweening authority over his party. And so it goes on. This tendency means that 'Congress' assumes very different forms in different states. This has been true since the 1980s[14], but it should perhaps trouble the national Congress leaders.

Finally, it is worth noting that when Congress loses substantial ground at the state level to regional parties, it eventually becomes weak enough to make it a non-threatening coalition partner for some regional parties. This tends to occur when it becomes the third or fourth strongest party in a fragmented party system—or when (as in Maharashtra) a four-party system develops.[15]

Efforts to Regenerate the Congress Organisation

By 1990, the Congress organisation—which once had both sinew and reach—had degenerated severely. This was mainly the result of Indira Gandhi's abandonment of intra-party democracy, her systematic undermining of the party organisation in the interests of personal rule—and then of Rajiv Gandhi's inconsistent management of party affairs. The weakness of the Congress organisation invited and facilitated challenges on the 'backward caste' issue, from the Hindu right, and from regional parties.

Once those challenges emerged, perceptive Congress leaders— and there have always been some in key posts—saw that the

---

practice systematic extortion as the BJP/Shiv Sena government of the 1990s did. But the predominant pattern is for Congress to come to resemble its adversaries.

[14]See chapter five of this book.

[15]This argument was first made in E. Sridharan, 'Electoral Coalitions in the 2004 General Elections: Theory and Evidence', *Economic and Political Weekly*, 18–24 December 2004. Swaminathan Aiyar made this case in the *Times of India*, 13 July 2008.

organisation required regeneration. Narasimha Rao had known the Congress in better days—before 1970—when it had been a democratic institution and a formidable political machine capable of cultivating broad popular support. He saw the degeneration as alarming.

He therefore tried to rebuild it. He knew that this would be difficult and would require several years. He knew that serious factional infighting had reached epidemic proportions long before 1990. He specifically recalled one grotesque example in 1985 when Congress members gathered in Mumbai to celebrate the party's centenary.

Separate trains from West Bengal arrived simultaneously—each carrying members of a different faction within that state's Congress which were at daggers drawn. As they marched across Mumbai, they spotted one another on opposite sides of a park. The importance of the centenary was forgotten and they threw themselves into a violent, embarrassing melee.[16]

Narasimha Rao saw the root cause of degeneration as the abandonment of intra-party democracy. He sought to re-introduce elections, every two years, to fill all party posts. He knew that the early elections would be untidy, but he believed that eventually, incapable figures would be marginalised and regeneration would occur. He saw this as 'the only realistic way to revive the organisation'.[17]

Rajiv Gandhi had announced plans to hold elections on fourteen occasions,[18] but none occurred in his time. Narasimha Rao was more determined and in 1993, an election was held. It was a disaster. Factional conflict soared. Massive sums were committed to vote buying, and voters' lists grew bloated with phoney names. Violence between Congress factions was widespread. In some cases, Congressmen murdered Congressmen, and there was even

[16]Interview with P. V. Narasimha Rao, New Delhi, 11 February 1992.

[17]His arguments were nearly identical to those made to this writer in the mid-1980s by Myron Weiner. (As far as I know, Weiner never put these ideas into print.) But Narasimha Rao said that he was unaware of Weiner's views in the matter. Interview, 11 February 1992.

[18]This figure is based on the monitoring of such announcements by A. G. Noorani and this writer.

an instance of Congressman *biting* Congressman. He eventually concluded that no further elections should take place. This was a deeply difficult moment for him, and it left him rudderless as party leader. He soon reverted to sly machinations which did him and the party no good.[19]

Readers of euphoric reports in the Indian and international media after the re-election of a Congress-led alliance in the 2009 national election might conclude that this problem has been solved. Commentators claimed that Rahul Gandhi, son of Rajiv and Sonia, had rejuvenated Congress and Parliament, attracted the youth vote and rebuilt the party organisation. All three claims are false. The new Parliament was the fifth oldest of the 15 since 1952, younger people voted less often for Congress and its allies than did their elders in 2009,[20] and Congress strategists—including Rahul Gandhi himself—agreed that organisational reconstruction had not yet occurred.[21]

Not *yet*. Rahul Gandhi is determined that it should happen. But the immensity of the challenge becomes clear when we consider what he has achieved so far, and what (in mid-2009) he planned to do next. He has held genuine elections within the Youth Congress. But these only occurred in two small states, Punjab and Uttarakhand which contain 3.2 per cent of India's population. He attempted an election in Gujarat but was thwarted. He planned to extend this process to all states by 2014. But that meant that democracy will have to be restored only to a minor front organisation—and only after a further five years.

In theory, the Congress Party already holds periodic elections for all offices, but party organisers consistently concede that these are

[19]I am grateful to Sanjay Ruparelia for stressing this last point.

[20]This is based on data from the post-poll survey of the Centre for the Study of Developing Societies (CSDS). I am grateful to K. C. Suri for assistance on this issue.

[21]Interviews with Congress strategists from Uttar Pradesh, Madhya Pradesh, Andhra Pradesh and Karnataka in New Delhi, Hyderabad and Bangalore between 19 May and 3 June 2009. Rahul Gandhi was not interviewed, but it was apparent that he decided not to accept a ministerial post and to focus on regenerating the party because he knew that that task had not been completed.

fictitious. Close advisors and observers of Sonia Gandhi indicate that she knows this—since she has expressed scepticism about whether genuine elections, which she favours, are feasible.[22] Redemocratising Congress will be exceedingly difficult.

Rahul Gandhi also recognises that the party's habit of choosing election candidates at the last minute has given opponents, who select theirs well in advance, a valuable head start. He has therefore insisted that candidates be named as much as a year in advance—a process which began after the 2009 national election. (In state elections thereafter, this did not occur; nor has it occurred prior to the national election of 2014.)

He favours a shrewd change in the structure of the Congress. Units of the party at lower levels have always conformed to *administrative* units (districts and sub-districts) and not to *electoral* arenas (parliamentary constituencies, state assembly constituencies). This made sense when Congress was dominant, since it enabled the party to exert pressure on bureaucrats at lower levels. But this has prevented it from concentrating its energies on winning electoral contests. The proposed change will facilitate that. (In early 2014, this had not occurred.)

Rahul Gandhi has also lent support to a strategy which can earn Congress popularity and strengthen its organisation in places where rival parties govern—mounting protests against parties in power. Until recently, this approach had rarely been adopted. But it has considerable promise. Consider two examples.

In Andhra Pradesh in the late 1980s, the Telugu Desam Party (TDP) held power. The leader of the state Congress, Chenna Reddy, selected issues on which the TDP had become unpopular and cajoled Congress members from rival factions to launch protests against these injustices. Since the TDP was always quick to resort to police action, many Congress protestors were swiftly jailed. This gained Congress public sympathy. It weeded out unreliables from the organisation since they declined to risk incarceration. And when members of warring factions were incarcerated together,

---

[22]These comments are based on interviews with four Congress strategists and two leading journalists, New Delhi, January and June 2009.

many of their suspicions of one another dissolved. Chenna Reddy was adopting a device which produced similar results before independence—*satyagraha*.[23] Congress won the ensuing state election.

More recently, Digvijay Singh who oversaw the Congress organisation in Bihar asked party activists to divide the state into small segments, to conduct social audits in each to identify popular resentments, and then to mount protests on those issues. He personally led agitations in certain localities, to shame others into action. By mounting protests, Congress appeared to be good for something (a departure from before), and party members were drawn together in constructive action (another astonishing change for them).[24]

The use of protests while in opposition can help revive the organisation, image and prospects of Congress. Rahul Gandhi proposes to adopt this approach more widely. Indeed, he began during the 2009 national election campaign by joining a *dharna*[25] in Jhansi—a seat which Congress then won. He has more recently backed a search within various states for what one colleague describes as 'street fighters'. This term does not imply that violence will be used, but rather that the party will now support leaders who are prepared to mount challenges in the streets to governments headed by rival parties.[26] If this approach is widely adopted, it will begin to regenerate the Congress organisation. (However, by early 2014, it had seldom been used.)

That strategy holds far greater promise than a second option, the deployment of the alleged 'charisma' of members of the Gandhi family. Some media reports claimed that Rahul and Sonia Gandhi had excited mass enthusiasm at the 2009 national election, but interviews with reliable observers on the ground in areas where

---

[23]Interview with Chenna Reddy, Hyderabad, 2 April 1990.

[24]Interview with Digvijay Singh, New Delhi, 11 July 2007.

[25]A *dharna* is a protest, often involving fasting, which demands action to correct a perceived injustice.

[26]This section is based on interviews with Congress strategists in New Delhi in November 2008, and in January and June, 2009.

they addressed rallies contradict this.[27] The limited potential of this option was vividly apparent during the Uttar Pradesh state election of 2007, when Rahul Gandhi played the pivotal role in the Congress campaign. The party was embarrassed when its vote share declined from the previous election, from 8.9 per cent to 8.6 per cent. Rahul's own popularity increased during the campaign, but only from 5 per cent to 7 per cent. He was less popular than his party.[28]

One last approach offers greater promise, and has been adopted by Sonia Gandhi in recent years. It entails efforts to negotiate and to enforce from above, uneasy unity among squabbling Congress factions at the state level. Serious factionalism at that level is an enduring legacy of the Indira Gandhi years, when infighting was systematically fomented to undermine regional leaders.

Sonia Gandhi has supported efforts to forge unity within the party, of the kind which occurred before state elections in Madhya Pradesh (1993), Karnataka (1999) and Andhra Pradesh (2004). Two processes must run simultaneously. Serious efforts at sinking factional differences must occur, and faction leaders must be *seen* to be doing this—as they were, for example, during the 1999 Karnataka election campaign when all major Congress figures boarded the same bus and toured the state—demonstrating unity and propelling the party to victory. When Congress governments are formed in various states, Sonia Gandhi lends solid support to her chief ministers. She tells delegations of dissidents to back their chief ministers until she acts—which she has almost never done. This helps to quell squabbling, even though in nearly all states, factional tensions remain. The management of the Congress has changed for the better, but the composition of the Congress has not, and still gives cause for deep concern.

If Rahul Gandhi succeeds in making protests a widespread practice, the composition of the party will begin to change.

[27]This is based on interviews with over thirty perceptive political activists, civil society leaders and analytical journalists from Maharashtra, Madhya Pradesh, Uttar Pradesh, Andhra Pradesh and Karnataka in May and June 2009.

[28]Interview with Yogendra Yadav, Delhi, 20 July 2007.

Unreliables will find the rigours of street demonstrations and possibly jail too much to bear—and they will be marginalised. But at this writing, this is only an idea, and it will be difficult to implement.

The Role of—and the Systemic Need for—Dynastic Rule within Congress

Members of the Nehru-Gandhi family have loomed large atop the Congress since independence. Narasimha Rao's attempt to reintroduce intra-party elections in 1993 was intended to give party structures more substance as *institutions* at a time when it appeared that the *personal* ascendancy of family members might not be restored. But then Sonia Gandhi emerged, the pre-eminence of the family was re-established, and Rahul Gandhi's more recent rise to prominence brings a fourth generation into play.

The family is commonly described as a 'dynasty'. That term is accurate in physiological terms, but it is misleading in terms of politics, party management, and policy. On all three fronts, there were radical differences between Nehru's approach and that of Indira and Rajiv Gandhi. But astonishingly, it has lately become apparent that the approach of Sonia and Rahul Gandhi differs markedly from that of Indira and Rajiv. They have substantially reverted to something close to Nehruvian ways. Congress activists and leaders find it impossible, even dangerous to acknowledge this, but it is true.

Nehru sought to strengthen democratic institutions within India's new political system after independence, and to sustain democracy within Congress which had prevailed since 1919 when Mahatma Gandhi introduced it. As result, he yielded to regional elites within the party on key issues, despite his disagreement. He was also a social democrat who believed that the government should strive to promote social justice. Indira Gandhi differed from her father on both issues. She abandoned intra-party democracy and filled all important posts from above. She also undermined democratic institutions more generally, in the pursuit of personal rule. And while she won her first major election victory in 1971 by promising to 'abolish poverty', she did little to translate the slogan into reality.

Sonia Gandhi emerged as a leader at a time when the inability of any single party to win a parliamentary majority had triggered a massive dispersal of power away from the once-dominant PMO—horizontally to other institutions at the national level, and downward to the state level. She has done little to recentralise power. Even in states which Congress governs, she has left the chief ministers largely undisturbed—like Nehru, but unlike Indira Gandhi. And lately, she and especially Rahul have shown an interest in rebuilding and redemocratising the Congress organisation. Finally, since 2004, she has presided over the creation or expansion of an array of programmes which seek to benefit poor people,[29] spending on which exceeded \$57 billion under the Congress-led alliance between 2004 and 2009—with similar amounts disbursed thereafter. On all of these fronts, Sonia and Rahul Gandhi have operated in the manner of Nehru, and in striking contrast to Indira Gandhi.

On another key issue, however, Sonia Gandhi's view is identical to Indira Gandhi's. The predominance of the 'dynasty' must be sustained. Nehru would have viewed this with the same contempt that he exhibited towards the princely order. For him, the hereditary principle was patently unsuited to a democratic republic.

All systems of dynastic rule are liable to change, since much depends on the capabilities and predilections of successive rulers. This is apparent from the marked differences between the approaches of Nehru and Indira Gandhi, and now in the substantial revival of Nehruvian strategies by Sonia and Rahul Gandhi. Devotees of the 'dynasty' should consider what might have happened had Indira Gandhi been succeeded by her son Sanjay whose harebrained schemes during the Emergency earned Congress a humiliating defeat at the 1977 election, and whose unbridled behaviour posed a grave threat to democratic institutions.

[29]They include the National Rural Employment Guarantee Scheme (NREGS), Bharat Nirman, Sarva Shiksha Abhiyan (SSA), the Mid-day Meal Scheme, the National Rural Health Mission (NRHM), the Total Sanitation Campaign, Integrated Child Development Services (ICDS), the Jawaharlal Nehru National Urban Renewal Mission (JNNURM), and Polio Eradication.

The dominance of the 'dynasty' persists because there is a *systemic need* within Congress for it. Factional conflict was thoroughly institutionalised within the party under Indira and Rajiv Gandhi. The latter sometimes complained about it,[30] but many of his actions encouraged it. Narasimha Rao's abortive attempt to use intra-party elections to overcome it showed how deep the rot had gone. Because factionalism is rife, the party desperately needs an unquestioned, autocratic arbiter atop the organisation whose rulings will be meekly accepted by contending forces.

But while Congress needs the 'dynasty', it is also imperilled by it. If hereditary rule is essential to maintaining order within the party, it has proved damaging and it poses serious risks.

Consider the damage. Dynamic regional leaders whose ambitions have been blighted by dynastic dominance have left Congress in dismay. Sharad Pawar in Maharashtra and Mamata Banerjee in West Bengal are key examples. Their importance was apparent from Congress' dependence upon them as allies, for its survival in power in New Delhi since 2004 and for its future prospects. The requirement that Rahul Gandhi succeed his mother has also proved damaging. Congress chief ministers may have suffered little interference from Sonia Gandhi, but their achievements are seriously under-played, lest they appear to rival Rahul.

There are also future risks. What if a hereditary ruler turns out to be incompetent, destructive or unpopular? What if Sonia and Rahul Gandhi, like Rajiv Gandhi before them, suddenly become unhappy with their strategies, reverse themselves in mid-course, and alienate important interests?

The pathologies that afflict Congress—especially factionalism, partly concealed by the order imposed from on high, but a seething reality everywhere—and the dubious remedy of dynastic rule, may not prove terminal. The party may muddle along for many years

---

[30]For example, he once lamented the infighting in his party by telling the story of '... a merchant who exported crabs packed in uncovered tins without any loss or damage, to the amazement of the importer. The Indian crabs, he explained, pulled one another down and prevented them from moving up!' *The Hindu*, 11 February 1990.

yet. But its fortunes depend dangerously—for compelling systemic reasons—upon a single bloodline.

Congress Today

How might Congress muddle along for some time yet? Rahul Gandhi's proposed changes in the party offer some hope of organisational revival, but the decay runs so deep that he may make only limited headway—and in any case, it will take a long time. Congress will struggle to emerge from obscurity in several hugely important states. In several states where it remains strong, its main rivals are regional parties which it therefore cannot include in alliances needed to win national elections. It may be unable to prevent rival parties at the state level from poaching the credit for constructive programmes it initiates from New Delhi.[31] It relies on the hereditary principle which is inherently unreliable over the long term.

How can a party that faces such difficulties hope to remain a major force? The answer lies in the difficulties and incapacities of its adversaries, and certain other things. Congress benefits from the tendencies of the 'backward castes' to come into conflict with other disadvantaged groups and to fragment—so that they cannot become a sustainable anti-Congress force.

Its principal adversary, the BJP, faces immense problems. Its Hindu nationalist agenda has generated popular enthusiasm either for very limited periods (as in the six months after the destruction of the Babri Masjid[32]) or in limited areas, notably Gujarat. Its complicity in the anti Muslim pogrom in that state produced a state election victory in 2002, but deep and lasting suspicion throughout India.

---

[31]Surveys by the CSDS have found that in some states, Congress at the national level received most of the credit for the massive NREGS while in others, parties opposed to Congress which headed state governments were given credit.

[32]This writer argued—to widespread disbelief—that its effects would be highly temporary just before the destruction occurred, in *The Independent*, 8 December 1992.

Outbursts of bigotry and violence have (thus far) had little staying power as devices for inspiring mass support.

Its party organisation lacks the capacity to penetrate below the district level.[33] Its national election campaigns in 2004 and 2009 were both inept. The generation which must now lead the party lacks promising figures. One potential future leader, Narendra Modi, would make the BJP's already difficult task of attracting parties to its alliance extremely difficult.

The regional parties which oppose Congress at the state level also face daunting problems. Taken collectively, they pose a greater threat to Congress than does the BJP. But they can seldom be 'taken collectively'—they cannot develop collective coherence, as their disarray at the 2009 election demonstrated. A few leant towards the BJP, others towards an unconvincing 'third front', and still others towards a fourth front. And nearly all regional parties lack the organisational capacity to penetrate effectively to the local level.[34]

With adversaries like that, Congress does not need immense strength. We have here a contest among parties which all suffer serious disabilities.

Two other things help Congress. First, if one party is perceived as the main villain in the political drama, others will combine against it—often with devastating results. Congress has been so restrained at the national level since 2004, and so helpful to its allies—one source close to the prime minister complained that 'it gives them whatever they want'[35]—that it has avoided this. And as long as Modi looms large, the BJP will appear the more nefarious national party.

Second, not just the 'backward castes' but other social blocs which have sometimes opposed Congress tend to disintegrate over time. That happens because Indian voters tend strongly to shift their

---

[33]This is discussed in more detail in chapter seven of this book.

[34]The great exception to this is the Communist Party of India-Marxist (CPI-M), but it is strong only in three states. The DMK in Tamil Nadu retains some penetrative capacity. The TDP in Andhra Pradesh sought with limited success to acquire this capacity between 1995 and 2004, but its organisation has since degenerated somewhat.

[35]Interview, New Delhi, 11 July 2007.

preoccupations from one of the huge number of identities available to them to another, and then another—often and with great fluidity.[36] They do not fasten permanently and ferociously on one identity—as in Sri Lanka. This prevents tension and conflict from building up along a single fault line in society. That hurts parties that seek to fix voters' attention on one fault line. The main losers are the Left which focuses on class divisions and the BJP which focuses on the division between Hindus and others. This fluidity benefits parties whose lack of ideology enables them to shift their emphases as the popular mood swings—like Congress.

When Congress took power in New Delhi in 2004, its strategists were concerned about disenchantment among disadvantaged groups who had been largely left behind by liberalisation and growth. Congress analysts recognised that their victory in the 2004 general election had not—as the media claimed—been the result of a revolt by the rural poor against liberalisation and globalisation. They saw that Congress had gained a higher proportion of votes in urban than in rural areas. And they saw that in (for example) Haryana and Punjab—two adjacent states with similar numbers of poor people in similar circumstances—the Congress and its allies won impressively in one and were crushed in the other. Such things could not have happened if the rural poor had actually revolted. It was a myth.

But Congress leaders chose not to challenge it. It was a useful misperception, since it made Congress and its allies appear to be more humane than their opponents. Their 2004 government sought to cultivate support from a diverse array of interests. It was able to provide substantial benefits to prosperous groups as a result of a spectacular rise in government revenues after 2003. But it also proceeded as if the myth were true, by committing even more massive resources to new initiatives for small farmers, the rural poor and near-poor who have great numerical strength. The steep increase in revenues meant that Narasimha Rao's social democratic

---

[36]For more detail, see chapter eight of this book. Recent survey data collected by *Lokniti* in Delhi indicate no diminution in this tendency.

hope that growth would enhance state resources and capacity had been realised.[37]

The result is an impressive array of initiatives—some of which made a potent impact. But it is important to stress that the party's leaders sought to make their main impact through *government programmes* rather than through the *Congress organisation*. They recognised that, given its weakness, the organisation could not play a constructive role. One senior advisor to Congress recently said that the only thing most of that party's members know how to do is to shout 'Sonia Gandhi Zindabad'. A leading Congress strategist toured India in 2007 and found that the condition of the organisation was 'terrible, terrible'. When a political scientist visited various party offices across Uttar Pradesh during the 2007 election campaign there, he found BSP activists brimming with ardour. He saw that at least half of the BJP activists were working flat out because 'in their guts' they were burning with spite towards the minorities. But in Congress offices, he found 'only listlessness—cronies and relatives of candidates, and political pimps'. When he told party leaders in New Delhi of this, they agreed that it was an accurate description.[38] It is thus logical that Congress leaders should have relied not on the party but on government programmes.

[37]The comments above are based on extensive interviews with key strategists—on terms of anonymity—close to Manmohan Singh and Sonia Gandhi in New Delhi in July 2007, November 2008 and May and June 2009.

[38]These comments are based on interviews in New Delhi in July 2007.

— *s e v e n* —

In Part, a Myth
The BJP's Organisational Strength

This paper appeared in 2005, after the defeat of the BJP at the national election the previous year, and long before its return to power in New Delhi in 2014. It explains that while the party has a stronger (and more democratic) organisation than nearly all of its rivals, its strength has one important limitation. It lacks the capacity to penetrate effectively into rural areas where elections are won and lost. It carried that disability into the election in 2014—when its victory owed more to an innovative and extremely effective campaign strategy, to the efforts of Hindu nationalist sister organisations, and (not least) to mass discontent with the ruling United Progressive Alliance (UPA).

I n 1999, a visitor called at the offices of three political parties in Patna. Bihar's State Assembly was in session, so he expected the parties' headquarters to be more active than usual.

He first went to the Congress Party office. It was open, but not a single person was present during the hour that he waited there. Then went to the office of the state's (then) ruling party, the Rashtriya Janata Dal (RJD). Here one man was present, but sound asleep on a mat on the floor.

Then he moved on to the office of the BJP. More than a dozen people were busily conferring, writing and talking on the telephone. When they were asked about the party's activities in the state, they provided an extremely cogent, detailed explanation of their clearly defined roles, and the organisational structure within the state headquarters. Then the visitor asked about how well the organisation extended out into various districts and beyond, to rural areas where most voters live. The answers became rather tentative and vague. He was told—thrice—that 'we are a cadre-based party'. But little more of substance was provided. This seemed odd, but the vibrant scene at the BJP office offered such a stark contrast to the other two that he saw little reason to question a widely held belief. This is the notion that in Bihar and most other Indian states, the BJP has a stronger organisation than its rivals—a penetrative structure, consisting of full-time activists or cadres,[1] which is capable of reaching down effectively below the district level into sub-district and local arenas.

Its allegedly strong organisation is sometimes seen as a factor that can help the party to compensate for other problems that it faces. Three of these are especially important. The first is the failure of the Hindu nationalist agenda to attract broad popular support— across India generally, and in most individual states. The second is the rather poor performance of many of its chief ministers atop

---

[1]Christophe Jaffrelot has explicitly described the BJP as 'a cadre-based party' in 'BJP and the Challenge of Factionalism in Madhya Pradesh', in T. B. Hansen and C. Jaffrelot, *The BJP and the Compulsions of Politics in India* (Oxford University Press, Delhi, 1998), pp. 267–90. This chapter argues that such claims tend strongly to be over-stated. Jaffrelot also states, convincingly, that divisions within the BJP should be seen as 'groupism' rather than 'factionalism'—because the latter word implies struggles *between individuals to whom local activists pay allegiance*' (the emphasis is Jaffrelot's). He contrasts the BJP's cadre-based character with that of other 'aggregative parties' which cash in on the influence of local politicians and notables, although he rightly notes that the BJP has become somewhat more aggregative in recent years (pp. 275–76).

state governments. The third is its difficulty in winning popular support across much of eastern and southern India.

But is its organisation actually all that strong? Despite the initial impression from those visits to party offices in Patna, the BJP organisation in Bihar is actually rather weak when one looks beyond the capital and certain other urban pockets. Later investigations revealed that in Madhya Pradesh—where the BJP looms larger than in Bihar, as one of the two main parties—its organisation again had few cadres and failed to penetrate into rural areas effectively.[2] And it has long been apparent that the BJP in Karnataka has a frail, poorly led organisation.

So let us look more closely at the strength of the BJP organisation in a number of important states. It turns out that in a large number of states, the BJP is weaker, less well led, and penetrates less effectively into rural areas where elections are won and lost than is normally supposed. In many, it has a solid organisation in some urban enclaves—but only *some*—and in a few eccentric rural pockets. Indeed—most astonishingly of all—in many (and probably most) states, its organisation is weaker than that of at least one other party, *even where* other parties also have insubstantial organisations. This chapter sets out evidence on these issues, and then considers some of the implications of this—for the BJP, for other parties, and for democracy and communal accommodation in India.

It should be stressed that this study is exploratory and does not purport to be definitive. It is intended as an invitation to others to examine these matters in greater depth. Such studies are badly needed because the BJP's organisation has received remarkably little attention in recent years. Analysts have concentrated instead on the party's strategies, its discourse, the images that it projects, its leaders, its social base, its share of the votes in various elections, its outreach to groups that have not traditionally supported it, the tension between pragmatism and purity—among other issues. All of these things are important, and several of them bear directly on

---

[2]This comment is based on visits to the state in 2002 and (twice) in 2003.

its organisation. However, so far we have heard surprisingly little about the BJP organisation *per se*.[3]

The Type of Organisational Weakness Analysed Here

This chapter concentrates on one particular aspect of the BJP's organisation. It questions the widespread notion that the party has a cadre-based structure that is capable of penetrating into sub-district and local arenas across rural India. It does not argue that the party's organisation is weak *in general*. In certain other—but in electoral terms, less important—ways, its organisation tends to be strong in many parts of India. The idea that its organisation is strong is in part a myth, but *only* in part. Let us consider some of its genuine strengths.

The BJP's internal processes are more genuinely democratic and institutionalised than are those of most other parties in India. The degree of institutionalisation is, however, sometimes overstated. Its organisation is also comparatively well disciplined—although we need to be clear about the kind of discipline we are discussing. Certain kinds of indiscipline have at times loomed large in recent years. In Madhya Pradesh, for example, conflicts developed over the award of tickets for the state election of 1993. Two years later, internal party elections could not be held there because 'tensions were so acute'. In 1997, party elections were delayed in places owing to 'intense infighting' which, in Bhopal District, led to violent clashes.[4] Then, as the 1998 Lok Sabha election approached, violence over nominations within the BJP's state headquarters office reportedly led to over 50 people being hospitalised.[5] That is serious indiscipline, even by the sorry standards of the Congress Party.

---

[3]For example, most of the contributors to the most wide-ranging recent assessment of the BJP in several states (who include this writer) tend to deal with the party's organisation by implication or barely at all. Hansen and Jaffrelot, *The BJP and the Compulsions of Politics in India*.

[4]Ibid., pp. 278, 284 and 288.

[5]Interview with reporters at the *Hindustan Times*, Bhopal, 6 December 2003.

In some other respects, though, discipline within the BJP has remained impressive. Its organisation is more capable than those of most other parties of maintaining control over what may be politely termed 'fundraising'. It manages this in a more centralised and disciplined manner, in order to provide more resources for the party and less to individuals. For instance, one well-informed source in Madhya Pradesh explained that in the Congress, fundraising and profiteering are decentralised—leaders at the state level 'loot, but share the loot' with party colleagues at lower levels. 'In the BJP, that is not allowed. Certain key figures in a state government, at high levels but not at the top, are in charge of it. The party retains most of the money.'[6]

The BJP is also remarkably effective at persuading its state-level units to accede to instructions from national leaders. But as we shall see, this strength is also one source of its weakness as a penetrative force.

Finally, the BJP's organisation is also harder to break than are other parties. The 'breaking' of party organisations—that is, the process by which party's members are induced to defect to other parties—has been a significant theme in recent years in several states. The BJP has suffered from this at least once—in Chhattisgarh after Ajit Jogi became chief minister in 2003—but that was an unusual instance. The difficulty in breaking the BJP organisation was apparent in late 2003, particularly in Uttar Pradesh, when Chief Minister Mulayam Singh Yadav managed to break other parties to secure his majority in the state assembly, but not the BJP.

As Jaffrelot shows, there are two main reasons that the BJP is difficult to break. First, people who have left the party tend strongly *not* to flourish outside it. Second, and more importantly, it deploys people with Rashtriya Swayamsevak Sangh (RSS) backgrounds as *sangathan mantri's* (organising secretaries). They form the core within the organisation, and maintain more coherence than is found

[6]Interview with a famously incorruptible legislator, Bhopal, 16 December 2003.

in most other parties—although that coherence has diminished in recent years.[7]

It should be stressed, however, that this writer's research in Madhya Pradesh in early 2003 indicated that by then, the BJP did not possess such an organisational presence at the *local* level across most of that state. Two things may explain this. First, the 'dense network' may not have extended as far as party leaders would have wished, and over time, it may have decayed—partly as a result of groupism. Second, many RSS activists in Madhya Pradesh had cooled in their enthusiasm for the BJP, because they were dismayed by said groupism and by the national leaders' de-emphasis of the Hindu nationalist agenda since the mid-1990s. It is plausible to assume that similar things have happened in a number of other states.

So, to reiterate, this discussion deals with just one type of organisational weakness. This is the BJP's failure in most parts of India to develop cadre-based structures that are able to penetrate effectively into sub-district and local arenas in rural areas—*where election outcomes in almost all states are decided*. This weakness leaves the party with a limited capacity to convey messages from the national and state levels to important interests, and to deliver goods and services to them. It also makes it difficult for the party to convey information upward about the concerns, preferences and problems of interest groups. So it damages not only the electoral prospects of the BJP, but also the party's capacity to govern effectively and responsively when it takes power at the state or national level.

Before we turn to a state-by-state discussion of the BJP's organisation, it is necessary to comment briefly on one specific issue—the degree to which it is justified to speak of the BJP and the RSS as distinct entities. We sometimes hear it said—in the Indian press and in some academic analyses—either that these two bodies are one and the same, or that the RSS controls the BJP. There is no doubt that there is some overlap between the two organisations. Many people in the BJP organisation are currently members of the RSS, or have had close ties to it in the past. And the BJP often seeks

[7]Hansen and Jaffrelot, *The BJP and the Compulsions of Politics in India*, pp. 269–72.

proactively to insert RSS operatives at key points in its organisation, or at times even to draw RSS cadres *en masse* into its activities. But it is a mistake to claim either that these two organisations are identical and interchangeable, or that the RSS controls the BJP. It has exercised considerable influence over the BJP at certain times, and in certain places. But its influence varies greatly from time to time and place to place, and it almost always falls well short of outright 'control'. This is apparent from the research of many leading authorities on Hindu nationalism and from this writer's studies of politics in several states over the last decade.[8]

Organisational Weakness—State by State

Let us begin with the regions in which the BJP is weakest: the south and the east. In two southern states—Tamil Nadu and Kerala—the BJP's organisation is decidedly frail. In Tamil Nadu, party-building has progressed less far than in the other three southern states. It has only a tenuous reach beyond a limited number of urban pockets. In Kerala, the RSS is solidly established in certain urban centres and some sub-regions, but the BJP *per se* has far less strength. As its new leading mobiliser in Kerala recently said, 'The BJP (has) had a negligible presence in the state's polarised polity'.[9] In both these states, the party has never won a significant share of the popular vote.

In the other two southern states, it has at times attracted substantial numbers of votes—9 per cent in Andhra Pradesh at the state election in 1999 and 28.8 per cent in the 1991 parliamentary election in Karnataka—although nothing approaching that on most other occasions. (The BJP has gained a greater share of both votes and seats in Karnataka since this analysis appeared in 2005, but the

[8]Those states are Haryana, Uttar Pradesh, Bihar, Orissa, Rajasthan, Madhya Pradesh, Chhattisgarh, Andhra Pradesh, Tamil Nadu, Karnataka and Kerala.

[9]This was Krishna Kumar, former Congress minister in the Central government, who defected to the BJP and was assigned the task of building the party in Kerala. *The Hindu*, 12 October 2003.

penetrative power of its organisation outside some urban centres and below the district level has not increased.)

In Andhra Pradesh, the BJP's electoral alliance with the Telugu Desam Party (TDP) at the 1999 state election did not yield benefits that could facilitate organisation building. The ruling party starved it of advantages. After a membership drive in 2001–02, the BJP managed to develop networks of activists in most cities and in a small minority of rural arenas. But the TDP refused to permit it to contest elections from those areas in 1999, and a similar pattern prevailed in 2004. The state-level unit of the BJP initially declared itself in favour of statehood for the Telangana sub-region, in order to enhance its popularity and organisation-building efforts there. But the party's national leaders then compelled it to abandon that posture—in part because it was inconvenient to the TDP. This undermined the standing of the BJP in Telangana and damaged morale within the state unit more widely. It thus remains a rather marginal force in Andhra Pradesh, albeit one whose vote share may exceed the difference between those of the TDP and its main rival, the Congress Party (as it did at the 1999 state assembly election). (The BJP has experienced ups and downs in Andhra Pradesh and Telangana since this study first appeared, but the penetrative capacity of its organisation has not been enhanced.)

Until the 2004 state assembly election in Karnataka, the BJP played a marginal role there.[10] At times, it *appeared* to be reasonably strong. It was the official opposition for a brief period after the 1994 state election, and again after the 1999 state election. Despite this, other opposition parties—the Congress between 1994 and 1999 and the Janata Dal from 1999 to 2004—were far more plausible alternatives to the ruling parties than was the BJP.

Thus, at the 1999 state assembly election, the Congress— which had been badly mauled in terms of seats at the previous state election, but which had an organisation of far greater substance, reach and penetrative power than the BJP—swept back to power

[10]Much greater detail is provided in J. Manor, 'Southern Discomfort: The BJP in Karnataka', in Hansen and Jaffrelot, *The BJP and the Compulsions of Politics in India*, pp. 163–201.

on the basis of popular disenchantment with the Janata Dal. The BJP's national leaders forced the state-level unit of the party into an illogical, last minute alliance with the Janata Dal. That contributed to the scale of the Congress victory. However, no serious analyst should believe that if the BJP had been free to oppose the Janata Dal in 1999, it would have had a chance at capturing power. Its organisation was, and is, too weak—concentrated in urban areas and eccentric rural pockets—most notably Coorg (Kodagu) and the two coastal districts. It has also been incompetently led at the state level for over two decades, which has undermined organisation building.

The BJP ceased to be a marginal force at the Karnataka state assembly election of 2004. It gained the largest number of seats in a hung assembly, although it still came second to the Congress in total votes received. It was then denied the chance to govern by the formation of a coalition between the Congress and the Janata Dal-Secular (JD-S). On close examination, this improved performance turns out to owe little to the organisational strength of the BJP. Indeed, it still lacks penetrative capacity in nearly all rural areas of the state. Its gains at that election are mainly explained by its success in winning support from Lingayats in *part* of northern Karnataka—in Bombay Karnataka—something that it accomplished despite this organisational weakness. It should also be noted that the BJP failed to win many seats in the *other* northern sub-region, Hyderabad Karnataka, because the JD-S captured most of the anti-Congress vote there *despite* a rather frail organisation.

The decision of the other two parties in Karnataka—both of which have more penetrative organisations than the BJP—to form a coalition government in May 2004, following the state assembly election, will probably qualify as an historic miscalculation that will enable the BJP to take power at the next state assembly election. By combining, they leave the BJP as the only alternative available to disgruntled voters if they govern poorly. The early evidence of infighting within the governing coalition strongly suggests that they will indeed govern badly. The Congress and the JD-S would have been better advised to permit the BJP to form a minority government, and then to have thwarted most of their initiatives by using their majority in the state assembly. They could then have won a subsequent state assembly election by arguing that the BJP had provided wretched government, but short-term calculations blinded the leaders of those two parties to this opportunity. The main point to stress, however, is that both the BJP's rise in Karnataka and the likelihood that it will form the next government there do not imply that its organisation is capable of penetrating into rural arenas. It is weaker in that connection than either of the other two parties in the state.[11]

Let us now turn to the eastern states. In Bihar, the picture is somewhat brighter for the BJP. Over the last 15 years, it has made some headway in developing its organisation, so that it is no longer dominated—as it was in the 1980s—by urban trading castes. During the 1990s, the party attracted activists from a wider array of upper caste groups. This enabled it to capture much of the old upper caste base of the Congress, and to penetrate into rural areas across much of the state. Activists' relative inexperience still limits its impact, but the RSS (which is especially strong in tribal areas), and the informal higher caste networks of BJP operatives, compensate somewhat for this deficiency.[12]

When we turn to Orissa, we encounter the kind of dismal situation for the BJP that it faces across most of the south. In that state, the BJP formed an alliance at the last state election with the Biju Janata Dal (BJD), and they governed the state in a coalition led by the latter party thereafter. But the BJP's efforts since 1999 to strengthen its badly under-developed organisation have been damaged by its association with a ramshackle ally led by a capricious Chief Minister, Naveen Patnaik. So the BJP organisation in Orissa remains quite insubstantial.

One study Gillan of the 1998 Lok Sabha elections in West Bengal initially provides rather surprising news—namely, that 'the BJP has improved its once insignificant organisational base to the extent that it has a party structure in place *throughout all localities* of the

---

[11]These comments are based on interviews with activists from all three parties, and with analysts, in Bangalore, 7–14 May 2004.

[12]I am grateful to Shaibal Gupta for these points.

state'.[13] But a careful reading of what follows indicates that, however extensive this organisation was, it lacked efficacy. It amounted to 'an organisational foothold' which enabled the party to gain only 'a limited following in a number of districts, particularly in the border areas of the state'. Although the BJP won one seat at the 1998 Lok Sabha election West Bengal—its first—it could not be said to have 'built up to the victory ... by means of consistent organisational and electoral growth'. Instead, Gillan argues, 'the BJP vote share (in that constituency) has fluctuated over several elections'. The party's organisation also exercised a rather tenuous hold over its activists, given 'the frequent instances over the last ten years of party workers moving between' the BJP and Congress.[14] So in West Bengal once again, the party's organisation appears to lack the capacity to penetrate effectively below the district level.

Let us now turn to northern, central and western India, where the BJP has long had greater organisational strength and electoral success. As state elections approached in Rajasthan and Madhya Pradesh in late 2003, the BJP's organisation was seen by many analysts to be so incapable of penetrating below the district level that it could only win if it drew RSS cadres into the campaign. It was not just independent observers who took this view. The national leaders of the BJP agreed, and decided to sideline the party's traditional leaders at the state level, and thus much of its organisation.[15] Relative outsiders were projected as the pre-eminent figures in the campaigns. Senior party operatives from New Delhi were inserted as the campaign coordinators. A senior RSS leader in Madhya Pradesh told a journalist that the party's organisation 'was in a messy state', so that from mid-2002, 'the RSS took over the reins of the election'[16]—as it did in Rajasthan (and apparently Chhattisgarh).

[13]M. Gillan, 'BJP in 1998 Lok Sabha Elections in West Bengal: Transformation of Opposition Parties', *Economic and Political Weekly*, 5–12 September 1998, pp. 2391–95 (emphasis added).

[14]Ibid., pp. 2392 and 2395.

[15]Interview with Amitabh Singh, Bhopal, 8 December 2003.

[16]*Hindustan Times*, 6 December 2003. The quotations are from the reporters' summary of the interviewee's words.

Large numbers of RSS activists from other states were also brought in, so that these states witnessed RSS campaigns, rather than BJP campaigns. In all three cases, they succeeded in ousting incumbent Congress governments.[17] The case of Rajasthan deserves a little more comment. How do we explain the failure of the BJP to develop a penetrative organisation there? The party there was long dominated by one adroit leader—Bhairon Singh Shekhawat—twice chief minister of the state (see chapter twelve of this book). Both in government and in opposition, he succeeded in maintaining his pre-eminence within the BJP by pursuing two main strategies, neither of which lent itself to the construction of a penetrative party organisation.

First, he cultivated cordial personal ties to leading figures (and even to individual legislators) in other parties. This minimised resistance to his initiatives, and helped him to maintain his image as a moderate. To lend credence to this image, he needed to play down communal issues. That impelled him to remain somewhat aloof from the efforts of RSS activists at the grassroots, especially among tribals—efforts which bore political fruit, especially at the 2003 state assembly election, after Shekhawat had left state politics. He also restrained himself and BJP activists from organisation building in rural areas—partly because a strong, penetrative organisation would threaten his personal pre-eminence, and partly because it would alarm politicians in other parties with whom he had developed congenial ties that served him well.

Second, within the BJP, Shekhawat projected his influence through highly *personalised* networks. He selected individual members of the party who were close to him and helped them to develop political bases within various sub-regions of the state. Some of these people developed networks that enabled them to make their influence penetrate downward in rural areas, but these tended

[17]On Madhya Pradesh, see J. Manor, 'The Congress Defeat in Madhya Pradesh', *Seminar* (February 2004), pp. 18–23. A close reading of press reports from Rajasthan and Chhattisgarh indicates that similar things happened in all three states.

to be personal structures with the BJP label attached to them, rather than the other way round.[18]

The available evidence on Uttar Pradesh is limited, and we badly need further research on this crucial state. It is clear that in some parts of the state, the BJP possesses some penetrative capacity. For example, in the area around Agra, it has greater strength than in the neighbouring districts of Madhya Pradesh.[19] The same appears to be true in some, but not most other parts of Uttar Pradesh. But the dependence of the BJP upon the influence of certain caste leaders—not least Kalyan Singh—indicates that the party's organisational strength in rural parts falls well short of what it requires.

In Punjab, the BJP organisation is reliably seen to be less strong than in several other northern states, for example, Madhya Pradesh where it is distinctly weak. The party in Punjab is largely dependent on RSS cadres during election campaigns. It is strong mainly in urban areas, but it also has modest strength in the Majha region (Gurdaspur and Amritsar districts) and in the Doaba regions between the Sutlej and Beas rivers. It has only a few pockets of strength in the state's largest region, Malwa. Its electoral prospects depend on whether or not it has an alliance with the Akali Dal.[20]

In Haryana, the BJP organisation is in a shambles. It has never been a cadre-based party with a wide network. It was captured right from the beginning by what is called pejoratively 'the GT Road party' (that is, by Punjabi refugees who settled close to the Grand Trunk Road that passes through Haryana). As a result, the party never developed a strong organisational presence among the local Haryanvis and was confined to Punjabi pockets, mainly in urban areas. Whatever strength it has is on loan from the RSS.[21]

[18]I am grateful to Rob Jenkins and Sanjeev Srivastava for evidence on Rajasthan.

[19]I am grateful to Rob Jenkins for this observation. It was corroborated in an interview with Digvijay Singh, former Congress chief minister of Madhya Pradesh, New Delhi, 15 May 2004.

[20]I am grateful to Harish Puri for this information.

[21]I am grateful to Yogendra Yadav for these insights.

In Gujarat, the behind-the-scenes influence of Narendra Modi, while Keshubhai Patel was chief minister after 1995, caused a split in the BJP organisation into RSS and non-RSS factions.[22] Modi's subsequent takeover of the BJP government in the state and his centralised style made the BJP popular without bolstering the party's organisational substance.

In quite recent times in rural Maharashtra, the BJP has missed significant opportunities to acquire the penetrative capacity that it has always lacked in most parts of the state. When it governed during the late 1990s, it was mainly its coalition partner, the Shiv Sena that made inroads into the influential sugar cooperatives in western Maharashtra which had long been a Congress stronghold. This was done, in part, by changing the boundaries of zones within which cooperatives can deliver their produce to sugar mills. That required very visible action by the state government, so the process was plainly known to BJP leaders there. But they did far less than the Shiv Sena to follow up with efforts to insert their own loyalists into the cooperatives. The BJP may have been somewhat complacent in this connection because it believed that the RSS possessed that capability, in some parts of the state.[23]

It is also worth briefly considering the BJP's organisational problems in comparative context. In how many significant states do other parties have stronger, more penetrative organisations than the BJP? The answer is 'in a very large number'.

This is, not surprisingly, true in the four states where other parties have quite strong or very strong organisations. In West Bengal, the CPM's organisation is very strong. In Kerala, the CPM is less formidable than in West Bengal, but still quite strong.[24] In Andhra Pradesh, the TDP under Chandrababu Naidu after 1995

[22]G. Shah, 'The BJP's Riddle in Gujarat: Caste, Factionalism and *Hindutva*', in Hansen and Jaffrelot, *The BJP and the Compulsions of Politics in India*, p. 262.

[23]I am grateful to Rob Jenkins for this evidence from Maharashtra.

[24]This comment is based on T. J. Nossiter's comparisons of the CPI-M in these two states, and on discussions with numerous specialists in the politics of the two states.

developed a solid, penetrative organisation that is undoubtedly quite strong.[25] In Tamil Nadu, the DMK has an organisation that is still surprisingly (after many years in the wilderness) strong. The BJP organisation in these states is much weaker than those of these four parties.

But when we look further afield, to states without strong parties, it is remarkable how often the BJP comes off second best, compared to its rivals. Indeed, in several states, it is weaker than not one but two other parties. In Karnataka, it is clearly less strong (at present and at all times in the past) than the Congress, and at most times over the last 20 years, than the Janata Party/Janata Dal. It is also certainly weaker than two other parties in Orissa, Haryana, Punjab and Tamil Nadu. To say that it has less penetrative capacity than the wretched BJD in Orissa, the chaotic AIADMK in Tamil Nadu, or the severely faction-ridden Congress state unit in Andhra Pradesh[26]—is to point to serious difficulties.

The BJP's position, in comparative terms, is more encouraging in Bihar. One party has a stronger organisation, but it is the Communist Party of India-Marxist Leninist (CPI-ML) which plays little part in electoral politics. The BJP there has a superior organisation to that of the Congress which, according to Shaibal Gupta, 'is in very bad shape', and to the ruling RJD of Laloo Prasad Yadav. The RJD, argues Gupta, 'is really without any organisation', but it compensates with its strong, informal networks among disadvantaged castes and Muslims.[27] (This chapter was written before the emergence of Nitish Kumar in Bihar.)

If we consider states that have something close to two-party systems, in which the BJP is one of the two parties, the picture that emerges is only somewhat brighter for the party. In Madhya Pradesh over the last ten years, the Congress has had a rather weak organisation, but it has consistently had more substance and reach

[25]I am grateful to Benjamin Powis and K. Srinivasulu for insights on this topic.

[26]For an example of divisions within the Andhra Pradesh Congress (a very old story), see *The Hindu*, 6 January 2004.

[27]This again is based on comments by Shaibal Gupta.

than the BJP. The same is true across most of Rajasthan. If the BJP organisation is on level terms with that of Congress in Chhattisgarh, this is not saying much since the latter has been greatly damaged by former Chief Minister Ajit Jogi's breathtakingly unwise over-centralisation of power while in office in the period before the 2003 state election. (Since this chapter appeared, the BJP has gained much greater strength in Madhya Pradesh and Chhattisgarh.)

This leaves only a small number of states where the BJP's organisation is (or at times has been) stronger than its rivals. In Delhi, for example, the BJP—unusually—has a reasonably strong organisation. However, we would expect that in a predominantly urban arena. It is compatible with the argument set out so far.

The BJP's National Leaders and the Problem of Organisational Weakness

One last question is worth considering here. How aware are the BJP's national leaders of the kind of organisational weakness discussed here: their party's lack of penetrative capacity? We have clear evidence that *at times*, they have recognised this and taken action to remedy the problem. This was apparent during the state assembly election campaigns in Rajasthan, Madhya Pradesh and possibly Chhattisgarh in late 2003. They systematically marginalised the old-line leadership of the party in these states, parachuted in alternative leaders and organisers, and took pains to draw RSS cadres into the fray.

But that is not the whole story. At other times, their actions have done further damage to already weak organisations at the state level—to promote good relations with regional parties in the interests of building coalitions that can yield majorities in the Lok Sabha. We have seen that this has happened in Karnataka and Andhra Pradesh, and it may have occurred in Orissa, Bihar and elsewhere. The compulsions of alliance-building have taken precedence over the strengthening of the BJP's organisation. Similarly, national-level politics have taken precedence over the BJP's interests at the state level.

That may be a rational decision by the BJP's senior leaders, and does not imply a failure to recognise organisational weakness at the state level. It does not call their competence into question. But something else does. In some states, they have persisted for exceedingly long periods with state-level leaders who are unimaginative and sorely lacking in political skills. This has, for example, long been true in Karnataka—the party's most promising state in the whole of the east and the south. In that state, the BJP's national leaders have given control of the party unit to a man (B. S. Yeddyurappa) who is inept, autocratic and either unwilling or unable to engage in organisation building.[28] Cases like that—and there are others—raise questions about whether the party's national leadership has at times allowed itself to be deceived by the myth that the BJP has a cadre-based organisation with penetrative capacity.

This chapter has argued that the BJP's organisation is weaker than many people believe in at least one important respect. In most Indian states, it lacks a cadre-based structure that can penetrate below the district level. Its organisation is reasonably strong in several other respects, although these strengths do not entirely compensate for this particular weakness. For example, the BJP is able to ensure that state-level units comply with instructions from the national level. This helps the party to develop coalitions at the national level, but it undermines the credibility and organisational strength of the BJP in some important states. Moreover, the BJP organisation is harder to break than are other parties. That is important, but it does little to make it more capable of winning elections or of governing effectively once elected.

Organisational discipline enables the BJP to raise funds in a more efficient and centralised manner than other parties—funds are for the party rather than for individual profiteers. This again is helpful to the BJP, but money does not suffice to win most elections. If it did, then more incumbent state governments—which almost always have more money than their challengers—would have been re-elected over the last 30 years.

[28]For a later analysis of the results, see J. Manor, 'The Trouble with Yeddyurappa', *Economic and Political Weekly*, 26 March 2011, pp. 16–19.

The BJP can call upon an auxiliary force, the RSS—the like of which is available to no other party—to help win elections at the state level when incumbent parties other than the BJP are vulnerable. This occurred in December 2003 in Madhya Pradesh, Rajasthan and Chhattisgarh. Nevertheless, there are limitations to the advantage that this provides to the BJP. The RSS cannot help to unseat incumbent governments that are not vulnerable—as we saw in Delhi on that same occasion. In many states, (especially, but not only in the east and the south) the RSS lacks the strength to ensure election victories.

We also need to ask whether the RSS can help the BJP, once it is elected in such states, to govern more effectively and responsively. Will it help the BJP to gain re-election in such places? The answers are unclear, but there are good reasons to doubt the utility of the RSS on both fronts. It is worth recalling the sole occasion on which a BJP government at the state level was re-elected (before 2003) thanks to its record on governance and development—Rajasthan in 1993. The RSS played little role there. The explanation had much more to do with the skills of Chief Minister Shekhawat and with the imaginative programmes that he and his team had created. There is no evidence that the RSS can assist in generating and implementing such programmes.

So even though the BJP's organisation is weak only *in part*, the part in question is vitally important both in winning elections and in governing effectively, imaginatively and responsively once it takes power at the state level—and perhaps also at the national level.

— eight —

'ETHNICITY' AND POLITICS IN INDIA

This paper explains the problems that arise when one word, 'ethnicity', is used to discuss several quite different things which often cut across one another: linguistic, religious, caste and other identities. It was mainly written for readers outside India, but Indians may find some useful ideas here. Among them may be the emphasis on the fluidity and frequency with which Indians have shifted their preoccupations from one to another (and then another) of the many identities available to them. This habit, which shows no signs of abating, prevents tension and conflict from building up along a single fault line in society—as has happened, with ghastly results, in places like Sri Lanka. It also analyses leaders' management of various 'ethnic' or (more accurately) social conflicts, which sets the scene for the discussion in the following paper. The penultimate paragraph acquires greater importance in the wake of the 2014 national election.

To make sense of our world, we need words that can be applied to roughly comparable phenomena in diverse settings. 'Ethnicity' is one of these. It is indispensable if we are to discuss similar trends in very different places, but it is also unsatisfactory. By attaching this one word to quite varied things, we risk obliterating subtle and not-so-subtle differences between them. When it is used indiscriminately—as it often is—it can produce

PART III *Managing Political and Social forces*

more distortion than understanding. This article seeks to exploit the patent utility of the word while paying careful attention to its limitations.

There are particular problems in analysing 'ethnicity' in India, the most heterogeneous and complex society on earth. Indeed, that complexity makes it harder and more risky to apply this word there than almost anywhere else. The discussion below will show that the cavalier use of the term threatens to distort our understanding of variations not just between nations but within nations as well; but also that there is still plenty to be learned from an assessment of 'ethnicity' in India.

This chapter is divided into three parts. The first part briefly summarises the most useful mode of analysis in developing an understanding of 'ethnicity' in India and perhaps beyond. The second part applies this approach to the complex social and political realities of India. It begins by identifying and discussing a range of identities in India which may be described as 'ethnic', calling attention to their tendency to cut across one another. It then examines the remarkable fluidity with which Indians frequently shift their preoccupations from one to another of the many identities ('ethnic' and otherwise) that are available to them in this heterogeneous society. After a further section on the most important 'ethnic' identities in India— those based on religion and language—it considers the problem of 'ethnic' violence and, finally, post-modernist analyses of religious conflict there. The third part assesses the political management of ethnicity in India.

A Mode of Analysis Appropriate to India

Given the current popularity of the term 'ethnicity' in discussions of public affairs, it is surprising how many analysts of post-Independence India avoid using it. A few have wrestled seriously with it, but many more have been reluctant to confront the huge practical difficulties that arise when this term is applied to the subcontinent. Witness, for example, one study by Robert L. Hardgrave, Jr.[1] He was asked

[1] 'India: The Dilemmas of Diversity', *Journal of Democracy* (October 1993), pp. 54–68.

to contribute an analysis of India to a discussion of 'The Challenge of Ethnic Conflict' in diverse settings. His discomfort with the assignment is apparent from the fact that he makes use of the term at only two places in his essay and then rather gingerly. This is not to accuse him of timidity. There are, as we shall see, good reasons for his unease.

Given the complexities of India, one mode of analysis appears to be particularly helpful. It has been set out by Paul R. Brass, an India specialist, in a book on ethnicity in all contexts. Let us consider, rather briefly and simplistically, the main elements of his approach to social groups who share one or more of the following things: 'language, territory, religion, color, diet (or) dress'[2]—that is, to potential 'ethnic' groups.

Brass is an 'instrumentalist' rather than a 'primordialist'. He regards the formation of an ethnic identity among any such group, and (to go one long step further) the transformation of that identity into ethnic nationalism, as by no means inevitable. When either or both of these things happen, it is the result of (1) actions taken by elites within the group to promote the change(s) and (2) favourable conditions which arise from the broader political and economic (and, we might add, social) environments rather than from the cultural values of the ethnic groups in question. This implies that 'ethnic identity is itself a variable rather than a "fixed" or given disposition'. Brass also stresses 'the critical role of the relationships established between elites and the state', either as 'collaborators with [or] opponents of state authority and state intrusions into regions inhabited by distinctive ethnic groups'. In other words, he sees elite competition as an important force in shaping historical outcomes: 'Elites seeking to mobilize the ethnic group against its rivals or against the centralizing state strive to promote a congruence of a multiplicity of the group's symbols.... Elites seeking to challenge the authenticity of an ethnic group's claim for individuality will do the opposite....' This further implies that 'the process of ethnic identity formation

---

[2]P. R. Brass, *Ethnicity and Nationalism* (Sage Publications, London, New Delhi and Newbury Park, CA, 1989), p. 18.

and its transformation into nationalism is reversible'.[3] He accepts the insights in the well-known book *The Invention of Tradition*,[4] but he adds that when ethnic consciousness is crystallised, 'the community or nation created ... does not necessarily constitute an entirely new entity but one that has been transformed, whose boundaries have in some ways been widened, in others confined'.[5]

This approach seems to me to ring true. It offers a useful means of analysing both the Indian case, where 'ethnicity' has not become an unmanageable and deeply destructive force, and another—Sri Lanka—where it has wrought ghastly damage.[6] Brass's mode of analysis helps us to answer several key questions. Where and to what extent has the formation of ethnic consciousness, and perhaps even the further process of the transformation of such consciousness into ethnic nationalism, occurred in India? How often do we see something less dramatic: 'the mere persistence of ethnic differences in the population'?[7] Where ethnic consciousness has been formed and perhaps even transformed into ethnic nationalism, how durable have these changes been? Have they been undermined or even reversed over time?

Understanding 'Ethnicity' in India

Cross-cutting 'Ethnic' Identities

When used in the Indian context, the term 'ethnic' can imply at least five quite different types of identities.

1. *Identities grounded in religion*: This usage refers mainly to Hindus (roughly 82 per cent of the population), Muslims (12 per cent) and Sikhs (2 per cent). They are not separate *racial* groups. For example, many Indian Muslims are descended from converts

[3]Ibid., pp. 13–17.
[4]E. J. Hobsbawm and T. O. Ranger (eds), *The Invention of Tradition* (Cambridge University Press, Cambridge, 1983).
[5]Brass, *Ethnicity and Nationalism*, p. 17.
[6]See J. Manor, *The Expedient Utopian: Bandaranaike and Ceylon* (Cambridge University Press, Cambridge, 1989).
[7]Brass, *Ethnicity and Nationalism*, p. 63.

from Hinduism, and many Sikhs and Hindus have long practised intermarriage.

2. *Identities grounded in language*: There are at least nine major languages in India as well as a huge number of minor ones.

3. *'Tribal' identities among adivasis or 'Scheduled Tribes'*: Adivasis are a difficult category to define. Put crudely, such people tend to stand outside or on the margins of Hindu society, inasmuch as they tend not to follow conventional Hindu religious practices, and many do not organise themselves into *jatis* (endogamous castes).

4. *'Tribal' identities among people in Himalayan or remote northeastern areas*: This usage refers to people who are racially distinct from the people of the Indian plains. In some northeastern states in India's federal system, single 'tribal' groups enjoy heavy numerical predominance. In others, 'tribal' minorities sometimes agitate for autonomy within or separation from their state.

5. *'Aryan' and 'Dravidian' identities*: Some early scholarly writings on India made much of the division of the subcontinent into two main clusters of linguistic groups: the Indo-European in the north, east and west, and the Dravidian in the south. Little has been heard of this classification over the last generation, for several good reasons—not least because it scarcely surfaces as the basis of a meaningful political identity. A regional movement in Tamil Nadu (but not in the other three Dravidian language regions) stressed it heavily until the 1960s, but even there it has largely fallen into disuse.[8] We therefore, set it aside during the rest of this discussion.

The first four of these types of identities can be assessed as 'ethnic' in character. But each is unlike all of the others, and each fits into Indian society and politics in a distinctive way. Types 1 and 2 are discussed in the section below on 'Religious and Linguistic Identities'. But the two types of 'tribal' identities (3 and 4) differ markedly from each other. These groups occupy areas that are spatially separate, and they therefore neither reinforce nor cut

[8]That is explained in chapter nine of this book.

across one another—indeed, they almost never encounter each other. Most of the 'tribals' in type 4 tend to be geographically cut off from most other Indians of any description. Most in type 3 live in discrete underdeveloped areas within states on the plains, but suffer incursions by non-'tribals' from their regions which are often exploitative in character.

When a group belonging to any of these four types is caught up in strife, it is possible to say that 'ethnic conflict' is occurring. But the groups themselves and the types of conflicts in which they become involved are so variegated that it is more confusing than enlightening to lump them together under a single label. The first three types of 'ethnic' consciousness listed above usually cut across and undermine one another. *Adivasis* (type 3) are found in greater or lesser numbers in most Indian states, and—insofar as they fix on their 'tribal' identities—they erode the solidarity of the regional linguistic group. The two most important of these 'ethnic' categories—religious and linguistic groups—almost always cut across one another and almost never (except in a few tiny northeastern states) reinforce one another.

In India, therefore, we tend not to find the kind of rough congruence between them that we find in Sri Lanka, where most Sinhalese are Buddhists, nearly all Buddhists are Sinhalese, most Tamils are Hindus and nearly all Hindus are Tamils. That is a very different story from that, say, of India's Punjab, where an 'ethnic' Sikh secession struggle arose. Nearly all Sikhs speak Punjabi, but a substantial minority of Indian Punjabis are Hindus. Many Sikhs also reside outside the Punjab, and other social cleavages—most notably caste—undermine solidarity among them. In the troubled Kashmir valley (although not in the larger state of Jammu and Kashmir which contains it) we see less a congruence of religious and linguistic identities than a religious group predominating very heavily in numerical terms within a discrete territory—so even that is not a good example of different types of 'ethnic' identity reinforcing one another.

Heterogeneity and Fluidity

The reference above to caste raises a further and very major issue. 'Ethnicity' in India runs up against two realities which undermine its potency and, especially, its staying power. The first of these is the unparalleled heterogeneity of Indian society. The second is the tendency of most people there to shift their preoccupations from one identity to another, frequently and with great fluidity.

Because Indian society is so heterogeneous, people there have a wide array of identities available to them. These include at least three different kinds of caste identities (*varna, jati*-cluster and *jati*), religious identities (including *sub*-identities: loyalties to sects within larger religious groups), and identifications with clans and lineages— as well as linguistic, class, gender, party, urban/rural, national, regional, sub-regional and local identities, and sometimes varying types of 'tribal' identities too. Most of these cannot be described as 'ethnic' identities and—as we have seen—those which can be often cut across one another. The crucial point is that Indians tend not to fix on anyone of these identities fiercely and permanently, as groups in places like Sri Lanka have done. They tend instead to shift their preoccupations, readily and often, from one identity to another, and then another, in response to changing circumstances. As a result, tensions do not become concentrated along a single fault-line in society, and do not produce prolonged and intractable conflict— 'ethnic' or otherwise—that might tear democratic institutions apart.

Religious and Linguistic Identities

Let us consider the two most important 'ethnic' identities—religious and linguistic. The frequent shifts in people's political and social preoccupations are bad news for the Hindu nationalist forces which seek to focus attention on divisions between Hindus and religious minorities, especially Muslims. They are also bad news for leftist parties that focus on class divisions. They also make it easier for parties near the centre of the political spectrum, which have vaguer ideologies, to gain popular support. They find it easier to shift their emphasis from one issue to another, in line with peoples' changing preoccupations.

We also need to understand that one of the main impediments confronting the Hindu right faces is, ironically, traditional Hinduism. Hinduism differs from the world's other great religious and cultural traditions in that it is not univocal: it is not focused upon a single sacred text and a single god or historical figure. Muslims look to the Qur'an, the Prophet Muhammad and Allah; Jews to the Torah and the God of Abraham and Isaac; Christians to the Bible, Christ and the Trinity; Confucians to the 'peerless sage of ten thousand generations'. By contrast, the Hindu sacred texts are numerous and varied, and Hindus worship a great variety of gods. Many village temples are devoted to one of the more prominent deities, but many also focus on divine figures that are known only locally. Different caste groups in the same locality may worship different gods. Different figures among the prominent deities attract popular devotion in different regions of India. A south Indian who visits Bengal on the day devoted to the goddess Saraswati will be astonished to find shops and offices closed and mass acts of worship in progress, since in the south, little heed is paid to this occasion. Bengalis visiting Bombay during the festival of the god Ganesh will be similarly surprised, for the same reasons.

Efforts by politicians on the Hindu right to make the god Ram the pre-eminent figure all across India have met with huge difficulties because of this diversity. In seeking to homogenise a tradition which is so heterogeneous, they are not appealing to traditional Hinduism, but seeking to transform it into something more like Islam or Christianity. They have a long way to go yet.

What of linguistic identities? Table 8.1 lists the languages that are spoken by over 25 million people, along with the names of the major states in which most residents speak them, moving from south to north.

Hindi is spoken by a large minority of the population, but efforts to make it a national language have not succeeded among the majority. English (which, after Hindi, is India's second official language) also helps to integrate the country; but since it is understood by only about 5 per cent of the population, it cannot perform this role adequately. Nor does India have a common written language like Chinese, which uses symbols rather than a phonetic script, enabling most of China's linguistic groups to communicate on paper. Indian languages have phonetic scripts, many of which differ radically.

TABLE 8.1:   Major Indian Languages and Corresponding States

Language	State
Tamil	Tamil Nadu
Malayalam	Kerala
Kannada	Karnataka
Telugu	Andhra Pradesh
Oriya	Orissa
Marathi	Maharashtra
Gujarati	Gujarat
Bengali	West Bengal
Hindi	Rajasthan, Madhya, Pradesh, Delhi, Uttar Pradesh, Bihar, Haryana

These variations have led some to say that India is not one country and that it is bound to break up. This has never been a serious possibility. Nehru shared some of these anxieties, and consequently resisted pressure from within his Congress Party in the 1950s to redraw the artificial boundaries between states which the British had imposed, to make them conform to divisions between linguistic regions. He feared that if all of the speakers of each separate language, such as Tamil or Gujarati were placed within a single state in the federal system, they might then become more inclined towards separatism. In the event he was unable to prevent the revision of boundaries; but after it happened, he realised that his fears had been groundless. Once the speakers of a single language were thrown together within a state, they discovered all of the things that divided them: caste, class, religious, sub-regional, urban/rural and other cleavages. So the regional solidarity which is necessary to fuel secessionism within individual states is unattainable because there is too much diversity within each region. While the great linguistic, cultural and other variations between states mean that the Indian federation is more loosely integrated than federations in more homogeneous countries like the United States or Australia, heterogeneity *within* individual states means that serious threats to break away seldom arise.

Several exceptions to this have, however, cropped up since the early 1980s, with secessionist movements emerging in a few small states—in tiny states in the north-east, in Punjab from 1983, and in Kashmir from the late 1980s onwards. As we shall see in chapter nine which follows, the Indian authorities have manageable (with the exception, so far, of Kashmir) to 'manage' these although in some cases, the excessive use of coercion has caused concern and left a legacy of bitterness.

To return, then, to our basic theme, the complex social divisions in India—religious, linguistic, caste, class, regional, etc.—produce a confusing picture which has led many commentators to argue that such complications will destroy Indian democracy. In fact, the opposite is actually true. Some of these many social divisions do on occasion reinforce each other. For example, conflict between lower and higher castes has strengthened class conflict between poorer and richer groups, some of the time. But usually these divisions have the opposite effect, cutting across and undermining each other. Conflict among castes subverts Hindu solidarity and makes Hindu-Muslim conflict less likely. Regional divisions undermine inter-regional alliances on religious and class lines. Caste, class and religious conflicts damage regional solidarity. Urban-rural rivalry weighs against most other types of conflict. The essential point here is that the complexity of Indian society tends to prevent tension and conflict from building up along a single fault-line in ways that might threaten national unity and the democratic process. So conflicts which have their roots in India's social and cultural diversity are unlikely to wreck democracy.

The Problem of 'Ethnic' Violence

Let us look carefully at patterns of violence in recent times. We often read that India's democracy is imperiled by a relentlessly rising tide of strife. However, much of this conflict is a sign of the vibrancy of Indian democracy—although it also poses problems for democracy—since it is triggered by demands for justice from disadvantaged groups who are responding to the logic of competitive politics.

The tiny number of meticulous analyses of this topic show that violence has waxed and waned quite markedly. For example, violence at the parliamentary election of 1989 was quite serious in certain regions, but it was less in evidence at the election of 1991 (despite the murder of Rajiv Gandhi by foreigners from Sri Lanka), and the numerous state elections between 1993 and 1995 witnessed little strife.

Similar patterns can be seen when we consider, more specifically, 'ethnic' violence. We have noted that there has been little violence in recent years between linguistic groups. If we consider violence between religious groups, we find radical variations from year to year. Philip Oldenburg has shown that at no time between 1964 and 1987 did either the number of communal incidents or the number of persons killed in them reach anything like the levels seen in 1962–63—not even during 1984, when Sikhs were massacred after the assassination of Indira Gandhi.[9] Since 1987 (the last year covered in his study), India has experienced severe Hindu-Muslim rioting in late 1990 and in late 1992 and early 1993. But the levels have been quite low during most of that period—between 1988 and mid-1990, from early 1991 until December 1992, and again since April 1993. The evidence from recent years does not add up to an inexorable march towards disaster.

These marked fluctuations in levels of religious violence are intimately connected to the fluidity with which people in India shift their preoccupations from one identity to another. During periods in which religious antagonism is whipped up, many people in areas of tension fix their attention on their religious identities. But time and again, it has been evident that this kind of antipathy has little staying power. When the excitement and violence wane, and fresh events call attention to other issues, most people's preoccupations shift to other identities which those issues affect. Hence, the recurring dramatic declines in levels of violence between religious groups.

[9] P. Oldenburg, 'Assessing State Activity at the Grassroots in India', paper presented at the Association of Asian Studies Conference, San Francisco, 1993.

We also need to maintain a sense of scale when we assess 'ethnic' conflict in India. Even if we add up the entire populations of all of the northeastern states (which have never all been alienated and disrupted simultaneously), the entire state of Jammu and Kashmir (some of which has largely been free of strife) and Punjab (which is now grudgingly reconciled to 'normal' politics) we arrive at a grand total of just 7.7 per cent of India's population. Those parts of India which have experienced persistent—although usually intermittent—'ethnic' conflict constitute a small and geographically marginal portion of the country.

Post-modernist Analyses of Religious Conflict

Finally let us consider post-modernist analyses of 'ethnic' conflict in India. Ashutosh Varshney has helpfully identified three main arguments advanced by post-modernists in this connection, in these words.

1. There is no 'scientific knowledge' ... about the (historical) origins, rise and spread of Hindu-Muslim antagonisms; rather, there have only been 'discourses' or 'narratives'. In the hands of the British, a primordial antagonism between Hindus and Muslims dating back centuries became the 'master narrative', even though there was evidence of Hindu-Muslim coexistence.

2. The master narrative has over time become the lens through which even small clashes between Hindus and Muslims have been interpreted.

3. It is impossible to establish the truth about what happened (during contemporary religious conflicts), about the cause and effect of communal violence. Indeed, facts and representations cannot be separated. The claim is not that facts don't exist, but that the most important facts necessary to make causal arguments simply cannot be culled from the morass of representations.[10]

---

[10]A. Varshney, 'Master Narratives, Local Narratives, and Communal Violence: Hindu–Muslim Relations in Two Indian Cities, Hyderabad and Lucknow', paper presented at the Association of Asian Studies Conference, Washington, 1995, pp. 4–5. The historians to whom he refers include

Like Varshney, I find much both to accept and to criticise in these arguments. It is true that most of the evidence that we have on religious conflicts—historical and recent—reaches us through 'narratives' which are coloured by unhelpful 'representations'. The 'master narrative', developed under British influence, contributes mightily to these distortions and patently under-emphasises plentiful evidence of Hindu-Muslim amity. It is thus perverse to expect to develop 'scientific' explanations of these episodes. However, one need not be a post-modernist to be sceptical of any claim to 'scientific' or indeed rigorous proof of anything when India's history, society and politics are being examined. Also, as the work of some of these post-modernist scholars itself demonstrates, some of the available evidence is reasonably reliable and makes it possible for us to develop highly plausible (although certainly not 'scientific') explanations of much that has occurred.[11]

Again, like Varshney, I do not accept that when people fix on religious identities, they are experiencing feelings that are somehow less authentic than their feelings at other times. As Varshney writes, although the British may have constructed the 'master narrative', 'the construction itself does not quite explain why the masses responded to it.' We do not have reliable grounds for categorising religious identities as less genuine than others. Nor do we have grounds for asserting that religious identities are more authentic than others, as both religious extremists and those who loathe them

---

Gyan Prakash, Nicholas Dirks and Gyanendra Pandey. Those involved in more contemporary political studies include Partha Chatterjee, Sudipta Kaviraj and Paul R. Brass, although they do not entirely fit the usual 'post-modernist' descriptions.

[11]See e.g., G. Pandey, *The Construction of Commmunalism in Colonial North India* (Oxford University Press, Delhi, 1990) and the account of Sri Lanka's 1958 riots in J. Manor, *The Expedient Utopian: Bandaranaike and Ceylon* (Cambridge University Press, Cambridge, 1989), pp. 284–97. The latter book, which appeared before the publication of the former, offers quite similar analyses of the emergence of 'ethnic' identities and conflict, although it is not an example of post-modernist scholarship.

sometimes suggest.[12] We do know from the evidence that at most times—thanks mainly to the fluidity discussed above—most Indians are mainly preoccupied with identities other than their religious (or any other 'ethnic') identities.[13] Varshney does not attempt—as this discussion and Oldenburg have done—to show that such cases (and periods of relative calm) are more common than cases in which people are intensely preoccupied with religious identities.

Managing 'Ethnicity' in India

In assessing the 'management' of ethnicity in India—a theme which is paralleled by the discussion of the management of Centre–state relations in chapter nine which follows—we must be aware that we may be referring to one or more of three quite different things.

1. *Accommodationist management, to prevent ethnic consciousness from becoming too intense and destructive to national unity and the democratic process.* This is the way in which the term is most commonly used. The main device used by accommodationists like Jawaharlal Nehru, Lal Bahadur Shastri and P. V. Narasimha Rao is political bargaining, which implies a substantial sharing of power and resources with people at regional and sub-regional levels.

2. *Polarising management, to intensify ethnic consciousness to the point where 'ethnic transformation' occurs.* The main practitioners of this strategy are the forces of the Hindu right. They seek to dilute the content of the diverse traditions within the Hindu population in order to fix the attention of Hindus on a common, minimalist set of symbols and issues which will unite

---

[12]Varshney, 'Master Narratives, Local Narratives, and Communal Violence', pp. 6–7. The quotation is from p. 7. He develops his arguments more fully in A. Varshney, *Ethnic Conflict and Civic Life: Hindus and Muslims in India* (Yale University Press, New Haven and London, 2002).

[13]Varshney, 'Master Narratives, Local Narratives, and Communal Violence', p. 7.

them against minorities.[14] They intend to govern India (or states within it) in a more centralising, homogenising, commandist manner than the accommodationists.

3. *Manipulative management, to stimulate ethnic awareness for short-term political advantage.* Indira and Rajiv Gandhi engaged in this type of 'management' (another form of commandist, centralising rule), intermittently but with powerfully destructive effect. They used it in the hope of short-term gains within specific regions of the country, although when the ensuing strife mushroomed (as it usually did), it had deeply damaging results well beyond the region in question. This regional specificity implied a lack of consistency in the groups to which they appealed. Thus, we saw Indira Gandhi encouraging resentments among Muslims in Assam at one point, and at another her son doing things which were intended to win his party support from anti-Muslim Hindus in Uttar Pradesh. At one point Mrs Gandhi secretly encouraged Sikh extremism in Punjab in order to split the Sikh opposition to her Congress Party there. But when the extremists became too strong, she risked a ghastly conflict (which duly followed) by sending the army into the Golden Temple, an act which was aimed in part at gaining support from Hindus across north India.[15]

The Gandhis did these things on the basis of two assumptions— which were both naïve and cynical. (Naivete and cynicism may appear to be polar opposites, but often coexist and they tend to produce similar results.) The first assumption was that 'ethnic' provocation was safe in their hands, that it would only prove destructive when practised by genuine extremists. The second was that manipulative

[14]Sudipta Kaviraj has done most to educate me about this process. It is consistent with Brass's formulations. See in particular Brass, *Ethnicity and Nationalism*, p. 16.

[15]A leading member of the Janata opposition to Indira Gandhi once characterised her manipulative activities quite perceptively. Ramakrishna Hegde, talking with the journalist E. Raghavan and me, said: 'Mrs Gandhi could set you against me, me against him, and him against you, and take support from all three of us'. Interview, Bangalore, 11 August 1984.

actions that were intended to produce political benefits within one region of India would not do damage in others. The appalling results of the attack on the Golden Temple for the whole of India (and for Indira Gandhi, who paid with her life) demonstrate that both these assumptions were ill-founded. So do the hair-raising consequences of Rajiv Gandhi's machinations in Kashmir, without which the ensuing crisis there would probably not have occurred.

Let us now focus on the first of these types of management, which is the most important and the only one with any promise for India's democratic future. It alone is consistent with the aspirations and efforts of M. K. Gandhi, Nehru and the other architects of India's political order. (We need to remember, when we hear loose talk of a 'dynasty' extending from Nehru through daughter and grandson, how inconsistent the actions of Indira and Rajiv Gandhi were with those aspirations.) As Bhikhu Parekh has argued, Gandhi, Nehru and company (despite important differences among them) were not engaged in an attempt to make India into a variant of the modern European nation-state. They chose instead, as the basis for the new order, the 'politically more relevant and, to them, morally more acceptable concept of civilisation, and argued that not race, ethnicity, language, religion or customs but the diffused, plural and relatively heterogeneous traditional Indian civilisation best suited the Indians'.[16] The new India was designed in ways that sought to foster that heterogeneity, especially among 'ethnic' groups. To quote Parekh again:

> India has a uniform body of criminal but not civil laws. Muslims continue to be governed by their personal laws, which the state enforces but with which it does not interfere. The tribals too are governed by their separate laws, and the state has committed itself to making no changes in the practices and laws of Christians without their explicit consent and approval. Minority educational institutions enjoy many legal privileges and receive generous state assistance. The Indian state is thus both an association of individuals

[16]B. Parekh, 'Ethnocentric Biases of the Nationalist Discourse', conference paper, School of Oriental and African Studies, London, October 1995, p. 4.

and a community of communities, recognising both individuals and communities as bearers of rights.[17]

How, then, have those engaged in accommodationist management operated, and how difficult is their task? All social conflicts were easier to manage in Nehru's time than in recent years. In his day, Indian society was more self-regulating and less prone to conflict than it has been since the late 1960s. Caste and class hierarchies were challenged less often than of late. Severe Hindu-Muslim convulsions happened, but rarely.

Two main political trends, which have unfolded gradually but have progressed quite considerably, changed this situation. The first was a political awakening within all sections of Indian society. People, even in disadvantaged groups, became more aware of their rights and of the egalitarian implications of a political system in which each person had just one vote. They grew more assertive, more inclined to apply pressure on politicians to give them benefits, and more impatient and inclined towards conflict when the response was inadequate. This awakening made India both a more genuine democracy and a more difficult country to govern. The second was the decay of political institutions—both the formal institutions of state and crucial informal institutions like the Congress Party. This decay was partly the result of ossification, but was mainly attributable to efforts by politicians—above all by Indira Gandhi—to centralise power and weaken institutions in the interests of personal and dynastic rule (a theme which may arise again after the 2014 national election). Its effect was to damage the instruments which politicians had once used to gather information, distribute goods and services, and mediate social conflict—at a time when the political awakening was making those instruments more, not less necessary.

There is, however, another trend which weighs against decay and prevents the recent history of India's democracy from being merely a downward spiral leading to collapse. This is the capacity for the regeneration of damaged institutions (see chapter four in this book), and of minimally civilised social relations in areas that have

[17]Ibid., p. 8.

experienced extreme conflict.[18] When 'ethnic' or other conflicts cause 'normal' politics—the politics of elections, bargaining, resource distribution, coalition-building, etc.—to break down in one region (and these episodes have so far failed to turn into nationwide convulsions), the authorities' first response is to deploy coercive force to quell disorder. This often (and, thanks to institutional decay, increasingly) entails excesses by the security forces, but it is only a first step. It is swiftly followed by accommodationist management, with actions designed to entice the groups involved in conflicts back into 'normal' politics. Ameliorative gestures and the distribution of goods and services are undertaken to ease their sense of alienation. Elections are eventually arranged to draw these groups back into the business of mobilisation for purposes other than violence, often in the (frequently realistic) hope that more moderate elements in the aggrieved groups will form a government at the state level. (For more on this, see chapter nine of this book.) This approach has worked, imperfectly but substantially, most of the time: witness, for example, repeated episodes in the northeastern states where leaders of movements and even insurrections have become state chief ministers. It has even worked—despite ghastly scars—in Punjab, which suffered a decade of vicious conflict after 1984.

The efficacy of this formula rests on several things. First, severe conflicts have tended not to arise in too many places at once. Most regions (and most Indians) have not witnessed extreme convulsions. Second, the fluidity with which most Indians shift their preoccupations from one identity to another, in response to changing circumstances, greatly facilitates the process. Third, India's federal system tends (as Myron Weiner saw long ago) to quarantine and confine most severe conflicts within single regions. Fourth, there are in all parts of India many political activists—including 'fixers' (see chapter ten of this book)—who have the skills

[18]For fuller discussions of these three themes see chapter four of this book and J. Manor, 'The Electoral Process amid Awakening and Decay', in P. Lyon and J. Manor (eds), *Transfer and Transformation: Political Institutions in the New Commonwealth* (Leicester University Press, Leicester, 1983), pp. 87–116.

and the inclination to make 'normal' politics work. This is a major national resource which is the product of nearly half a century of experience with democracy, and which very few other developing countries possess. Finally, nearly all political parties in India contain senior figures who are adept at the politics of bargaining, and who create conditions in which these skilled activists can work effectively. Witness Chief Ministers Antony (Congress) in Kerala, Shekhawat (BJP) in Rajasthan, Basu (Communist) in West Bengal, and Deve Gowda (Janata Dal) in Karnataka. None of these five things is likely to disappear soon.

Another portion of the literature on India needs attention here, since it reminds us of the importance of the *actions* which accommodationist 'management' of 'ethnicity' entails. The distinguished social scientist, T. N. Madan has argued that the rise of the Hindu right has revealed how inappropriate Nehru's Westernised secularism was to conditions in the subcontinent. Madan focuses on Nehru's speeches and writings, which in his view set out a hopelessly alien vision that could never provide a basis for managing social conflict in India. Madan's analysis is unhelpful, not because what he says about Nehru's pronouncements is entirely wrong, but because he frames the problem incorrectly. He focuses on *discourse*, the words which express Nehru's vision and values, when he should be looking at the *actions* which Nehru and many others who exercised power in India took to promote political accommodation, not only among 'ethnic' groups, but among castes, classes and other interests. Political action has always been more important than political rhetoric in determining outcomes in India.[19] The alien character of Nehru's vision is a problem, but it is not the essential

[19]Others have also tended to over-emphasise ideas and to undervalue actions and transactions in discussions of related topics. See especially T. N. Madan, 'Secularism in its Place', *Journal of Asian Studies* (November 1987), pp. 747–59. See also the critique of Myron Weiner's writing on elite-mass integration in J. Manor, 'The Dynamics of Political Integration and Disintegration', in D. Dalton and A. J. Wilson (eds), *The States of South Asia* (Hurst, London, 1982), specifically p. 93. It should be stressed that Weiner is less guilty of this in many of his other writings.

problem here. The main explanation for the emergence of 'ethnic' conflict as a destructive force is not that leaders have persisted with Nehru's theories, but rather that they—not least his daughter and grandson—abandoned Nehru's accommodationist practice. What is needed is not a reformulation of high theory, although that is a worthy aim, but a return to the mundane politics of bargaining.

Prime Minister P. V. Narasimha Rao understood this. As a good Congressman, he would never criticise Indira or Rajiv Gandhi openly, nor would he challenge the myth that they represent continuity with the Nehru tradition. But much of what he said and did implicitly carries these messages. Most of his actions, after taking power in 1991, were intended to undo the damage done by the Gandhis and to revive the accommodationist approach. He set out to de-dramatise politics, to lower the political temperature, to provide a broad array of interests with enough warm words and material concessions to soothe their anger and alienation. He was not entirely successful in this. His government lacked the funds to forge bargains with the excessively wide range of interests that he had targeted. (His economic reforms were intended to change that by generating growth, although, as he well knew, that would take time.[20]) His Congress Party's organisation was so grievously damaged by the commandism of the Gandhis that it could not be for him, as it was for Nehru, an effective instrument for practicing the politics of bargaining. (His insistence in 1991–92 on elections at all levels of the party—the first in 20 years—was intended to begin a revival of the organisation; but he felt unable to persist with elections every two years, as he initially intended.) Yet until the destruction of the Babri Masjid at Ayodhya in December 1992—which was partly the result of his overly optimistic pursuit of accommodation with the Hindu right—he was remarkably successful. In that period, nothing gave him greater satisfaction than that during his premiership India

[20]For more on this see J. Manor, 'The Political Sustainability of Economic Liberalization in India', in R. H. Cassen and V. Joshi (eds), *India: The Future of Economic Reform* (Oxford University Press, Delhi, 1995), pp. 343–60.

had witnessed far less caste and religious conflict than during the previous decade.[21]

Since 1992, things have degenerated somewhat, but only somewhat. The convulsions which followed the events at Ayodhya were succeeded by election defeats in late 1993 for the Hindu right in three of the four states where they had previously governed. It is significant that the only state in which they avoided defeat— Rajasthan—was the one which had been governed by a brilliant, Congress-style accommodationist, Chief Minister Shekhawat (see chapter twelve in this book). 'Ethnic' polarisation cannot now give the Hindu right a thumping majority in Parliament. They may eventually achieve that, but if they do so, it is likely to owe more to voters' negative reactions to poor government by the other major forces in national politics than to mass enthusiasm for their brand of 'ethnic' politics.[22] If their record in government at the state level is any guide, their efforts to use their control of the institutions of state to forge an 'ethnic' Hindu identity will yield results that will disappoint them deeply. They will be thwarted yet again by their old enemies: socio-cultural heterogeneity, the resilience of caste (especially *jati*)—and especially by two other things: traditional Hinduism, and the frequency and fluidity with which Indians shift their preoccupations from one identity to another.

Some scholars, including Donald Horowitz,[23] have argued that ethnic conflicts in Asia and Africa are more deep-seated than those in Europe, and that consociational or other accommodationist devices are therefore less likely to assist in managing ethnic conflict there. That view is difficult to sustain. Horowitz was, admittedly, writing long before recent nightmares in the Balkans and the former Soviet Union emerged; but the horrors in Northern Ireland and the Basque region were already plain to see. The evidence from South Asia

---

[21]These comments are based on an extended encounter with the prime minister in New Delhi during the second week of February, 1992.

[22]That sentence was written many years before the 2014 parliamentary election.

[23]D. Horowitz, *Ethnic Groups in Conflict* (University of California Press, Berkeley, 1985).

suggests that it is more accurate to consider Europe and the non-Western world in similar terms. There are caustic, profound conflicts in both, as Bosnia and Sri Lanka indicate. But the world outside the West can also offer cases like India where 'ethnic' conflicts are more easily managed and where the political instruments for managing them are more readily available than in Europe's worst cases. The details of Indian 'management' strategies are discussed further in the next chapter of this book.

— *nine* —

POLITICAL BARGAINING AND CENTRE–STATE RELATIONS IN THE FEDERAL SYSTEM

This paper builds on the discussion in the previous chapter on 'ethnicity'. It analyses different strategies used by leaders in New Delhi towards states in this federal system. It explains why these have usually helped to make Centre–state relations manageable, but also how in some cases, things have gone badly wrong. It re-emphasises a key argument made elsewhere in this book (see especially chapters five, six and fourteen), that senior politicians make their influence penetrate downward in this complex polity and society by way of bargaining and accommodation rather than by diktat.

How are the demands of groups in Indian society for greater power, resources, autonomy, and—let us not forget— respect dealt with in this complex, culturally heterogeneous democracy? How and to what extent do politicians, parties, and governments accommodate these demands? Insofar as they fail to do so, what sort of frustrations develop, and what impact does that have on the democratic process? With these broad questions in mind, this chapter examines Centre–state relations.

Much of this discussion focuses on informal rather than with formal political institutions. 'Formal' institutions are entities of state created by India's laws and Constitution. They include legislatures, the federal system including the instrument known as President's Rule, the bureaucracy, the courts, etc. 'Informal' institutions include, most importantly, political parties—but also movements, factions, patronage networks, and the vast army of political activists and 'fixers' (see chapter ten of this book) who drive and sometimes disrupt the democratic process. That category also embraces non-official institutions which are both actors and arenas of contestation—cooperative societies, the boards of private trusts, schools, colleges, and temples, plus other institutions devoted to the furtherance of religion or social welfare—as well as organised interests such as caste associations, unions of farmers, workers, and other voluntary associations. Informal institutions stand between and integrate the state and society, but they also intermingle very substantially with society and with 'civil society' (defined here as 'associations of a voluntary nature, standing between the household and the state, with a significant degree of autonomy from the state').

Two main questions are addressed here. First, why have relations between New Delhi and the various state governments usually remained manageable? Second, why in some cases have things gone spectacularly wrong, so that violent separatist movements have developed and Centre–state relations have broken down?

In part, the answers provided here cover the same ground as an analysis offered by Atul Kohli which focused on two 'proximate variables'—'the level of institutionalization of the central state, and ... the degree to which the ruling strategy of leaders accommodates demands for self-determination'.[1] In part, however, this discussion goes beyond that state-centred approach and considers social, cultural, geographical, historical, political and economic elements that are (in varying degrees) external to the state. We shall see first that these latter elements exercise a potent influence over events, and second that economic conditions have had less importance than the other elements noted above.

---

[1] A. Kohli, 'Can Democracies Accommodate Ethnic Nationalism? Rise and Decline of Self-Determination Movements in India', *Journal of Asian Studies* (May 1997), p. 329.

The answers to our two questions change somewhat over time. During the first twenty years or so after independence in 1947, society in most of India (especially in rural areas) was sufficiently self-regulating that it posed few serious problems for political institutions—formal or informal. And in that early period one informal institution—the Congress Party's cluster of regional political 'machines'—possessed the substance and the reach to manage most of the social tensions that arose.

Since the late 1960s, things have become more difficult on both the socio-cultural and the political fronts. Interest groups have crystallised and have become increasingly well organised and aware of their political concerns. They have pressed harder for resources, power, and respect, and have exhibited growing impatience with mere tokenism. This has made India a more genuine democracy and a more difficult country to govern.

At the same time, political decay has afflicted most formal and informal political institutions. This has partly resulted from ossification, but its main cause has been attempts by politicians to erode the substance and autonomy of institutions in the interests of personal rule. Decay has damaged the instruments which politicians need to manage such a lively polity. This has sown frustration among organised interests and has produced far more strife of a destructive sort that occurred in the first two decades after independence.

In very recent years—since the passing from power in 1989 of the Gandhi 'dynasty' which was the main source of attempts at deinstitutionalisation—an important counter-tendency to decay has become particularly evident. Numerous damaged institutions— informal and especially formal—have been rebuilt, at least to some degree, and have begun to function in more autonomous and non-partisan ways. The federal system is one example—thanks in part to a 1994 Supreme Court ruling setting down guidelines for the imposition of President's Rule[2] and to the disinclination (and perhaps the inability) of most national governments in the hung parliaments

[2]A. Mozoomdar, 'The Political Economy of Modern Federalism', in B. Arora and D. V. Verney (eds), *Multiple Identities in a Single State* (Konark, New Delhi, 1995).

which existed between 1989 and 1999 to be as commandist as their predecessors. The courts have become far more assertive, as has the Election Commission. We have also seen the creation of new formal institutions which hold considerable promise—most notably the *panchayats* and municipal bodies which have emerged after the 73rd and 74th amendments to the Constitution came into force in 1993.[3] These and other tendencies make it possible to speak not only of decay but of political regeneration in India (see chapter four of this book).

This does not mean that India's institutional difficulties are at an end. But they continue to be eased by elements of the political sociology and the political culture to be found in most (though not all) Indian regions—which lend themselves to the functioning of open, liberal politics generally and to a federal system in particular. There are, nonetheless vivid (indeed hair-raising), exceptions to this generalisation. Both the generalisation and the exceptions will be explored here.

This chapter tackles these issues mainly by examining events in a number of specific Indian states. The first two, 'mainstream' states Andhra Pradesh and Tamil Nadu—illustrate the generalisation that Centre–state relations have been reasonably manageable. We then turn to three 'troubled' states or areas—Punjab, Jammu and Kashmir, and the Northeast—which represent exceptions. More attention will be devoted to the exceptions than to the generalisation. This might seem somewhat misleading, since states where Centre–state relations have never degenerated into severe crisis greatly outnumber those where breakdowns have occurred. So let us note here at the outset that the exceptions are just that—unusual cases which help to inform us about the more general tendency.

The exceptional, 'troubled' cases assessed here fall into two categories. The first two—Punjab, and Jammu and Kashmir—are states where Centre–state relations were bound to be difficult, but where creative 'management' from New Delhi could have

---

[3]R. Crook and J. Manor, *Democracy and Development in South Asia and West Africa: Participation, Accountability and Performance* (Cambridge University Press, Cambridge, 1998).

prevented the breakdowns which occurred. In the other case—the Northeast—breakdowns were and remain unavoidable. New Delhi's 'management' there has sometimes left much to be desired, but even if it had been impeccable, it would have been impossible to prevent breakdowns from occurring.

'Manageable' Centre–state Relations: Socio-Cultural Conditions and the Politics of Bargaining

Centre–state relations have tended strongly to remain 'manageable,' though not trouble-free, for four main reasons. First, powerful group demands seldom take the form of states' (or *statewide* elites') demands which impinge mainly on New Delhi and which—if frustrated—might generate secessionist sentiments. Demands tend far more often to arise out of *intra*-state conflicts, so that the resulting pressure is felt mainly or exclusively at the state level. This supplements Myron Weiner's insight that the formal structures of the federal system tend to quarantine conflicts within regional arenas.[4]

The second reason provides the main explanation for the first. The social and cultural complexity and heterogeneity—indeed, heterogeneities within heterogeneities—that we encounter within most states are so formidable that they make it exceedingly difficult to develop the kind of statewide solidarity which secessionism requires.

Third, this socio-cultural complexity and heterogeneity have contributed to a strong tendency among Indian citizens to shift their preoccupations from one to another of the many identities which they have available to them—often and with great fluidity. Depending upon circumstances and recent events, they may fix for a time on their *jati, jati*-cluster, *varna*, on their local, sub-regional or national identities, on their class, linguistic, communal identities, on sectarian identities which fragment Hindu, Muslim, and other communal identities, etc. But they seldom fix ferociously and tenaciously

[4]M. Weiner, *The Indian Paradox: Essays in Indian Politics* (Sage, New Delhi, London and Thousand Oaks, 1989), p. 36.

on any one of these, as people in, for example, Sri Lanka have done. This fluidity reduces the severity and longevity of most conflicts within most states—and undermines the threat of secessionism which requires sustained solidarity round regional identities—*because it prevents tension and conflict from building up along a single fault line in society* (see the previous chapter in this book).

Fourth, despite the decay which formal and informal political institutions have suffered in recent decades, they often remain capable of making the politics of bargaining work. This comment refers mainly to political parties (and occasionally to factions within them) and to the organised interests with which they interact. Most of these informal institutions still contain enough people with appropriate skills and attitudes to sustain the bargaining process, imperfectly but at least adequately. A small army of political activists and 'fixers' (see chapter ten of this book) constitute a major national resource that is unavailable to most other countries in Asia, Africa, and Latin America. This capacity to practice the politics of bargaining prevents the socio-cultural heterogeneities noted above from creating such political chaos that accommodations within states, and between centre and states, unravel. (We will see that this generalisation cannot be applied to the Northeast, but it is valid in most of the rest of the country.)

One further comment is in order here. Rob Jenkins' has stressed the importance of the number and diversity of arenas in which political conflict occurs within individual Indian states. Contests take place frequently for seats in the national parliament and in state assemblies, for seats on councils in the multiple tiers in the *panchayati raj* system (since 1993), and for positions of influence in a number of quasi-official and non-official boards, cooperatives, associations, etc. The existence of so many opportunities to capture at least some power persuades parties and politicians to remain engaged with the politics of elections and bargaining, even when they suffer defeats in some contests.[5]

---

[5]R. Jenkins, *Democratic Politics and Economic Reform in India* (Cambridge University Press, Cambridge, 2007).

On those rare occasions when separatism is contemplated by powerful regional interests, the coercive power of the Indian state tends to discourage such thinking. But separatism seldom comes into play, for the reasons set out above and because those interests tend to the view that the political bargaining—within individual states, and between states and the Central government—offers them sufficient incentives to make open revolt unpalatable.

What constitutes a creative 'management' approach by the Government of India to Centre–state relations, and in particular to disenchanted regional groups which have turned or might turn to separatism and/or violence? It contains several strands. It entails a visible willingness to listen to the grievances and discontents of regional groups, and to change some policies in response to them. Policy changes are sometimes accompanied by political enticements, such as promises to include such groups in ruling coalitions if they moderate their more extreme demands. At the very least, groups which have been disinclined to take part in 'normal' electoral politics are commonly encouraged to abandon their reluctance. They are told that if they succeed in such elections, the central authorities will welcome them as the new government of their state. Packages of economic assistance and new development programmes are often offered at the same time—indeed, they may precede negotiations, as a sign of the Central government's good intentions.

Such initiatives sometimes have to be pursued at the same time as Indian security forces are engaged in conflict with members of such disenchanted groups. That can cause problems for attempts at accommodation, but the Central government has succeeded often enough with such attempts to make this twin-track approach worth trying—as many people in New Delhi understand.

Finally, on occasion, the creative 'management' of Centre–state relations entails the imposition of President's Rule—direct rule from New Delhi, after the suspension or dissolution of a state assembly. This comment will raise hackles, because this constitutional provision has often been abused by commandist national leaders to uproot legitimate state governments headed by their opponents. But we need to consider the reasoning that led the framers of India's Constitution to arm the Central government with these powers.

They concluded that occasions would arise when state governments would prove incapable or unwilling to cope with severe conflict. They thought that, in such circumstances, New Delhi might justly conclude that to quell disorder, or to prevent it from reaching ever more dangerous levels, President's Rule needed to be invoked.

In this writer's view, they were correct. Such occasions have indeed arisen. It would be very surprising if they had not, since the stresses that attend an adventurous experiment with democracy in a society like India's are bound to overwhelm liberal institutions—not often, but occasionally. (Doubters should consider the hair-raising array of problems faced by the authorities in India's Northeast, which are surveyed below.) The extravagant abuse of these powers by both the Congress and Janata governments of the 1970s and 1980s, and any future abuse which may occur, should not blind us to this patent fact.

D. A. Low, who knows both India and Africa well, has noted how much destruction might have been avoided if the Organisation of African Unity (OAU) had possessed such powers to snuff out strife in member nations before it reached grotesque levels. This would have made it possible to revive 'normal', minimally civilised politics and relations between warring social groups, using the constructive management approaches outlined above. The aforementioned decision by India's Supreme Court in 1994, requiring the Central government to justify more systematically its use of these powers, establishes welcome safeguards against their misuse. More safeguards may be needed, but the legitimate use of these provisions should not be excluded from a menu of creative approaches to extreme (if unusual) problems.

Case Studies of Individual States

Mainstream States

To examine these themes in more detail, let us consider a mainstream—that is, a reasonably typical—state. Note that we turn for our 'norm' not to New Delhi, but to a *state*. The reason is that politics at the national level and in Parliament are abnormal, in that they differ from most states and their state assemblies in important ways, and most crucially in one.

Caste has far less importance at the national level than in the politics of any single state. This is because India has not one caste system but many. Roughly speaking, each linguistic region has its own distinctive caste system. And since most state borders (the Hindi belt excluded) conform, again roughly, to the boundaries of linguistic regions, politicians in each major state share not only a common language but a common traditional social system which differs (slightly or radically) from those of other states.

Being a Brahmin in, say, Bihar or Uttar Pradesh, where these groups have considerable numerical strength, land and economic power, means something very different from being a Brahmin in the four southern states where Brahmins comprise only 3 or 4 per cent of the population and own little land. And there are no indigenous Kshatriyas or Vaishyas in the southern part of India. So when members drawn from the four *varnas* meet in the Lok Sabha, they find their common caste status to be of little relevance. The only caste bloc which constitutes an approximately similar proportion of the total population in nearly all of India's major states (Gujarat excepted) are the Scheduled Castes (SCs). So national-level politics cannot provide us with the kind of 'norm' that a state can.

To explore the 'norm', let us consider the only Indian state with a population of over twenty-five million where a 'movement' for secession from India has *appeared* to acquire real force: Tamil Nadu. When the so-called Dravidian 'separatist' movement there is subjected to careful examination, major doubts arise about whether it amounted to much

There are three fundamental reasons for these doubts. First, it was never clear exactly who was supposed to do the seceding— so 'nationalists' in the state were confused about what their actual 'nation' was. Second, there were always doubts about how much popular support this 'nationalism' commanded. Finally, the alacrity with which Dravidian party leaders abandoned separatism, and their disinclination to revive it at their moment of greatest conflict with New Delhi (the anti-Hindi riots of 1965), inspire scepticism about whether they had ever been firmly wedded to the idea at all. Let us briefly consider these issues.

What 'nation' was supposed to be served by this 'nationalism'? At first—in 1914—an organisation called 'the Dravidian Association' sought 'a Dravidian state under the British Raj', which would 'safeguard the political, social, and economic interests of the Dravidian people'. But this 'people' was defined entirely in *caste* terms. The association was seeking 'a government of, by, and for the non-Brahmin'[6]—on the assumption that south Indian Brahmins were outsiders. The 'movement' at this point did not desire separation from India, but rather the destruction of Brahmin influence within south India—or, more precisely, within that portion of south India covered by Madras Presidency.

It is difficult to regard this as 'nationalism', and that difficulty persisted into the next phase—the 1920s and 1930s, the era of the Justice Party—and beyond. The Justice Party was, like its Dravidian party successors, so 'riddled with factionalism'[7] that it lacked the solidarity that is necessary to drive nationalist movements. And its overwhelming emphasis was not on 'nationalism', but (again) on anti-Brahmin grievances.[8]

In the next phase of the story, E. V. Ramaswami Naicker—who generated something that we can justly describe as a 'Dravidian movement'—confused things further. He came to prominence in 1937–38 by organising protests against the Congress government's introduction of Hindi as a compulsory school subject in Madras Presidency. As Robert Hardgrave accurately reports, he saw this 'as a subjugation of Tamil peoples which could only be avoided through the creation of a Dravidian State'.[9] But this comment plainly illustrates the confusion. Was it the *Tamils* who needed to be rescued, or the Dravidians—that is, the people in the four Dravidian

---

[6]R. L. Hardgave, *The Dravidian Movement* (Popular Prakashan, New Delhi, 1965), p. 12.

[7]Ibid., p. 24.

[8]Ibid., chapter three.

[9]Ibid., p. 27.

regions: the Tamils, Malayalis, Telugus, and Kannadigas? No one quite knew.

Ramaswami Naicker backed the call for Pakistan because it might assist with 'the creation of Dravidisthan' or 'Dravida Nadu'—a term that embraced all four linguistic groups. But the party which he eventually formed, the Dravida Kazhagham (DK), 'brought the message of *Tamil* nationality to the masses'.[10] These are different things.

I have, during twenty-five years of research in south India, sought in vain to identify a single political figure among the Malayalis, Telugus and Kannadigas who ever identified with the notion of a Dravidian 'nation'. Few had even heard of the idea. Tamil leaders made next to no effort to carry the message to their Dravidian brethren. Why? Because they were not serious about pursuing this alleged dream; because this was an entirely Tamil affair. And yet—presumably because it was a more grandiose bit of pretence or bluff than talk of an independent Tamil Nadu—these leaders continued to press on with the confusing call for an 'independent', a 'sovereign' Dravida Nadu.[11]

The high water mark of this campaign came during the mid- to late-1950s. The Dravida Munnetra Kazhagam (DMK)—which by then had taken over from the DK as the main bearer of this theme—made 'a separate Dravida Nadu' its central issue during the Tamil Nadu state assembly election of 1957 (soon *after* the creation of that state within the Indian union). But again, there are reasons to doubt their seriousness about this. The theme was seized upon in large part out of convenience. It offered 'a *convenient* focal point for elaborating DMK ideas about social reform' which enabled the party to 'appear to stand for something concrete'. Had they fought the election on their main concerns—'that caste prejudices and religious "superstition" should be eliminated'—they would have run

---

[10]Ibid., pp. 27 and 31.

[11]M. R. Barnett, *The Politics of Cultural Nationalism in South India* (Princeton University Press, Princeton, 1976), pp. 93 and 109.

up against efforts by the ruling Congress Party in Tamil Nadu to promote both justice within the caste system and secularism.[12]

The view that Dravida Nadu was stressed more out of convenience than conviction gains credence when we see how swiftly the demand was abandoned soon thereafter. It became inconvenient for several reasons. No support for the idea had emerged from the other three southern states. Tamil Nadu might still have sought independence on its own, but DMK leaders feared that 'it might not be economically and militarily viable'. And if the Government of India banned separatist parties—which at the time seemed 'likely'— it could have been disastrous for the DMK which, after the 1957 election, had only 15 of the 205 seats in the state assembly.[13]

The demand was informally abandoned in 1961 and formalised in 1963.[14] It is worth stressing that it was *not* revived during the anti-Hindi riots of 1965 in Tamil Nadu, even though that marked the low point in the state's relations with New Delhi. It cropped up again among some DMK activists in 1968, one year after that party took power in Tamil Nadu. But party leaders ignored it, relegating it to the status of an 'undercurrent' in Tamil politics that was 'vitiated but not eradicated'.[15] Little has been heard of it since.

Separatism was always undermined by the confusion over the composition of the so-called Dravidian 'nation'—was it all south Indians, all non-Brahmin south Indians, all Tamils or all non-Brahmin Tamils? No clear answer ever emerged. DMK leaders were intimidated by the coercive potential of the Indian state—but it must be stressed that this never had to be brought into play, mainly because separatism's mass appeal was nonexistent beyond Tamil Nadu and weak within it.

This meant that it did not pose a serious 'management' problem for India's central authorities. Relatively little in the way of a 'management' approach to Tamil Nadu emerged in the period up to the late 1960s. Instead of a coherent 'approach' from New

[12]Ibid., pp. 93–94.
[13]Ibid., pp. 94 and 109.
[14]Ibid., pp. 89 and 110.
[15]Ibid., pp. 89, 110 and 114.

Delhi, what we saw in those years was a rather haphazard mixture of neglect, accommodation, and occasional acts of insensitivity. The most notable such act was the attempt to impose Hindi, but when it triggered rioting, the Central government soon backed off and accommodated Tamil sensibilities. In other words, when serious trouble occurred, New Delhi swiftly adopted a concerted strategy towards the state—an 'accommodationist' approach, to use a term set out late in the previous chapter.

The Central government's most important initiative, which was not a response to separatist demands, was the decision in 1956 to redraw the boundaries of Tamil Nadu and numerous other states along linguistic lines. By bringing nearly all Tamils together in a single state, this compelled Tamils (and people in all other new linguistic states) to confront all of the things which divided them. Given the heterogeneities within heterogeneities that existed within this and other regional societies, these were immensely formidable. In most Indian states—and in all of the large states—they undermined the kind of solidarity which is necessary to mount a credible separatist movement. This largely explains why no regional movement in any large Indian state except Tamil Nadu has ever become avowedly separatist, and why in Tamil Nadu separatism never became a serious threat.

It is fortunate for India as a whole and for Tamil Nadu in particular that the system of mono-linguistic states had taken firm root long before the early 1980s when Indira Gandhi adopted a new, deeply destructive 'manipulative management' approach to use a term discussed at the end of the previous chapter. This entailed efforts to foment suspicion between 'ethnic', especially religious, groups and then to deploy coercive force in response to the very ructions which she had catalysed—on the dubious assumption that this would yield short-term partisan advantages. Had the central authorities adopted this posture towards the likes of Tamil Nadu in the 1950s and 1960s, it might have produced disastrous outcomes. But by the 1980s, most 'mainstream' states had evolved to the point where such initiatives would not have wrought havoc. Perhaps sensing this, Mrs Gandhi targeted other more susceptible states— mainly but not only Punjab—with ghastly results. It is to Punjab and two other troubled regions, outside the 'mainstream', that we now turn.

Troubled States

We must consider three areas in which severe conflicts between the Central government and groups in various states have led to breakdowns in relations: Punjab, Jammu and Kashmir (or more precisely, the Kashmir Valley), and India's Northeast. It was never going to be easy to maintain congenial relations with any of these areas—for reasons set out below—but there are important differences between these cases. Creative 'management' could probably have avoided breakdowns with Punjab and Kashmir. But at least occasional breakdowns in relations with most states in the Northeast were (and remain) unavoidable, no matter what approaches New Delhi tried.

Punjab: The ghastly crisis that gripped Punjab for more than a decade from the early 1980s was plainly avoidable. It would not have occurred if leaders in New Delhi had restrained themselves from meddling in potentially explosive disputes within the majority Sikh community there, and from exploiting anti-Sikh feelings among Hindus once the explosion occurred. This episode demonstrates what should have been obvious—that social diversity within religious minorities (along caste and class lines in the case of the Sikhs) will not suffice to prevent them from reacting ferociously, and in numbers, to perceived affronts to their faith.

In the late 1970s, Indira Gandhi's son Sanjay and her senior political lieutenant from Punjab, Zail Singh (himself a Sikh), sought to undermine the strength of their main opposition in the state— the Akali Dal (an overwhelmingly Sikh party)—by encouraging the emergence of the Sikh extremist Sant Jarnail Singh Bindranwale. When lethal violence broke out in 1978 between Bindranwale's group and a 'heretical' Sikh sect, the Nirankaris, Mrs Gandhi's Congress Party publicity machine backed Bindranwale. Zail Singh lent financial support to Bindranwale's newly formed political party, even though—as a government White Paper declared—it was 'established with the avowed intention of demanding an independent sovereign Sikh state'.[16] In 1979, Bindranwale's candidates failed miserably (despite support from the Congress) in elections to the committee which oversees Sikh shrines. But Congress support continued and, in return, Bindranwale campaigned actively for that party's candidates at the parliamentary election of 1980 which brought Mrs Gandhi back to power.

She made Zail Singh India's home minister, but—to keep him from establishing a dominant position in Punjab's politics—she named his arch rival, a more secular-minded Sikh, Darbara Singh, as the state's chief minister. The latter adopted a hard line against Sikh and Hindu extremists in Punjab, while Zail Singh continued to promote and defend Bindranwale from New Delhi. Mrs Gandhi oscillated between supporting each of these two leaders—a policy which alienated Sikh extremists, even as one section of her party encouraged them.[17] It is difficult to imagine a more dangerous approach to the problem.

When mounting violence from Bindranwale's group persuaded the Punjab government to seek his arrest, Zail Singh (whose job included oversight of law and order in India) arranged for a police car from neighbouring Haryana state to ferry him safely to his *gurudwara* (temple) in Punjab. Soon thereafter, an outraged Chief Minister Darbara Singh had Bindranwale arrested, an act which triggered massive violence including murders, train derailments, and an airline hijack. Zail Singh—acting on Indira Gandhi's orders—then had Bindranwale released from jail, telling Parliament that there was no evidence that he had been behind the crimes for which he had been detained.

This decision had appalling results. The Punjab police—who were now targeted for retribution by Bindranwale's assassins—were deeply demoralised. Bindranwale seemed a hero who had successfully challenged the might of the Indian state, and he was free to plot further atrocities. When one of his close allies was killed

---

[16]M. Tully and S. Jacob, *Amritsar: Mrs Gandhi's Last Battle* (Rupa, New Delhi, 1985), pp. 58–60.

[17]Ibid., pp. 60–66 and K. Nayar and K.Singh, *Tragedy of Punjab and After: Operation Blue Star and After* (Vision Books, New Delhi, 1984), pp. 36–39.

by a rival Sikh politician, Zail Singh and Rajiv Gandhi attended the memorial service and allowed themselves to be photographed in Bindranwale's company.[18]

There followed (from 1982 onward) a series of negotiations with Sikh extremists, first directly involving Mrs Gandhi, and then through intermediaries. She again oscillated between accommodation and obduracy—an inconsistent approach which solved nothing. In mid-1982, amid continuing violence, Bindranwale took refuge in the Golden Temple in Amritsar, the Sikhs' holiest shrine. By late 1983, his forces escalated their campaign of mayhem—slaughtering Hindus at random and committing outrages at Hindu temples. This led to the imposition of direct rule from New Delhi in Punjab. And yet Congress opponents of Zail Singh—whom Mrs Gandhi had by then made President of India (head of state)—have claimed that he remained in daily contact with Bindranwale thereafter. So, on frequent occasions, did Mrs Gandhi through an emissary, until less than a month before she sent the army into the Golden Temple in June 1984.[19]

That military action is sufficiently well known to require little retelling here, but two depressing points are worth stressing. First, it might not have been necessary had the will existed in New Delhi to let the Punjab police do their job properly much earlier. Second, the timing of the army's attack on a holy day—marking the martyrdom of Guru Arjun—ensured that many innocent pilgrims were killed in the fighting. This was an act of colossal insensitivity.

The attack caused severe damage to the shrine, deeply offended even moderate Sikhs, and provoked mutinies in several Sikh army units. It touched off years of terrorist activity by Sikh militants and led, on 31 October 1984, to the murder of Indira Gandhi by two of her Sikh bodyguards.

The severity of the crisis deepened as a result of vengeful responses to the assassination. Over 3,000 Sikhs were massacred during the days which followed, in Delhi and elsewhere. Much of

[18]Tully and Jacob, *Amritsar*, pp. 67–72 and facing p. 117.
[19]Ibid., pp. 73–105 and 121; and Nayar and Singh, *Tragedy of Punjab and After*, chapter two.

the slaughter was carried out by groups of Congress supporters, often led by prominent party leaders. The police were restrained by senior Congressmen from intervening to stop the carnage.

In the weeks followed the massacres, senior officials actively sought to thwart efforts to identify and apprehend the murderers. For example, a bureaucrat atop the Ministry of External Affairs (MEA) sought to bully a European diplomat into suppressing photographic evidence of an attempt by a mob including prominent Congressmen to torch the Sikh-owned house where he resided. An official of his seniority could only have been acting on orders from politicians at the apex of the system. The government refused to establish a commission to inquire into the massacres, so groups of eminent citizens felt compelled to do so independently.

During the parliamentary election campaign soon after the assassination, the Congress took out a full-page advertisement in national newspapers which offered a coded appeal to the fear of Sikhs. I attended an election rally in Delhi at which Rajiv Gandhi did nothing to prevent the crowd from shouting down the Sikh mayor of the city (a Congressman) and then spoke of taking revenge (*badla*) when discussing his approach to the crisis. Actions such as this only deepened the dangerous gulf between Sikhs and others, despite the fact that the country now faced its worst post-Independence crisis— which, among other things, had compromised the defence of India.

There followed nearly a decade of Sikh terrorism and severe counter-insurgency campaigns by India's security forces. The government adopted the time-honoured model for dealing with such breakdowns—coercive force to impose minimal order, coupled with accommodative initiatives to ease discontents and to persuade moderates to resume 'normal' representative politics. But the grotesque events of 1984 had so severely ruptured relations between New Delhi and the Sikh majority in the state that it took much longer than ever before, roughly a decade, to produce something resembling the preferred outcome. And terrible scars, many of them left by the draconian actions of the security forces over that decade, remain among the Sikhs.

The misguided actions of national leaders in this episode were based on a strange mixture of naiveté and cynicism. These may seem to be opposites, but they go together far more often than many suppose. And they tend to produce very similar, deeply damaging results.

The horrors of Punjab's recent history have yielded one positive result. Many senior figures in New Delhi now firmly avow what was obvious to most of their counterparts early on—but not to the leaders of the Congress—that it is dangerous folly to play politics with religious sentiments. It is politically insane to encourage extremism among religious minorities (and indeed the majority). The upheaval in Kashmir has, as we shall see presently, reinforced the message.

Jammu and Kashmir: The story of Jammu and Kashmir (or mainly of the Kashmir Valley) differs dramatically from that of all other states. It pains a friend of India to say it, but New Delhi's approach to Kashmir has—by India's own democratic standards—been excessively manipulative and destructive. This was true not just in the Gandhis' commandist and manipulative phase, but during the entire period from independence until very recent years. (An encouraging change of view began to emerge in the 1990s, as we shall see.) Coercion, electoral fraud, and much else have marked the Central governments' 'management' of Kashmir. This often happened because the central authorities were ill informed or maladroit rather than malevolent, but it happened nonetheless.

The first major departure from India's democratic norms and the then Indian government's accommodative approach to most regional problems came in 1953. One year after Nehru and Kashmiri leader Sheikh Abdullah had worked out an agreement that might have provided a basis for something approaching 'normal' representative politics, New Delhi—tiring of Abdullah's autocratic behaviour and his references to the possibility of complete independence for his state—arranged a split in the ruling National Conference there. Abdullah was jailed and one of his lieutenants, Bakshi Ghulam Mohammed, was inserted in his place at the head of the regional government. The widespread protests in the Valley which ensued were quelled by the security forces.[20]

---

[20]S. Bose, *The Challenge of Kashmir: Democracy, Self-Determination and a Just Peace* (Sage, London, 1997), p. 32.

The following year, the Indian government issued a constitutional order which effectively negated both Article 370 of the Constitution (which contains special provisions for the state) and the 1952 agreement with Abdullah. It gave New Delhi unlimited powers to legislate on all matters—including those that had been granted to Kashmir under Article 370—and severely curtailed basic liberties. The Bakshi government in Kashmir proved corrupt during its ten years in power (1953–63), but its willingness to accept these impositions ensured its survival. At 'elections' in 1957 and 1962, it won between 95 and 97 per cent of the seats in the state assembly. This was sufficiently unsubtle to persuade Nehru to ask Bakshi to lose 'a few seats' in subsequent 'elections', for appearances' sake.[21]

Bakshi was ousted on New Delhi's initiative in 1963, in defiance of the wishes of a majority in the state assembly, and replaced by G. M. Sadiq. An effort to pass a no confidence motion foundered after the arrest of Bakshi. Protests from people in the Valley—which *still* centred on democratic demands rather than separatism or a desire to join Pakistan—again received a coercive response.

In 1965, Sadiq transformed his National Conference into the state unit of the Congress Party and two years later won another dubious state 'election'. In 1972, however, Sheikh Abdullah's followers proposed to take part in the next assembly election. The then Congress Chief Minister, Mir Qasim—believing that they would win—banned their participation in the poll and arrested large numbers of their leaders. Congress then won the ensuing 'election'.[22]

Three years later, Sheikh Abdullah abandoned his demand for self-determination in order to be permitted—late in life—a further chance to take power. In 1977, his National Conference won well at the first genuinely free election to occur in Kashmir. The Congress Party lost every seat in the Valley.[23]

A further competitive election took place in 1983, a year after Sheikh Abdullah's death. His son and political successor, Farooq

---

[21]Ibid., pp. 33–34.

[22]Ibid., pp. 34–37.

[23]Mir Qasim, *My Life and Times* (Allied, New Delhi, 1992), pp. 106 and 132; and ibid., p. 36.

Abdullah, led the National Conference to victory again in an aggressively fought contest with the Congress. The Conference then joined other anti-Congress parties in a nationwide opposition front. Mrs Gandhi's response was to engineer yet another split in his party in 1984, only a year after it was elected. Defectors from the National Conference, with Congress support, formed a new government. Two years later, this government was dismissed and President's Rule under Jagmohan was introduced after 'carefully organized riots ... provided the pretext'.[24]

The next state election in 1987 saw a return to fraudulent practices. Farooq Abdullah, who the previous year had entered an alliance with Rajiv Gandhi, faced a popular backlash in the Valley. To ensure his 'election', rigging and muscle power were used. This, plus his government's corrupt and repressive ways and the chief minister's own foolishness, eventually provoked a widespread upsurge of protests. These were put down by force, and that triggered the start of serious armed resistance in the Valley.

One remarkable feature of this story is the great length of time it took for Muslims in the Valley to resort to outright resistance. This strongly suggests that accommodation at many points before the late 1980s would have worked—and may still have some promise. But opportunities for accommodation were repeatedly spurned. If future Indian policy makers want an object lesson in how *not* to manage relations with sensitive regions, Kashmir provides it.

Various New Delhi governments since 1991 have sought to apply the lessons of the Punjab 'solution' to Kashmir—where the story is far from over. They may or may not have been inappropriate, they have certainly been rushed, and the results have been mixed. More generous concessions to the people of the Valley and perhaps of the entire state of Jammu and Kashmir may be required before something approaching political 'normality' can be reestablished.

The Northeast: India's Northeast is the one region of the country where Centre–state relations have been and remain unmanageable much of the time. In most (though not all) of these states—Mizoram

---

[24]Bose, *The Challenge of Kashmir*, pp. 41–43.

in recent years is an important exception—relations are bound to degenerate from time to time into severe conflict. New Delhi's 'management' of the region has at times contributed to breakdowns. But even when this has not been true, the states of the Northeast and the Centre's relations with them are afflicted by so many excruciating problems that even the most effective management strategies were and remain bound to prove insufficient—again, much (though not all) of the time.

To say this is not to deny Dasgupta's observations that we need to pay attention to the positive aspects of community formation, the lineage of communities in wider political institutions as parts of the northeastern administration and representative systems, and the contributions of these processes to the national systems— and to the long history of peace, social collaboration, and political reconciliation, democratic participation, and innovations in institution-building and sustenance.[25] All of these things are impor- tant realities, but they have not yet succeeded in bringing extreme conflicts in most of the Northeast to an end, and it seems unlikely that they will do so anytime soon.[26]

Consider the problems that confront those who seek to manage the region through accommodation. When the British ruled India, they did not assert sovereign control over much of the Northeast. They relied instead on a policy of 'least interference' and permitted 'traditional institutions' to govern many of the more remote areas of the region. When disturbances or actions occurred which the British deemed unacceptable, they resorted to punitive responses which inspired a tradition of bitter resentment among groups in the Northeast towards India's central authorities and towards forces in the region which aided or acquiesced to the British. That resentment survived the transition to Indian independence and posed huge problems for New Delhi thereafter. The British approach to the Northeast also left a legacy of confusion about the borders between

---

[25]J. Dasgupta, 'Community, Authenticity and Authority: Insurgence and Institutional Development in India's Northeast', *Journal of Asian Studies* (May 1997), p. 345.

[26]Ibid., p. 347.

areas in which different 'tribes' and clusters of 'tribes' enjoyed pre-eminence.[27]

After independence, India's new rulers did not have the luxury of sustaining the British approach to the region. It now faced potentially (and often actively) troublesome neighbours—East Pakistan, China, and Burma. This left them no option but to fix and then police international borders, and to develop arrangements for the exercise of sovereign authority. But since the Central government's relationship with the Northeast was far less well institutionalised than relations with areas of 'mainstream' India,[28] immense difficulties ensued.

To make matters worse, the Partition of the subcontinent had severed traditional trade routes—most crucially down the valleys and rivers leading to the port of Chittagong (then in East Pakistan)—and had cut the Northeast off from most of its former markets. This made the economic development of the region, which might have eased resentments and the threat of turbulence there, exceedingly difficult. The Northeast now stood at the extreme end of poorly developed communication and transport lines which—since they ran through a narrow strip of difficult terrain up and over the hostile territory of northern East Pakistan—were vulnerable to disruption. This made and continues to make the commodities which must be brought in from the rest of India extremely expensive—another irritant.

The lack of clarity and consensus over informal demarcation lines between areas occupied by the diverse social groups of the Northeast has continued to bedevil the region—despite, or often because of, Indian efforts to formalise these lines into boundaries between states and union territories there. When a state or union territory is carved out in response to a demand for autonomy—usually from a cluster of 'tribes' which have developed a sense of common 'ethnicity', a tricky word in South Asia (see chapter eight of

[27]B. G. Verghese, *India's Northeast Resurgent* (Konark, New Delhi, 1996), pp. 103–04 and 137.

[28]Kohli, 'Can Democracies Accommodate Ethnic Nationalism?', p. 329.

this book)—other groups, that are not part of the cluster but which find themselves within the borders of the new arena, raise objections and sometimes resort to outright resistance. Entire clusters granted a state or union territory often remain unreconciled to the non-inclusion of others from their 'ethnic' group who stand beyond the state or even the national boundary. They may also resent the presence of other social groups within their new bailiwick, or the migration of 'strangers' into the area.

Squabbles and splits within 'tribal' clusters frequently develop which undo political accommodations that were forged in response to what had seemed a cluster's unanimous demands. Individual 'tribes' within such clusters sometimes complain of injustice. Even when such resentments have little force, strife can arise out of rivalries between leaders of different tribes, out of 'localism', or out of linguistic and even ideological disputes.[29] Religion sometimes provides groups in the region with a sense of common identity, but it can also sow division among them. And the list of religions which command devotion is remarkably long—Christianity, Hinduism, Buddhism, Islam, and even Judaism! None of the world's major religions is absent. Generational rivalries often develop between older sets of leaders and younger, better-educated elements— especially when there are large numbers of educated unemployed, but not only then. At times, these have been compounded by conflict over systems of collective ownership of land, to which older leaders cling but which impede the acquisition of institutional finance that is badly needed for development.[30]

The number, frequency, and complexity of such problems in the region is mind-boggling. This is vividly apparent from B. G. Verghese's long and bafflingly detailed account of all this. Even the most enlightened and sensitive attempts to 'manage' such areas by the Government of India can all too easily unravel as a result.

Here the states of the Northeast differ crucially from most 'main-stream' states—in a way which reminds us of something important about most of the rest of India. We noted earlier that in most states,

[29]Verghese, *India's Northeast Resurgent*, pp. 115–17.
[30]Ibid., pp. 120–23, 127–29 and 137.

internal heterogeneities undermine the state-level solidarity which might otherwise produce secessionist movements. The same can be said of the Northeast, but the heterogeneities that we encounter there tend to go further. They undermine not just state-level solidarity but the politics of bargaining and political stability more generally—so that accommodations, once established, tend not to hold.

When they break down, the door opens again to renewed calls for secession, sometimes from their state and sometimes from India. Groups in the region tend strongly to turn—far more quickly than their counterparts elsewhere in the country—to armed struggle against the Central government and/or one another. The proximity of the northeastern states to neighbouring countries which provide a ready source of weapons offers part of the explanation. So does the opportunity to generate funds to purchase arms by smuggling teak, narcotics, etc. But the main root of the problem appears to be the difficulty which most societies in the northeastern states experience in sustaining the politics of bargaining.

Enlightened Central government efforts to manage relations with states in the Northeast have often been admirable.[31] Openness to 'tribal' preferences, offers of elections, and a willingness to revise boundaries have all been apparent much of the time. Generous developmental assistance has raised per capita incomes in most northeastern states to quite high levels.[32] But there have also been mistakes. Early efforts often suffered from ad-hoc-ism. Nehru's postures on northeastern questions sometimes shifted unhelpfully, inspiring resentments among groups in the region. New Delhi's failure to deliver on some promises was and continues to be an irritant. The responses of the security forces have sometimes been excessive—particularly in the days when people were forcibly herded into 'strategic hamlets' on the British Malayan model, but not only then. Verghese's long catalogue of initiatives which might yet be tried suggests that more could have been done.[33] And yet—to

---

[31]Dasgupta, 'Community, Authenticity and Authority', pp. 362–68.

[32]Ibid., p. 349.

[33]Verghese, *India's Northeast Resurgent*, chapters 8 and 16–18.

reiterate—even if much more had been done, severe troubles would still have occurred.

★ ★ ★

To conclude, let us briefly consider first the sources of the difficulties that have afflicted Centre–state relations, and then the prospects for a more accommodative Central government 'management' strategy.

Little has been said here about the role of economic conditions in destabilising Centre–state relations. This is no oversight. Such conditions appear to have had far less importance than socio-cultural and political factors in generating these problems. It can be argued that the remarkable prosperity which Punjab experienced in the years before the early 1980s, or the economic hardship that has long afflicted Kashmir, contributed to the disasters that struck these two regions. There is something in both arguments. But the irresponsible actions of politicians at both national and state levels appear to have loomed much larger in both cases. So, surely, did socio-cultural realities like the majority status within each state of religious groups which were minorities in the country at large. In other states where such socio-cultural factors were absent, we find levels of prosperity or deprivation which match those in these two states—and yet they have not faced the kinds of grotesque breakdowns which have occurred in Punjab and Kashmir.

In Punjab, Kashmir, and especially in the Northeast, geography also matters greatly. All three regions share borders with troublesome neighbours who have often done their best to compound problems which the Government of India faced and—to varying degrees in various regions—created. The geographical isolation of the Northeast from the rest of India, and its separation from most of its traditional trading partners and markets as a result of Partition, have generated immense difficulties.

The mention of Partition reminds us of the negative impact of certain historical legacies—especially in Kashmir and the Northeast. When a Hindu maharaja in Kashmir decided to take his Muslim majority state into the Indian union in the 1940s, this was bound to generate long-term problems for New Delhi. The troubles in the Northeast have intensified as a result not just of Partition, but also of the British disinclination to exercise sovereign power over much of this region. The Indian government after 1947 had no option but to assume the sovereign's role, and that has led inevitably to excruciating dilemmas. The historical legacy in 'mainstream' India has posed far fewer problems. So historical, geographical, and socio-cultural elements—together with political achievements and miscalculations—have counted for much more than have economic factors.

To say this is not to rule out a link between continued economic growth and the survival of the politics of bargaining in India. P. V. Narasimha Rao clearly perceived a connection between these things. He recognised that the decay of political institutions and excessively confrontational political postures were major factors, during the 1980s, in the intensification of social conflict across India and in the mounting difficulties that confronted both Centre–state relations and the politics of bargaining more generally. But he also believed that sustained, and indeed accelerated, economic growth was required if the politics of bargaining was to survive amid rising demands from organised interests. This was an important consideration in his decision to liberalise the Indian economy (see chapter six of this book). The point here is not to deny that his views were justified, but to argue that non-economic factors appear to have had greater importance in the cases that we have examined.

The severe troubles that arose during the 1980s, especially in Punjab and Kashmir, have persuaded many in New Delhi that they need to pursue more accommodative approaches to Centre–state relations. Those inclinations resonate with movement towards a more economistic conception of security policy.

Despite grave developments in Kashmir since early 1999, long experience in coping with a diversity of crises, great and small, in a wide array of states, has equipped many Indian politicians and bureaucrats with the skills and attitudes that will help to make the politics of bargaining work—not perfectly, but tolerably well. They will also be assisted by a major, seldom recognised national resource—the vast army of political 'fixers' at all levels of the system who share those skills and attitudes. The Constitution rightly arms New Delhi with adequate powers to cope with breakdowns. And a

Supreme Court decision in 1994, which requires the Government of India to provide detailed justifications for the imposition of President's Rule, will help to curb overly aggressive actions that were once routine. All of this suggests that accommodative inclinations at the apex of the system might yield substantial benefits.

— *t e n* —

'Towel over Armpit'

Small-Time Political 'Fixers' in the Politics of India's States

Here we encounter small-time political entrepreneurs or 'fixers' who travel to government offices at higher levels in efforts to obtain benefits from official programmes for their villages. They are a major resource—for democracy and development—which India has produced in much greater measure than other developing countries. They have—amid many ambiguities—enhanced democratic competition, transparency and accountability in the political process, at and above the grassroots.[1] They serve as a counterweight to anomie in Indian politics which has long been a concern (see chapter three of this book), and to the centralisation of power in many state governments that has gathered momentum in recent years (chapter fourteen). They have often helped to undermine caste hierarchies in villages—but their increasing popularity in villages also tends to erode the authority of caste elders. Because (as we see in chapter fifteen) those elders have been crucial in arranging accommodations between castes amid the declining acceptance of the old hierarchies, the emergence of 'fixers' and the elders' loss of influence may open the way to greater inter-caste tension and violence.

---

[1] These themes are discussed in far more detail in R. Jenkins and J. Manor, *Politics and the Right to Work: India's Mahatma Gandhi National Rural Employment Guarantee Act* (London/New Delhi/New York, Hurst/ Orient BlackSwan/Oxford University Press).

You are waiting at a bus stand in a very small town in south India to travel to the nearby district headquarters town. You overhear fragments of furtive conversation from within a group of women standing next to you.

'Look, here he comes. Towel over armpit ... trying to look important ... travelling again.'

As they turn to look at a man striding toward them, stifled laughter breaks out among them. But one of the women dissents.

'He helped us', she says. 'Sometimes he is important.'

Her comment and the arrival of the man quell their laughter. He and they politely greet one another with the shy decorum that is customary in this socially conservative region. Then the bus pulls in, and niceties dissolve in the crush to board it. The only people who do not join in the scrum are you and the man who has just arrived, but there is room for everyone and you all get on. As the bus pulls away, he briefly converses with you in incomprehensible English. The women notice, as they are meant to do, and then the jolting of the bus kills all communication.

The phrase, 'towel over armpit', is commonly used in Kannada, the language of the southern state of Karnataka, to refer to members of a sizable army of small-time, freelance political 'fixers' who operate there.[2] They are called that because of their habit of draping a long cotton cloth, resembling a stole, over one shoulder. The towel gives them a rakish look, but it is also practical. They use it to wipe away sweat from their foreheads as they shuttle back and forth between grassroots communities and government offices at higher levels in the system, seeking benefits for the rural dwellers they represent.

These people are middlemen (and nearly all are still male) who serve as crucial political intermediaries between the localities and powerful figures (bureaucrats and, especially, politicians) at higher

[2]I am grateful to M. N. Srinivas for alerting me to this phrase.

levels. Their attire and their air of self-importance make them figures of fun, but they have their uses for local groups, as the latter well understand. They also provide critically important assistance to politicians, especially at election time. These 'fixers' are a major national resource which India possesses in greater abundance than just about any other less developed country.[3]

Only one serious study of political 'fixers' in India has emerged, a perceptive paper focused largely on one state (Andhra Pradesh) by G. Haragopal and the late G. Ram Reddy in 1985.[4] As they noted, 'fixers' operate at all levels, from local to international. But they (like this writer) focused on those who seek to represent local-level interests, since it is there that party organisations are weakest and, thus, that 'fixers' play their most crucial roles as enablers of the democratic process. These people are political operatives 'who do not hold any formal political or administrative positions', but who practice the art of approaching officials for favours and making the wheels of administration move in support of such favours as a profession that is an important source of livelihood and influence for them.[5]

'Fixers' tend to have modest educational qualifications—usually but not always secondary schooling and occasionally some post-secondary education. Many have lived at least briefly in urban centres, but a large majority of them have spent most of their lives in the rural areas where (again) a large majority of them operate and

[3]This became apparent during the research for a book, J. Manor, *The Political Economy of Democratic Decentralization* (Washington, The World Bank, 1999).

[4]G. Ram Reddy and G. Haragopal, 'The Pyraveekar: "The Fixer" in Rural India', *Asian Survey* (November, 1985), pp. 1148–62.

[5]Ibid., pp. 1149–50. In this study, I am largely ignoring three other, less important groups which Haragopal and Reddy mentioned because they occupy official or semi-official positions and thus tend not to function as substantially detached intermediaries. These are: (i) village officers, (ii) politicians higher up, and (iii) employees of government line ministries at and especially above the local level. I have 'largely' (but not entirely) ignored them because one particular set of line ministry employees—local school teachers—are sometimes part-time 'fixers'.

where most Indian voters reside. ('Fixers' are also active in urban areas, but there is less need for their skills there because of the proximity of government offices and a greater density of politically sophisticated citizens. Slum-dwellers, however, are badly in need of such middlemen and are often unable to benefit from their services.

Most of these middlemen practice their craft on a part-time basis, since it brings them income only intermittently—usually at election time when they are often well paid by a candidate and / or a party during a few weeks of campaigning. The 'commissions' that they receive or skim off for arranging bargains between elections— which are often spurned by 'fixers' or simply unavailable—are usually quite modest. So some other source of income—school teaching, agriculture, shop-keeping, salaried or occasional work—is usually required.

Many 'fixers' aspire to full-time careers in politics, especially to nominations to state legislatures, but relatively few appear to obtain this. Seats on elected councils (*panchayats*) at intermediate and local levels are another possibility, but since only five or six of India's states have adequately empowered and funded such bodies, this is usually an unattractive option. Despite these frustrations, many persist in their work—hoping eventually to make a living from politics, and meanwhile enjoying job satisfaction and esteem in the eyes of people at the grassroots.

Haragopal and Reddy noted in 1985 that 'fixers' 'come largely from middle income groups'.[6] This has become less true in the intervening years. People from middle income groups still predominate, but the 1990s have seen a larger minority of people from poor, low status backgrounds emerge as 'fixers'—often but not always seeking benefits for disadvantaged groups.

'Fixers' bring three important things to the political process in India: knowledge, skills and attitudes. Their knowledge includes some understanding—often a sophisticated understanding—of the conditions and problems faced by people at the grassroots. They are familiar with the distinctive informal mechanisms which groups at the local level use to manage their affairs and the resources available

[6]Ibid., p. 1152.

to them. They also have some knowledge of the social order and the informal economy in these localities. They tend to know when and how universalistic government programmes designed much higher up in the system are inappropriate to local conditions and felt needs. They are also aware that higher-level policymakers often commit massive funds to huge projects—large hospitals, dams and the like—which do little to benefit (and sometimes damage) grassroots groups, and which siphon off funds that might be used for small-scale local projects (irrigation channels, minor roads, primary health care centres, etc.) which local groups strongly prefer. Finally, of course, 'fixers' have some understanding of how the political system higher up (usually only *somewhat* higher up) works. This requires a knowledge of power relations between key politicians and bureaucrats.

As these comments indicate, their skills include the ability to operate in the 'idioms' of both local and supra-local politics, and to speak the distinctive political languages used at both levels—they are bi-lingual.[7] They do not survive long in their chosen line of work without knowing how to consult groups at the grassroots and how, on occasion, to help build local-level coalitions—both of which are sometimes delicate processes. They need to be able to extract information from people in authority about government programmes, and to represent local views to those higher up. That requires an ability to find out whom to contact and lobby, and how these things should be done—usually by way of a subtle mixture of deference and assertiveness, plus some salesmanship since they need to persuade higher-level politicians that a response to a request serves the latters' interests. Once a response is proffered, 'fixers' may also need persuasive skills to 'sell' it to grassroots groups, since they often bring back less than a full loaf.[8]

---

[7] W. H. Morris-Jones' time-honoured essay on this remains remarkably relevant today, amid greatly changed circumstances: 'India's Political Idioms', in C. H. Phillips (ed.), *Politics and Society in India* (London, Allen and Unwin, 1963), pp. 133–54.

[8] The similarity of this discussion of skills to that provided by Reddy and Haragopal in 'The Pyraveeker', p. 1153 indicates that little has changed on this front since the mid-1980s.

Their attitudes include an implicit awareness that political relations between local and higher levels do not amount to a zero-sum game, that they can provide much of the 'value-added' within those relationships, and that they can help to foster at least limited 'synergy' between levels.[9] They are not immune to the passions that often grip interests, castes or religious groups, but they tend to recognise that when passions are inflamed, it can get in the way of the mundane bargains which they seek to forge—by generating poisonous animosities and (more crucially) by creating unrealistic expectations that are the very bane of 'fixers' lives. They also tend to understand that many of those who seek to ignite such passions are members of tightly organised extremist groups who prefer to exclude free-booting 'fixers'.

The earlier reference to 'fixers' as—on balance—'enablers of the democratic process' does not imply a claim that they are committed, in some philosophical sense, to democratic principles. They are mostly rough and ready types who scarcely reflect on the meaning of their role or on the business of democratic government. But they are driven by gut-level understandings which—most of the time—serve the cause of democracy quite well.

They have their eyes firmly fixed on the main chance, and they know that their interests are best served by open, competitive, representative politics—by pluralism. They have an intense distaste for politicians who over-centralise, or who undermine informally and formally rule-bound governance in the interests of partisan advantage or personal domination.[10] They detest politicians and bureaucrats who are unresponsive or ineffectual, or who pay little heed to development programmes. Their distaste is anchored in an awareness that all of these things choke off opportunities for 'fixers' and for the people at the grassroots whom they seek to serve—whom (as we explain just below) they *must* serve if they are to get anywhere in their careers.

[9]P. Evans, 'Government Action, Social Capital and Development: Reviewing the Evidence on Synergy', *World Development* (June, 1996), pp. 1119–32.

[10]I am grateful to Sudipta Kaviraj for help in developing this point.

Most 'fixers' are not above acts of malfeasance. But again, in their gut they know that corruption undermines them. This is especially true of corruption inspired from above, but they know that it also applies to their own illicit acts. This serves as a potent check on profiteering by 'fixers', and as a solid reason for them to support higher-level politicians who restrain themselves and their subordinates from corruption.

So if we ask whether 'fixers' genuinely seek to serve the people whom they claim to represent, and whether they can actually make much of a difference to them and to the democratic process, the answer in each case is a qualified 'yes'.

Most of them tend to be more concerned with their own interests and careers than with the welfare of the people whom they serve, but they are not strangers to altruism. Many take real pride in having helped to arrange benefits for grassroots groups. More crucially, nearly all 'fixers' understand that villagers in most parts of India are now so politically aware and assertive that unless they can deliver something tangible, they will be unable to earn esteem at the local level on which their careers depend. So the distinction between their self-interest and their ability to assist rural dwellers is something of a false dichotomy.

Can they make much difference to people at the local level? Yes they can—in modest but significant ways—but only when conditions are right. Much of the detail which follows seeks to identify those conditions, but two stand out and are worth stressing here—even though they may seem obvious. It is crucial that ruling parties at the state level be interested in providing somewhat responsive government, and that their attitudes and approaches to governance do not cripple their capacity to achieve that. Most (though not all) of these ruling parties—despite many glaring failings—genuinely seek to be responsive. But many of them largely fail in this because they are too incompetent at political management, too inclined towards centralised control, too preoccupied with profiteering, with factional strife within the ruling party, with vengeful treatment of the opposition, or with something else. Many ruling parties fail because their organisations are too weak and ineffectual to respond adequately to pressures from below.

'Fixers' serve as important conduits for such pressures for greater responsiveness, by constantly acquainting power-holders with opportunities to respond to felt needs. They also provide, through their own services to higher authority, one means by which even incapacitated ruling parties can respond.

If we ask precisely whom 'fixers' seek to represent, the answers vary. Some attempt to obtain goods and services which would benefit entire communities at the local level. Others seek mainly or solely to assist specific groups within local arenas—often elites, but also specific castes or interests, including disadvantaged groups. There is insufficient space in a study of this length to delve into this complex issue.

It was understandable in the period up to 1970 or so that these middlemen should have received very little attention from analysts of Indian politics. In those years, the organisational strength of major parties, especially the Congress Party, left little room for largely freelance 'fixers' of this kind. But the decay of party organisations—again, especially that of the Congress Party—over the years since 1970 has created openings and a need for such 'fixers' (and for analyses of them).

Decay undermined the capacity of parties to penetrate into local arenas, and to respond to mounting demands from the grassroots. It also undermined the performance of ruling parties at the state level, and helped to cause frequent changes of state governments. Incumbent governments in major Indian states (those with populations over 25 million) have been thrown out by voters at well over 60 per cent of elections since 1980. (Incumbent governments have also lost six of the last seven parliamentary elections.) As a result, 'fixers' have not only performed roles which were once handled by party organisations, they have also tended to maintain loose and temporary associations with any single party, so that they can continue to operate when changes of government occur.

The present chapter considers evidence on these people during the 1990s.[11] It seeks for the first time to assess them in a *comparative* context, by considering their activities in a diversity of Indian states.

[11] It is based in part on discussions with analysts in various states who have knowledge of 'fixers', and with 'fixers' or ex-'fixers' themselves—over

It will become apparent that they face very different circumstances in the various states, and that these circumstances influence the supply of 'fixers', their activities, and their contribution to the politics of representation, accommodation and coalition-building.

A number of 'circumstances' are worth noting here at the outset, before we immerse ourselves in the politics of various states. They include:

(i)   the level of economic development in a state,
(ii) the nature of the state's party system, including the degree of antipathy between the main parties,
(iii) the relationship between various parties and their social bases,
(iv) the character and strength of various party organisations— including the degree to which they penetrate into grassroots rural arenas, and their openness to 'fixers',
(v)   the modes of governance (commandist, pluralist, etc.) which party leaders, especially those in ruling parties, employ,
(vi) the extent to which corruption and criminalisation characterise a state's politics, and
(vii) the strength of democratic decentralisation (*panchayati raj*) and of institutions that are intended to promote participation by local committees in the management of common property resources, schools, irrigation systems, etc., in each state.

We will return to these issues later in this study. But let us now consider the problems and opportunities which small-time 'fixers' encounter in a diversity of Indian states.

Andhra Pradesh

In the southern state of Andhra Pradesh, 'fixers' have emerged in strength in the more economically developed sub-regions— especially in the rich coastal belt. But across much of the state, in districts with large numbers of extremely poor people and severe inequalities, it is harder for them to arise. There are many such districts. Despite this state's (overblown) go-ahead image as a centre

---

the last decade and especially during field studies in eight Indian states during 1998–99.

for rapid development through high technology, its overall literacy rate at the 1991 census (32.7 per cent) was lower even than the supposed basket cases of north India, Uttar Pradesh (41.6 per cent) and Bihar (38.5 per cent).

Very poor (or no) schools in these poorer areas deprive most people of the good secondary education which most would be 'fixers' possess. Widespread deprivation makes civil society there both quiescent and, when it rouses itself, more inclined to drastic acts against exploitation than to polite appeals through 'fixers' for government benefits. The leftist insurgents who are active in many of these under-developed areas deal aggressively with those seeking to act as middlemen with the government, since the latter might demonstrate that armed resistance is less promising than political bargaining. So, many parts of Andhra Pradesh offer 'fixers' fallow ground.

Lively competition within a bi-polar party system—which this state certainly has (unlike India generally)—usually encourages the emergence of 'fixers'. This is true up to a point in Andhra Pradesh, but it is greatly outweighed but the (to 'fixers') inhospitable character of the present state government and ruling party.

Since late 1995, the chief minister of Andhra Pradesh has been Chandrababu Naidu who leads a regional party, the Telugu Desam. He is widely perceived to be one of India's most dynamic young leaders. But his management of his party's organisation, and (more crucially) his systematic and largely successful efforts to maximise his personal dominance, have severely undercut opportunities for 'fixers'. In contrast to more pluralistic chief ministers (see the section on Madhya Pradesh), Naidu substantially controls and makes fiercely partisan use of every possible extension of government into rural arenas.

Consider, for example, his approach to two sets of local institutions which are supposed to foster participatory governance at the grassroots. On the one hand, he has packed local water users' and education committees (which have a role in decisions in these fields) with party loyalists. He has generously funded and empowered these committees, precisely because they are dominated by loyalists. On the other hand, he has denied substantial powers and resources to elected councils at lower levels (*panchayati raj* institutions) because he cannot exclude representatives of opposition parties from them as effectively as he has done from the other committees. And he has set the water and education committees *against* the decentralised councils in order to weaken the latter further.[12]

All of this, and Naidu's efforts to close off access to the bureaucracy to non-members of his party, have curtailed opportunities for 'fixers'. They cannot remain outside but on congenial terms with the Telugu Desam, as most would like to do in case the government changes. To obtain benefits for local communities, they need to join the ruling party. Happily for them, the Telugu Desam has a reasonably porous organisation. Unlike Communist parties across India or the ruling Dravida Munnetra Kazhagam (DMK) in neighbouring Tamil Nadu, it does not usually require them to serve their time and adhere to an ideology before granting them influence.

But the strongly partisan approach of Chief Minister Naidu still makes many 'fixers' hesitate to become involved with the Telugu Desam. This is partly explained by their aversion to being rigorously manipulated by a politician like Naidu. And if they join his party in the present, intensely adversarial climate, they will incur the wrath of members of the Congress Party (the main opposition force which may take power after a future state election) and forfeit any influence under a future Congress government.

So 'fixers' in Andhra Pradesh, who are already in short supply as a result of economic under-development in much of the state, tend to remain aloof—in temporary retirement—until the political wind changes. The chief minister does not realise it, but this denies him the services of many activists who could enhance his government's and party's reputations for responsiveness.

Madhya Pradesh

If we want further evidence of how Naidu's attempts at excessive control can damage his interests, we can find it in the contrasting case

---

[12]These comments are based on field investigations in the state in March–April 1999.

of Madhya Pradesh. Its Chief Minister, Digvijay Singh, has adopted a much less partisan and more pluralistic approach to governance. (For more detail, see chapter thirteen of this book.) It earned him substantial political dividends at a state election in November 1998 when his government became one of only a tiny number in recent years to be re-elected after a full five-year term.

Like Naidu, Singh has encouraged the proliferation of local committees involved with schools, watershed development, forest management, etc. But unlike Naidu, he has not sought to pack these with party loyalists. He is content to see people from the main opposition party (in this state, the BJP) involved in such committees. Unlike Naidu, Singh has also devolved substantial powers and resources onto elected councils at lower levels (*panchayats*), and he has encouraged collaboration between both sets of institutions. He is more interested in responsive, participatory governance than in partisan control from above.

The implications of this are complicated for 'fixers'. On the one hand, the existence of so many potent bodies at the local level has reduced their opportunities to play their preferred role as middlemen between villagers and the government at higher levels. If villagers want a new school, or tubewells, or whatever, they now turn not to a 'fixer' but to one or more of these bodies—which have the power and resources to respond quickly.

On the other hand, canny 'fixers' were quick to recognise that membership in these bodies offered them splendid opportunities to develop and make creative use of their skills at representation, lobbying, etc.—so, many of them got themselves elected to these bodies. They could do so safe in the knowledge that, in the absence of the kind of intensely adversarial atmosphere that prevails in Andhra Pradesh, their long-term careers would not be damaged by association with the current ruling party. As a result, Singh's government in Madhya Pradesh has benefited far more than Naidu's from the skills of 'fixers' who can help to make open, representative politics work well. This contributed, along with several other things, to his re-election in 1998—despite the fact that low levels of economic development in much of Madhya Pradesh impede the emergence of 'fixers' in abundance.

Orissa

Less has been achieved by 'fixers' in Orissa than in any other state discussed here, for two main reasons. First, extreme poverty and the very low level of economic development in one of the state's two main sub-regions—western Orissa—have yielded an exceedingly quiescent civil society by the standards of most other states. This problem is compounded by the exploitative grip which outsiders exercise over 'tribal' groups across much of that sub-region, which again has few parallels in other Indian states. This chokes off opportunities for the small numbers of 'fixers' that arise there.

Even in the more developed coastal sub-region, however, political 'fixers' have achieved less than their counterparts in other states. This is mainly explained by the long-standing dominance of Orissa's major parties by an elite drawn mainly from numerically tiny high caste groups. It is well nigh astonishing that the numerically powerful cultivating castes, which control much of the land in coastal areas, have been largely excluded from influential posts in ruling elites at the state level. Such landed groups had achieved pre-eminence in the politics of most Indian states by the late 1950s, but (partly owing to fragmentation along caste lines) they have never achieved that in Orissa.

The elites which have largely excluded them have governed in a grossly overcentralised, unresponsive manner—which is bad news not only for landed groups but for 'fixers' as well. These elites have made 'tall promises' of industrialisation over several decades, but have achieved little in this vein because they have followed through only ineffectually on grandiose rhetoric and plans. And yet their dominance persists, for reasons which cry out for detailed analysis—little of which is currently available.

For a taste of this political elite's dangerous detachment—from 'fixers' and from important social forces—consider the two most prominent political leaders in the state today. The leader of the Opposition, Naveen Patnaik (son of the late Biju Patnaik who was twice chief minister), has spent most of his life outside the state and leads his party in a manner which is at once both highly autocratic and foppish. He does not speak the regional language, Oriya, and has stated flatly that he has no plans to learn it. The present Chief Minister, Giridhar Gamang, is a 'tribal', but he has spent several decades in the national Parliament, and is too poorly acquainted with political networks in the state to govern effectively. His intense faith in numerology, which guides him in many decisions, was greatly strengthened by a recent event. He was persuaded to change his name from Gomango to Gamang, since this was said by his advisors to make him more likely (for numerological reasons) to succeed in politics—and soon thereafter he was selected by Sonia Gandhi to be chief minister. He speaks English and a 'tribal' dialect, but he has great difficulty expressing himself in proper Oriya.

This leaves Orissa facing a situation which has no parallel in the history of independent India. The leaders of *both* main parties are unable to communicate directly to voters in the regional language! This and the over-centralised, ineffectual governance that comes with it leave 'fixers' in this state largely at a loss.

Tamil Nadu

As in Orissa, small-time 'fixers' in Tamil Nadu are a seriously under-developed resource, but for very different reasons. Unlike Orissa, Tamil Nadu is well developed economically, has long had a comparatively lively civil society and—apart from one five-year spell (1991–96) under a brutish government bent on plunder—has not experienced severe misrule.

The explanation for the sad condition of political 'fixers' in Tamil Nadu is rooted in the character of the state's two main political parties. The first of these is the Dravida Munnetra Kazhagam (DMK) which emerged from the strong pre-independence Dravidian movement against Brahmin domination of Tamil culture and public administration. It held power in the state from 1967 to 1977, between 1989 and 1991, and at this writing has been in power once again since 1996. The other major party is the All-India Anna Dravida Munnetra Kazhagam (AIADMK), an off-shoot of the DMK which was founded by the vastly popular matinee idol, M. G. Ramachandran (known as 'MGR'). It (and he) ruled the state from 1977 to 1988 when he died, and again from 1991 to 1996 after his sometime co-star and companion, Jayalalithaa had consolidated control over the party. Each of these two parties has made life difficult for 'fixers' in its own distinctive way. The DMK has a strong, disciplined organisation that penetrates down to or close to the local level in most parts of the state. Uniquely among explicitly regional parties, it has a well elaborated cultural and political ideology which retains much of its hold on party activists, despite a degree of erosion in recent years. Its organisation has also proved remarkably resilient, most notably during fully 16 years in opposition to the ruling AIADMK. The point as far as 'fixers' are concerned is that such a strong, penetrative organisation tends to exclude them and to channel the distribution of goods, services and funds through its network of card-carrying activists. When the DMK is in power 'fixers' have only the most minimal opportunities to 'fix' anything.

The AIADMK, by contrast, has a weak organisation. Under MGR and—to a far greater extent—under Jayalalithaa, it has been more of a cheering section for the adoration of the supreme leader than a genuine organisation. Governance, patronage distribution and (under Jayalalithaa) the looting of both the government and the state more generally have been highly centralised. This has left even devout party loyalists—never mind loosely associated 'fixers' at intermediate and local levels—with few chances to influence the delivery of goods and services.

With next to no opportunities to practice their craft under the main parties, 'fixers' have not developed as a significant resource in Tamil Nadu. This, together with the longstanding hostility of both the DMK and the AIADMK to democratic decentralisation[13] have meant that the deepening of democracy and the development of

---

[13]The leaders of the two main parties have been far more reluctant than their counterparts in most other states to devolve powers and resources onto elected councils at lower levels for two main reasons. They have had a strong faith in centralised modes of governance. And the intense, even vicious rivalry between the two parties has made the leaders of each exceedingly reluctant to provide the other party with opportunities to demonstrate its popularity at elections to decentralised councils.

responsive governance which have occurred in many other Indian states have not taken place here.

Maharashtra

In this (economically) highly developed state, small-time 'fixers' again face difficult, even grim conditions. But in Maharashtra, unlike Tamil Nadu or Orissa, their problems are temporary. At this writing, a state government made up of two parties of the Hindu right—the Shiv Sena and the BJP—is nearing the end of its five-year term. Its truly dire record has made it very unpopular. The electorate will throw it out at the upcoming state election, unless the two main opposition parties divide the anti-incumbent vote about equally—an extremely unlikely possibility.

The Shiv Sena/BJP government here has governed unwisely—making wild populist promises, none of which it has fulfilled. It has been ineffectual—with mostly bungling ministers alienating the state's very able bureaucracy by behaving (as one senior civil servant put it[14]) in 'arrogant, abusive, and atrocious' ways. It has been profligate—reducing what was one of India's two most fiscally sound state governments to near-crisis. And it has been corrupt—combining immense rake-offs of public funds with systematic exercises in extortion the like of which no Indian state has witnessed before.

'Fixers' face two different sets of problems from the two ruling parties. The BJP largely excludes them by working through its own activists. The Shiv Sena's organisation is grossly over-centralised and substantially criminalised. It therefore badly needs help from 'fixers', but it has thoroughly alienated them by exorbitant demands for bribes and by threats of and the actual use of violence.

As a result, 'fixers' have temporarily gone to ground, and have lent their efforts to the election campaigns of the opposition parties—two variants of Congress. Maharashtra's high levels of economic development, its lively civil society, and its tradition (throughout most of the period since 1947) of imaginative management of

[14]Interview, Mumbai, 2 April 1999.

'fixers' have given the state a potentially formidable resource to which ruling politicians will soon turn once again. But the Shiv Sena/BJP regime has made little use of it.

Uttar Pradesh

India's largest state, Uttar Pradesh contains several seriously under-developed sub-regions where political 'fixers' have consequently struggled to emerge in strength. But for many years until the early 1990s, such people found abundant opportunities to apply their skills to good effect. During the 1990s, however, the situation has—from their point of view—deteriorated markedly.

Four things have contributed at least modestly to this, and a fifth has been particularly damaging. The first four are as follows.

(a) The woeful condition of party organisations in recent years, and the constant turnover of district-level leaders in every party except the BJP, make it difficult for state-level leaders to exploit the skills of 'fixers'.

(b) A time-honoured tradition in this state of aggressively centralised leadership inclines state-level leaders to bully lower-level activists, which discourages the latter (including 'fixers') from constructive work.

(c) Serious corruption and criminalisation in the politics of Uttar Pradesh have eroded the accommodative skills of political activists at lower levels.

(d) The emergence in the 1990s of something akin to a three-party system has placed all state governments in a precarious position and has made it impossible for any party to provide carefully crafted political management (of, among other things, 'fixers') for very long.

More damaging than any of these things, however, have been the ferocious animosities that divide three social blocs which underpin the three main parties in the state, and hence the parties themselves. This has led governments here to concentrate far less during the 1990s on arranging political bargains across lines that separate social collectivities, than do their counterparts in other states. They have focused far less on development programmes with promise over the medium term than on symbolic actions which—over the short term—bolster the self-esteem of their respective social blocs and enrage people in other blocs.

Since 'fixers' flourish when governments pursue political bargaining and development programmes from which benefits can be extracted for people at the local level, this trend has seriously undermined their prospects in Uttar Pradesh.

Karnataka

For political 'fixers', the southern state of Karnataka offers a reasonably promising environment. This is the result of both positive and negative things that can be said about this state.

On the positive side, at most (though not all) times since independence in 1947, this state has been governed by relatively effective, enlightened political managers who have turned increasingly to free-booting 'fixers' as party organisations have become less effective. Even those managers with tolerably good party organisations—such as the present-day Congress Party which has recently been rebuilt—have usually been willing to augment the strength and reach of their parties by working extensively through 'fixers'. Along with comparatively enlightened political management has come a preoccupation with constructive development programmes, especially for rural areas where most of the votes are. This has again opened up opportunities for 'fixers' to arrange the delivery of goods and services to village-level groups.

Land and wealth are distributed comparatively equitably across much of Karnataka—particularly the southern half which has long had less landlessness than almost any other part of South Asia. Partly because of this (and because social reform movements, ancient and modern, have had a potent impact here), relations between social groups have been comparatively congenial—far more than in Uttar Pradesh in the 1990s and in those areas of central India affected by leftist insurgency, and rather more than in most other states. This has persuaded all major political parties to seek support from a very wide array of interests and castes, and thus to build 'rainbow' coalitions. Such coalition-building, even by strong parties, is greatly facilitated by working through 'fixers'—as most Karnataka politicians understand well.

To turn to a set of concerns which might be read positively or negatively—Karnataka has never been governed by a political party with a strongly exclusive party cadre in the manner of the DMK in Tamil Nadu. Nor has any state-level leader since 1972 sought the kind of thoroughgoing partisan control over the distribution of patronage or over government agencies and programmes which Chief Minister Naidu in Andhra Pradesh has exercised in recent years. Politicians of all ruling parties in Karnataka (like Chief Minister Digvijay Singh in Madhya Pradesh) have been more inclined toward a pluralistic approach to governance.

On the negative side, Karnataka has retreated somewhat since 1992 from the remarkably strong system of democratic decentralisation (*panchayati raj*) which prevailed there after 1987.[15] That system denied 'fixers' many of their former opportunities, although many of them saw that it implied this and got themselves elected to decentralised bodies. It also enhanced the appetite of rural dwellers for quick, effective government responses to felt needs at the local level. Since the (moderate) dilution of the powers of decentralised councils, that appetite can only be satisfied by the extensive use of 'fixers' by ruling parties, as most party leaders recognise. The result has been greater opportunities for 'fixers'.

★ ★ ★

What are the implications of all of this for small-time 'fixers', and for our understanding of the democratic process at the state level in India? We have long known that great variations—political, social and economic—exist from state to state. This study indicates that there are at least a few more variations than we have fully recognised previously. This is true in at least two senses.

---

[15]R. C. Crook and J. Manor, *Democracy and Decentralization in South Asia and West Africa: Participation, Accountability and Performance* (Cambridge University Press, Cambridge, 1998), chapter two.

First, different socio-economic conditions—variations in the level and character of economic development, in the intensity of antagonism between social groups, etc.—can impede or facilitate the emergence of 'fixers' who are a potentially crucial political resource. They also influence the extent to which the politics of bargaining and representation (in which 'fixers' specialise) can develop, and the character of such politics.

Second, the political management styles of state-level leaders and ruling parties vary greatly, as do leaders' capabilities as managers. Two important elements of this are their *willingness* and their *ability* to work through 'fixers'. These things obviously have a potent impact on the opportunities and frustrations which 'fixers' face. We can, with some simplification, identify six types of leaders at the state level in India. (There is, as we shall see, some overlap between some of these types.)

(i) *Pluralists*: They adopt (in varying degrees) a relatively relaxed approach to political management, in that they do not seek to impose much in the way of partisan control over state-level political systems. They create highly favourable conditions for 'fixers'—by actively seeking their help, and by concentrating on development programmes on which they base their bids for re-election and which provide abundant opportunities for 'fixers'.

Pluralists, however, vary greatly in their capacity to cultivate popular support and win re-election. This group includes successful leaders like Chief Minister Digvijay Singh (Congress) of Madhya Pradesh who was re-elected in late 1998 after a full term in power—a rare achievement in India over the last decade. But it also includes leaders like Ashok Gehlot (Congress) in Rajasthan since 1998, whose performance cannot yet be adequately judged, and J. H. Patel (Janata Dal, now disintegrating) in Karnataka since 1996 who has been so relaxed that he has allowed events to spin out of control.

(ii) *Partisan 'control freaks'*: They seek to turn every programme and extension of government into an instrument to further the interests of their party. People and institutions that stand outside their control are starved of power and resources. Since they regard most 'fixers' as insufficiently partisan, they tend to exclude them from their tightly controlled patronage systems. The main example of this type in Chief Minister Chandrababu Naidu (Telugu Desam) in Andhra Pradesh.

(iii) *Leaders of penetrative, disciplined and ideologically focused parties*: The main examples of this are the Communist Party of India-Marxist (CPI-M) governments in West Bengal and Kerala, and the DMK in Tamil Nadu. They tend to exclude fixers, albeit in different ways. The two CPI-M governments have acted forcefully to empower and fund elected councils (*panchayats*) at lower levels, in which their party activists loom large—although opposition parties also have opportunities within them. This catalyses extensive participation and decision-making at lower levels, but it also greatly reduces the need for freelance 'fixers' since their traditional tasks are largely performed by *panchayats*. The DMK, by contrast, operates in a centralised manner and has starved *panchayats* of power and funds—so that DMK leaders bear some resemblance to Naidu in Andhra Pradesh, although their party organisation has more institutional substance than his does.

(iv) *Vastly corrupt leaders*: Two striking recent examples are Jayalalithaa in Tamil Nadu (1991–96) and the Shiv Sena/BJP government in Maharashtra since 1995. They offer 'fixers' little other than exorbitant demands for bribes and menacing postures. Jayalalithaa's system was highly centralised, the Shiv Sena/BJP's is less so—but both drive 'fixers' underground and inspire widespread popular resentment.

(v) *Leaders incapable of delivering goods, services and development*: Two examples are the current Congress Party leadership in Orissa and Lalu Prasad Yadav in Bihar.[16] 'Fixers'—who have emerged only in small numbers in both states as a result of low levels of economic development—find it well nigh impossible to operate under such leaders because the latter make little effort to promote development

[16]The Shiv Sena in Maharashtra (although not its coalition partner there, the BJP) is also largely incapable of delivering goods and services. But corruption outweighs and is the source of that incapacity, so it falls mainly into type iv.

programmes with which 'fixers' can engage, or to deal with such middlemen.

Here again, however, these leaders have produced different outcomes. The incapacity of all recent Orissa governments has been rooted in an elitism which makes it oblivious to the need to follow 'tall promises' with purposeful action. And at present, the problem is compounded by the inability of the current chief minister (a long-time absentee from the state) to understand conditions and the political networks which exist there. Lalu Prasad Yadav, by contrast, has won re-election once despite his (and virtually everyone's) ignorance even of the funds available to each government department, and his near-total neglect of development programmes. He won thanks to theatrical gestures to raise the self-esteem of disadvantaged groups, and his extraordinary ability to split opposition parties. Whether he can do so again, amid scandal, is another matter.

(vi) *Leaders preoccupied with the politics of spite*: They offer little in the way of concrete development programmes with long-term promise. Instead, they concentrate on largely symbolic acts with short-term impact, which are designed to inspire triumphalism among the social groups that form their base and to insult groups opposed to them. In such circumstances, 'fixers' find very few openings. Lalu Prasad Yadav bears some resemblance to this type, but the main example is the present government (and all governments during the 1990s) in Uttar Pradesh where no party has a broad enough social base to govern securely or for long.

In most Indian states, those where ruling parties lack organisational substance and reach, there will continue to be a great need for 'fixers' and the services which they can provide. That need can be reduced by either of two developments, but in most states, neither is likely to occur anytime soon.

The first of these is the creation and maintenance of a strong penetrative party organisation which is responsive to felt needs at lower levels. But only the CPI-M in West Bengal and (to a lesser degree) in Kerala, and the DMK in Tamil Nadu appear capable of this—and in the case of the DMK, responsiveness remains a problem. (It is possible that the BJP has this sort of organisation in certain states, but this writer's analysis of the available evidence raises doubts about this.) Elsewhere, state-level units of parties gain strength for a time—as we see at present with the Congress Party in Karnataka. But they tend eventually to lapse into decay.

The second development is the creation of well-funded and substantially empowered *panchayati raj* institutions. They perform the services in which 'fixers' specialise more systematically than informal networks of middlemen can. But only five or six of India's state governments have backed *panchayats* adequately. And some of them have later reversed course when jealous state-level politicians have clawed back power from decentralised councils. Partial reversals have occurred in Karnataka in 1992 and in Madhya Pradesh in early 1999.

So neither of these two developments appears likely to occur in the vast majority of Indian states. The need for 'fixers' will thus remain great across most of India. That does not mean, however, that most state-level politicians will create conditions that are congenial to 'fixers'.

If we leave aside those rare cases where penetrative, responsive parties exist (leadership type iii above), or where strong *panchayati raj* institutions have been created—and four of the remaining five types of leaders listed above tend not to do so: 'control freaks', corrupt leaders, leaders of incapable ruling parties, and leaders who pursue the politics of spite—we are left with only the pluralists. They consistently reach out to' 'fixers', but pluralists are in short supply, and some of them (like Chief Minister Patel in Karnataka) govern so ineptly that they cannot win re-election.

So even though there is a great need in most states for 'fixers', and even though they are present in some strength in most states, their services will in most cases be seriously under-utilised or completely squandered. This study, then, demonstrates both the creative potential of India's democracy and the failure of many leaders at the state level to make adequate use of it.

— eleven —

PRAGMATIC PROGRESSIVES IN REGIONAL POLITICS

The Case of Devaraj Urs

Between independence in 1947 and the late 1960s, the Congress Party—which was dominant at the national level and in nearly all Indian states—was itself dominated in nearly all states by landowning castes that exercised dominance at the grassroots. That left the disadvantaged majority in rural areas—where elections were (and still are) won and lost—ill served. Indira Gandhi won a huge victory at the 1971 national election by appealing to those disadvantaged groups with a promise to abolish poverty, but then she and most of the state governments that her party controlled did little to deliver on that promise. However, one of her chief ministers—Devaraj Urs in Karnataka—took effective action to benefit and mobilise the disadvantaged majority. He was inspired not by ideology but by pragmatic calculations. It was the only way that he could prevent the dominant landed castes, of which he was not a member, from ousting him. And he gambled (correctly) that the political awakening among disadvantaged groups was strong enough to ensure that they would support him. Other 'pragmatic progressives' emerged in later years (see the discussions of Bhairon Singh Shekhawat and Digvijay Singh in chapters twelve and thirteen), but as this 1980 paper argues, he was the first to succeed at this new type of political strategy.

One of the most promising regional experiments to develop in recent times is that of D. Devaraj Urs in Karnataka which ran from 1972 until his resignation as chief minister in early 1980. In assessing the historical importance of the Urs experiment we must arrive, as far possible, at conclusions on several key issues. We need to know whether he has proved that it is possible to break the control of dominant landed groups over regional politics. We need to know how successful his various programmes for reform have been in politicising the weaker sections of society at whom they were aimed. We need to know how much these programmes have given poor people new economic and political resources, so that they may begin to fend for themselves and the programmes may begin to take on a life of their own, even in the absence of a government to promote them. We need to know how successful Urs has been at generating broad popular support for his experiment and, specifically, how well he has done at building bridges between less prosperous caste Hindus and two other groups from whom they are often divided—Muslims and Scheduled Castes [SCs] (Scheduled Tribes [STs] being a very small group in Karnataka). We also need to know whether any Urs programme is likely in the long-run to prove counter-productive and, if so, whether the experiment as a whole can bear the strain.

Three other issues, which are raised by Urs's initiatives but which can only be settled on the basis of evidence from several regions of India, need to be borne in mind. First, to what extent must regional governments that expect to survive re-election campaigns include at least a significant proportion of the weaker sections of society within their circle of allies receiving spoils—substantive spoils, not just tokenism? Second, does Devaraj Urs, a patently self-interested and pragmatic man, signify not only that it is possible for a chief minister to become something of a progressive in his own interest, but that it is becoming *necessary* for pragmatists to turn progressive? And finally, what parallels are there between the Urs phenomenon and recent developments in other regions? Is he the wave of the future in mainstream India or simply an accident—an eccentric product of circumstance, of his own considerable talents, and of the peculiarly favourable social, economic and political conditions in Karnataka?

Constructing a Progressive Base[1]

One potential misunderstanding needs to be disposed of straightaway. The result of the 1980 Lok Sabha poll was not a negative popular verdict on the Urs regime. This must sound odd since the Urs Congress did not just lose the election in Karnataka, it was buried. The Congress (I) won 27 of the 28 seats (losing the last narrowly to Janata), 23 of which were won by an absolute majority. The Urs Congress came third, behind Janata, in 18 seats and nowhere was it close to victory. Nevertheless, this result should be read as a perverse endorsement of Urs's achievements. Voters believed that Indira Gandhi was the source of the post-1972 reforms and that Urs was merely her instrument. Urs himself had helped to create this impression, mainly because such slavish loyalty to Indira Gandhi was necessary to avoid the kind of irrational intrusions from the high command which have wrecked promising leaders and programmes in other states. The truth, however, is that Urs was principally responsible for the changes in Karnataka and—especially after 1974—he had accomplished these things not because of Indira Gandhi but in spite of her. He also largely protected Karnataka from the distasteful aspects of Emergency despite great pressure from the Sanjay caucus.[2]

The 1980 Lok Sabha result in Karnataka was thus a case of mistaken identity. The break between Urs and Indira Gandhi occurred in June 1979. The main cause of this was the intense pressure that was brought upon Urs by Sanjay Gandhi. When the break came, Urs believed that he had at least two years before the next election to establish in the voters' minds an identity distinct from that of Indira Gandhi. At the time, this was a reasonable assumption. But within a few weeks, the bizarre machinations of politicians in New Delhi had plunged the country into a parliamentary election. Urs had too

[1]This and other issues in this chapter are analysed in great depth in E. Raghavan and J. Manor, *Broadening and Deepening Democracy: Political Innovation in Karnataka* (Routledge, New Delhi and London, 2009).

[2]See J. Manor, 'Where Congress Survived: Five States in the Indian General Election of 1977', *Asian Survey* (August 1978). Interviews with four senior officials, Bangalore and Delhi, January 1980.

little time to carve out a separate identity for himself, hampered as he was by illness and the need to spend time outside the state. Voters generally had one of two reactions. Most were confused, not fully grasping that a split between Urs and Indira Gandhi had occurred. Thirty-eight of his election rallies closed with cheers for both him and Indira Gandhi. The second reaction was anger at Urs for his bad grace in attacking a woman and a person whom he had recently lauded. Even many Congress (I) workers in the state concede that Urs's record won Indira Gandhi the election. She polled many votes from those who opposed Urs, but her majorities were predominantly based upon the coalition of interests which Urs had constructed. One of the main aims behind Urs's unforced resignation as chief minister when the election trends became clear was to dramatise to voters that he and Indira Gandhi were now in opposite camps.[3] The widespread reports of shock among Karnataka villagers, that their votes for Indira Gandhi and the hand symbol had caused Urs to resign, lend credence to the view that most votes were not cast against Urs.

There can be no doubt that Urs has demonstrated that it is possible to break the control of dominant landed groups over state-level politics in Karnataka.[4] Put briefly, Urs became chief minister in 1972 after a quarter-century of Lingayat-Vokkaliga ascendancy in state politics. He was from a tiny *jati* that had no link to either of these groups. So in the interests of his own survival, he had to mobilise support among the less powerful sections of society who formed well over 60 per cent of the state's population. Both his selection and his survival during his early months in office owed much to the support of Indira Gandhi. But before long, Urs developed a broad range of reform and social welfare programmes which—together with his extraordinary talent as a political operator—won him

---

[3]Interview with Devaraj Urs, Bangalore, 16 January 1980.

[4]J. Manor, 'Structural Changes in Karnataka Politics', *Economic and Political Weekly*, 29 October 1977, pp. 1865–69. For background on the development of the system Urs displaced, see J. Manor, *Political Change in an Indian State: Mysore, 1917–1950* (Australian National University Press, Canberra, 1977).

broad support not only among the groups who had suffered the dominance of Lingayats and Vokkaligas, but also among poorer elements within those two dominant groups. His programmes hastened the erosion of vote-banks which was already occurring as a result of socio-economic change and growing political awareness. Urs's new alliance of the weaker sections of society provided a firm base for election victories in 1977, 1978 and, ironically, in 1980.

Land Reform

Let us begin by considering the most crucial of the Urs programmes, land reform. In 1955, when Daniel Thorner delivered his five classic lectures on agrarian India, he included Mysore among the 'areas of least change' since independence. Most of the other areas which came together the following year to form the composite state of Mysore (now Karnataka) witnessed some perceptible change. But neither the anticipation nor the enforcement of land reform laws had done much to alter the old agrarian structure.[5] In old Mysore, the inertia which prevailed was partly explained by the low incidence of gross inequalities in the distribution of land. The state had one of the highest proportions of owner-cultivators and lowest incidences of landlessness in the subcontinent. More important, however, was the preeminence enjoyed in state politics by representatives of the two dominant landowning groups, the Vokkaligas and the Lingayats.

In 1961, the legislature of the enlarged state passed a new Land Reforms Act. It created a common framework for the whole state, the constituent parts of which had previously been under five separate administrative authorities with rather varied land laws. The driving force behind the Act (which came into effect in 1965) was the Revenue Minister Kadidal Manjappa (a Vokkaliga), an idealist who had vivid memories from his youth of sufferings experienced by land-poor, and landless neighbours. On paper, the Act banned leases (with minor, insignificant exceptions) and gave tenants considerable security against takeovers by landowners of the plots which they

---

[5]Thorner's lectures were later published as *The Agrarian Prospect in India*, second edition (University Press, Delhi, 1976). See particularly, pp. 31–46.

work. It fixed a ceiling on holdings—with the excess to be distributed among the poor—and banned the acquisition of land by anyone except cultivators and agricultural labourers, unless a buyer planned to take up cultivation.

It was, however, a failure. Exemptions for co-operatives, sugar mills, joint farming societies and the like created loop holes which allowed many to escape the net of land ceilings which in any case were set rather high. The claims of tenants had to be dealt with by tribunals whose procedures were cumbersome and easily circumvented and, after 1968, by officials who were overburdened with other work and intimidated by politicians representing landed interests. Certain provisions of the new law were used by landlords to resume control of lands from tenants in ways unintended by the framers of the Act. There was also a failure of political will by politicians at the state level—excluding Manjappa and a few others—who depended on vote-banks in the gift of landed groups.[6]

Under Devaraj Urs, a new and substantially different Land Reforms Act was passed in 1973. Under it, the only persons eligible to hold land are those engaged in personal cultivation, with the sole exception of soldiers and sailors who are a tiny minority in Karnataka. Even widows, minors and disabled persons are barred from leasing land. Share-cropping is similarly abolished. The use of hired labour remains legal, but only through payment of wages (in cash or kind) and not in a share of the crop. Violators of the ban on the leasing of land are to be punished severely with, among other things, loss of the land to the government. Before 1974, landlords had the right—subject to certain restrictions—to resume control of tenanted land. The new Act forbids this. Where the old law merely strengthened tenants' rights to occupy the land that they worked, the 1974 Act gives the government ownership of all tenanted lands. The government is then to confer ownership of these lands to the tenants who worked them.[7]

[6]Interviews with Kadidal Manjappa, Bangalore, 6 July 1972 and 16 January 1980.

[7]M. A. S. Rajan, 'Land Reforms in Karnataka: Contexts and Relationships', manuscript, Bangalore, 1979.

Tenants obtain land by making application to land tribunals, of which there are now 193 across the state, with at least one per *taluk* (sub-district), varying according to the volume of applications. (There are 176 *taluks*.) Tribunals consist of an official as chairman and four non-officials including by law at least one member of the SCs or STs and usually a legislator. The tribunals are the pivotal element in the whole land reform process since their actions are not subject to prior approval by higher authority or to subsequent appeal. Urs put his Revenue Minister, B. Basavalingappa—an assertive SC— in charge of the composition of the tribunals. He packed them with supporters of both the Urs government and the land reform programme. In 1975, tribunals were further armed with special powers to vest land with tenants while cases awaited their attention. The Act also gives an agricultural labourer living in a house on land not belonging to him the right to own the house and 1/20th of an acre of land surrounding it.

The government is also committed to paying the landlord at a moderate level for lands taken away from him by a tribunal. All former tenants who become owners are required to pay the government twenty times the annual income in case of dry lands or fifteen times the annual income in case of irrigated lands. But payments are spread over a period of 20 years at low interest after a down payment of Rs 2,000, for which bank finance can be obtained.[8]

How well has the 1974 Act worked? The preceding discussion may have suggested that tenancies and not landlessness were the main target. Let us then first assess its impact upon tenancies. At the end of November 1979, 798,582 applications has been received from people claiming to be tenants who qualified for ownership of the lands they worked. Of these applications, 530,441 had been dealt with by land tribunals, 319,909 or 60.3 per cent of these cases had been decided in favour of tenants, with 1,249,174 acres being thus distributed. When we consider that the 1971 census stated that there

[8]Ibid., pp. 17–19, 26–28 and 35. Also, interview with B. Basavalingappa, Bangalore, 15 January 1980.

were only 397,042 tenanted holdings in Karnataka, these figures appear impressive. This is particularly true when we note that tribunals have processed only 66.4 per cent of the applications that have reached them. Indeed, if things continue at this rate, the tenancies awarded will easily exceed the total of tenancies in the census. There are at least three explanations for this, all of which are probably partly true. First, the census may have underestimated the number of tenancies (which may also have grown since 1971). Tribunals, which in a clear majority of cases are reliably reported to be pro-tenant, are in some cases awarding lands which are not true tenancies to people falsely claiming to be tenants, to the chagrin of landlords. And finally, tribunals are awarding tenancies to false claimants who have been set up by landlords to help them bypass the ceiling law. It is impossible to determine on present evidence the relative importance of these explanations.

A first glance at the average size of tenancies awarded in different districts suggests that the Act has been implemented rather unevenly. In the northern districts of Bijapur, Bidar and Gulbarga, the average sizes of awards to tenants are respectively 11.3, 10.9 and 10.3 acres. This is a far cry from Uttar Kannada, Mandya and Hassan where the average awards are 1.8, 1.8 and 1.5 acres respectively. But these figures are reasonably consistent with the average size of tenancy per district.[9]

The Act has had its most profound impact in the two coastal districts where the number of tenancies is high, and which together account for over one-third of the applications in the entire state. The incidence of tenancies outside these two districts is so low that official documents concede that 'the impact of land reform through tenancy abolition was of substantial significance in these

---

[9]These figures are extrapolated from interviews with officials in the land reforms section, Karnataka Revenue Department; a typescript on statistics on land reforms to the end of November, 1979 by H. N. Ranganathan, Assistant Special Officer for Land Reforms, Revenue Department (hereafter 'Ranganathan Typescript') and from Rajan, 'Land Reforms in Karnataka: Contexts and Relationships', p. 41.

two districts mainly'.[10] One corroboration of this is the absence of any interruption in growth in the agrarian sector during the land reform years.

The large number of cases decided in favour of tenants was impressive when set alongside the number of tenants in the state. But we should also take note of reports from the field which indicate that in a very small number of areas, the Act is not penetrating, in others relatives or allies of landlords are sometimes wrongly gaining land, weak tenants without links to powerful people are failing to gain land due to them (although there is no evidence of evictions on a massive scale), and tenants receiving lands sometimes remain under the control of landlords because of a continuing imbalance of resources. Many land tribunals (estimates range from 25 per cent to 35 per cent) are corrupt. Their decisions, especially in coastal districts, are often greeted with violent resistance which sometimes succeeds.[11] But having said all of this, nearly all sources indicate that very substantial gains have been made in the assault on tenancy.

What has been the impact of the Act upon the problem of landlessness? Earlier we stated that the incidence of landlessness in old princely Mysore, roughly the southern half of Karnataka, was comparatively low. But in the two northern districts of old Mysore (Shimoga and Chitradurga) and further north in the inland districts of Bombay, Hyderabad and Karnataka, the problem is quite serious. In these districts in 1971, an average of 49 per cent of the active population engaged in agriculture was landless labourers. In Dakshina Kannada District on the coast the figure was 45.8 per cent and in the state as a whole, it was 40 per cent.[12] The land reforms

[10]Rajan, 'Land Reforms in Karnataka: Contexts and Relationships', p. 4.

[11]This is based on interviews with a wide range of social scientists, journalists, civil servants, lawyers dealing in land cases and politicians of all parties in Karnataka. See also S. X. J. Melchior's reports, *Economic and Political Weekly*, 5 May and 18 August 1979.

[12]Rajan, 'Land Reforms in Karnataka: Contexts and Relationships', p. 43. We exclude Kodagu and Chikmagalur districts from this comment because the large plantations there which are excluded from the Land

have had little impact on this problem. By the end of November, 1979, only 37,812 acres of surplus land had been distributed among 7,127 landless people which is less than 0.3 per cent of the landless population.[13] Only 1,509 applications have been filed by landless agricultural labourers for ownership of houses they occupy on others' lands, and of these, a mere 47 have been processed by land tribunals—as opposed to over half a million tenants' petitions.[14] In aiding the landless, the Land Reforms Act is an abject failure.

Senior officials in Karnataka who were involved in the creation of the Act have plainly stated that it was never intended to aid the landless. Both they and Urs recognised that the Act was inadequate, that it could only be a first step in a longer and more radical process. But they believed that it was necessary to end tenancies first, to consolidate the government's base before proceeding to a marked lowering of ceilings and an assault on landlessness.

If we translate this into political terms, it gains considerable credence. Who would be most threatened if a vigorous assault were made upon landlessness? The answer is: the landowning, cultivating sections of the Lingayats in the northern districts of the state where landlessness is most pronounced.[15] It is at this point that the problem of land reform becomes entangled with another important policy of the Urs years—that of preferment for the 'backward classes' in education and government employment and promotion. The people who lost (and stand to lose) by far the most from this policy of preferment are Lingayats. (Vokkaligas, the other group formerly dominant in state politics, are included in the list of 'backward

---

Reforms Act (because of their economic importance) markedly distort the figure.

[13]Ranganathan typescript. Of the recipients, 3,966 were members of the Scheduled Castes and 3,161 were from other groups.

[14]'A Bird's Eye View of Land Reforms in Karnataka', Briefing Paper, p. 3.

[15]For a discussion of various occupational groups within the Lingayat category or sect, see J. Manor, 'The Evolution of Political Arenas and Units of Social Organisation: The Lingayats and Vokkaligas of Mysore', in M. N. Srinivas et al. (eds), *Dimensions of Social Change in India* (Allied, New Delhi, 1976), pp. 169–87.

classes', partly because they are less educationally advanced than Lingayats and partly because it would be politically risky to alienate them thoroughly.) But to say merely that 'Lingayats' will lose is to be far too unspecific. The Lingayats are a huge category spread over most of northern and western Karnataka and divided into various *jatis* and occupational groups which are often in conflict with one another. The most marked of the conflicts is that between the large 'Sadar' group whose main occupation is cultivating and the 'Banajigas' who are traditionally merchants and traders.

Who among Lingayats gained most in education and government employment before the arrival of Devaraj Urs as chief minister? In proportion to their total numbers, the small 'Jangama' (priestly) group and the Banajigas—both traditionally urban and literate—did far better than any of the cultivating groups, including the Sadars. One prominent Lingayat leader (from a neutral group) stated in 1971 that major gains among the Sadars in education and employment were limited to a few families which he proceeded to name. When his remarks were checked with others, they proved to be only a slight exaggeration. This uneven distribution of preferment added heat to the traditional conflict between Sadars and Banajigas and caused resentment among other cultivating groups as well. They had been promised a great deal by Lingayat politicians—not least by the presiding genius over the entire Lingayat political enterprise, S. Nijalingappa, a Banajiga. Those promises led many to perceive themselves as Lingayats first and as other things, second, and they evoked intense Lingayat chauvinism similar to that recently displayed by Jats in Haryana and western Uttar Pradesh. But during the Lingayat heyday in state politics (1956–1971), the actual gains in education and jobs for the numerically powerful but educationally less advanced Lingayat cultivating groups were disappointing. One of the principal reasons for the surprising ease with which Urs broke and replaced Lingayat-Vokkaliga dominance in Karnataka was this estrangement between the urban Banajigas and the cultivating Lingayats with their great numerical and economic strength. The latter were partially neutralised as a result of their estrangement.

Urs knew that this was a crucial factor in his favour and he was understandably reluctant to take any action which would drive the landed and the urban Lingayats together. A land reform programme which mainly attacked *tenancy* posed no serious threat to any major group outside the two coastal districts which are of marginal importance in the arithmetic of state politics. Indeed it would help many poorer Lingayats in rural parts. A policy of preferment for 'backward classes' in education would mainly hurt the elite urban Lingayat groups who were the only Lingayats who still harboured high expectations in this area. And predictably, it is from this quarter that the main protests against 'backward classes' preferment have come—led by a retired Jangama civil servant. But an assault on landlessness was quite another matter. It would have threatened the prosperity of Lingayat cultivators in the inland districts of northern Karnataka and could easily have revived their alliance with urban Lingayats. It is principally for this reason that no attack on landlessness was made in the 1974 Land Reforms Act. Urs and his closest advisers intended such an attack, but they preferred to solidify their support among ex-tenants before proceeding to that stage.

Preferment for 'Backward Classes'

There is a lesson in the Lingayats' experience with promises of preferment in education and government jobs for anyone who considers making such pledges. They are an effective way of crystallising the political consciousness of a group whose support a politician needs. For a certain period, they can be used to sustain the solidarity of the group. But in the long run, the expectations such promises generate cannot be fulfilled and disillusionment and anger are bound to follow. There are simply not enough government jobs to satisfy the aspirations of any sizeable group—and it is always to large groups that such promises are made. There may be enough reserved seats in secondary schools and in undergraduate colleges, but there are seldom enough in elite professional colleges to which so many aspire. Nor is there sufficient employment to assuage the appetites of those emerging from secondary and higher studies. Promising preferment is a double-edged sword offering only temporary advantage.

Devaraj Urs knows this. He shrewdly announced his acceptance of a report advocating reservations in schools and government service for Karnataka's 'backward classes' during the run-up to the 1977 Lok Sabha election. He chose that moment because he realised that the main result of such programmes is not the transformation of the lot of the 'backward classes' but rather a temporary surge in their political consciousness which he needed at that election.

The timing of this announcement was significant in one other way. It was made five years after he had taken office, after his various programmes for reform and social welfare had had time to make an impression, and fully three years after his main initiatives, the Land Reforms Act, had taken effect. In other words, by the time he announced his promises of preferment, he had already demonstrated by substantive action rather than mere rhetoric, that he was the champion of the groups which had previously been dominated by Lingayats and Vokkaligas. Because he had established this, he mortgaged far less of his prestige to the ultimately risky promises of preferment than those who *begin* their drive for power with such promises. If (when) the 'backward classes' found that the premises could not be fulfilled, their frustration would be tempered by the knowledge that they had gained from Urs in other ways.

This point about the timing of promises is important in discussing the analogies which are often rather loosely drawn between Urs's doings and those of Karpoori Thakur in Bihar. Thakur proclaimed his policy of preferment for the 'backward classes' soon after taking office. He did so in order to signify 'that the Backwards had displaced the Forwards as the dominant force in Bihar politics, that the old days of dominance in public affairs from village to Vidhan Sabha by the "twice-born" were gone forever'.[16] But he made this announcement before he had either consolidated 'backward class' control of the state-level politics or developed programmes to provide 'backward class' people with new economic and political resources in the form of substantive patronage from government.

[16]H. W. Blair, 'Rising Kulaks and Backward Classes in Bihar: Social Change in the Late 1970s', *Economic and Political Weekly*, 12 January 1980, p. 66.

His early offer of preferment inflamed feelings among both forward castes and SCs who felt threatened by it and led to the collapse of his government before it had time to achieve its major goals. It was replaced by a government which was dominated by 'Forwards and Jana Sanghis'.[17] In the words of Devaraj Urs, 'Karpoori climbed into the ring before he learned how to box'.[18]

Comparisons are also drawn between Urs's actions and the endeavours of Charan Singh to cultivate 'backward class' support, mainly in Bihar, Uttar Pradesh and Haryana. There are some parallels between them. Several of the occupational groups which Charan Singh sought to help were also among Urs's constituents, notably poorer cultivators, some artisans and service castes, and people engaged in animal husbandry. Most of these people are economically weak. Charan Singh sought to create programmes to aid these groups educationally, politically and economically. It would thus be wrong to overstate the contrasts between Charan Singh and Devaraj Urs.[19]

Nevertheless, important contrasts exist. A great many of Charan Singh's supporters are cultivators who have, over the last decade or so, made significant economic gains. Thus, in addition to uplifting certain economically weak groups, Charan Singh is also bolstering further the position of economically strong groups. Urs is engaged in something quite different and less ambiguous. His followers are overwhelmingly drawn from economically weak groups. Although Vokkaligas who formerly enjoyed political dominance are listed among Karnataka's 'backward classes', the criteria for the allotment of preferment (which, in addition to caste, give preference to the poor and to rural dwellers) favour the underprivileged among them. Urs is thus strengthening economically weak groups and forging them into a force that can maintain political ascendancy over more prosperous elements.

[17]Ibid., p. 67.
[18]Interview with Devaraj Urs, Bangalore, 12 January 1980.
[19]I am grateful to Francine Frankel for this information.

Bases of Support

There is one other important contrast between Urs and these north Indian leaders. Urs has maintained a firm alliance between less prosperous caste Hindus, the SCs and Muslims. This is not the case in north India. Karpoori Thakur's government fell in part because of SC fears about the 'backward class' movement. We witnessed blatant and widespread intimidation of SC voters in the 1980 Lok Sabha poll by Jats and others in Haryana, and western Uttar Pradesh.[20] Urs's careful cultivation of Muslim support through generous patronage to Muslim groups and Waqf boards stands in stark contrast to the rancid anti-Muslim diatribe that this writer had to listen to from high Lok Dal officials in the party's headquarters on the eve of the 1980 election. In north India, Madhu Limaye had developed a strategy, inclusive of Muslims, and some Muslim farmers appear to have backed the Lok Dal,[21] but most of their votes were lost.

The only genuine parallel in north India to the experiment in Karnataka, as Urs himself emphasises, is the Shekhawat government in Rajasthan. But it has not had time to develop its programmes fully and since it is a Janata Party enterprise, its days seem numbered in the wake of the Congress (I) victory in the 1980 Lok Sabha elections. (For more on Shekhawat in later years, see chapter twelve of this book.)

One further question is pertinent in the light of the failure of land reforms in Karnataka to assist landless people who are very often members of SCs. If preferment programmes in north India have been seen as threats by the SCs, how did Urs maintain an alliance between them and the 'backward classes'? He did so through a combination of symbolism and substantive action. On a symbolic level, he kept the SC leader, B. Basavalingappa, in the prominent role of revenue minister, more than doubled SC representation in the cabinet (with important portfolios), and had the Assembly Speaker chosen from among their number. Urs also sought, largely

---

[20]See for example, *The Statesman,* 4 January 1980 and *Indian Express,* 18 January 1980. These reports were confirmed by officials of the Election Commission, New Delhi, 29 January 1980.

[21]I am grateful to Bashiruddin Ahmed for this information.

successfully, by all accounts—to reassure the SCs that reservations for 'backward classes' meant no diminution of their statutory quotas. He drove the point home by energetic efforts to see that SC quotas which had never been adequately filled in the higher ranks of government service were more fully met during his tenure, and went to the extent of increasing representation over the statutory level to compensate for previous shortfalls. He did this despite considerable resistance from caste Hindu officials.[22] He expressed particular satisfaction about this when reviewing his time in office after his resignation.[23]

On a more substantive level, the Urs government sought to compensate for inaction on behalf of the landless by promoting social welfare programmes for the SCs. Such programmes were not as alarming to cultivating Lingayats in northern districts as an assault on landlessness would have been. Among the more important of these were schemes to aid small and marginal farmers, to grant house sites on unoccupied land, to build houses for the poor, and to increase scholarships and places in hostels for SC students. In urban areas, slum clearance boards often gave SCs first access to houses. Child development programmes extending from anti-natal care to school-going age were often aimed in large measure at the SCs and located in areas where they are found in large numbers. Old age pensions have also reached some of them. The government acted firmly in many parts of the state in an effort to get primary education to all children and brought pressure upon teachers to ensure this. Government vigilance and pressure on employers brought, for the first time, substantial compliance with minimum wages laws in 1977 and after. Significant inroads were made into the practice of bonded labour for the first time. A 1976 law liquidating rural debt and allowing former debtors to redeem pledged property made a tangible difference to the SCs, although government schemes to make alternative credit available were slow in making an impact.

[22]I am grateful to Mumtaz Ali Khan for this information. As further evidence at this effort, see 'Reservations in Promotional Vacancies—Defects: Remedies with Reasons', typescript, 1978.

[23]Interview with Devaraj Urs, Bangalore, 22 March 1981.

Urs, who had concentrated several key portfolios and enormous power in his own hands, maintained considerable pressure on officials to show greater sympathy to the SCs. To assist him in this, he appointed SC officials to the crucial post of Deputy Commissioner in several districts. The degrading practice of carrying night-soil on the head was banned, evidently with wide effect.[24]

Most of this information comes from Mumtaz Ali Khan, a longtime advocate of SC interests, and a frequent critic of government in the past. His surveys of SC villages in every *taluk* of Bangalore District (which contains both backward and developed areas) in 1970 and 1977 uncovered considerable gains for SCs in the struggle against untouchability. He also found them much more willing in 1977 to place cases of discrimination before the police (partly because under Urs, the police were fairer in their behaviour), demonstrably less afraid of once-dominant landed castes, and far more outspoken about their attitudes to political parties and candidates.[25] It must however be emphasised that in many places, these government initiatives failed to penetrate.[26] The story of Karnataka's SCs in the 1970s is of a transition, for some from wretched to slightly less wretched conditions and, for others of no transition at all. It is impossible on present evidence to quantify the extent of the transition. But serious efforts have been made on their behalf, and despite the Urs government's timidity on landlessness, which afflicts so many of the SCs, its record is on balance quite enlightened and reasonably effective.

The Durability of the Changes which Urs Introduced

We have seen that Devaraj Urs has demonstrated that it is possible to break the control of dominant landed groups over state-level

[24]Interviews with Mumtaz Ali Khan. Bangalore, 17 January 1980 and with Karnataka civil servants, 15 and 19 January 1980. Also, Mumtaz Ali Khan, 'Seven Years of Change: A Study of Some Scheduled Castes in Bangalore District', typescript 1979, pp. 184, 191, 194–215.

[25]Ibid., pp. 185–87.

[26]Interviews with G. K. Karanth and two Karnataka civil servants, Bangalore, 17 and 18 January 1980.

politics and to replace it with a solid alliance including most of the less powerful social groups. He sustained this for seven-and-a-half years and his resignation was not caused by any fracturing of this alliance. How durable will it prove in his absence?

Most of the initiatives enumerated above which helped the SCs also, aided less prosperous caste Hindus (and, in many areas, Muslims). These programmes, taken together, form on paper an impressive range of initiatives. Others can be added to the list—bank finance to artisans (a traditionally deprived section in Karnataka), special programmes to assist handloom weavers, free legal aid, a restructuring of co-operative societies to break the dominance over them of small groups of rich people, the 'socialisation' of some urban land nutritional schemes for children, a programme (which pre-dated the Centre's Food-for-Work programme) to provide up to 100 days employment for seasonal labourers, an effort to provide villages with drinking water and another to supply electricity in under-served rural areas.[27]

Serious reservations must be registered about some of these programmes. Some were conceived too late to have any substantive impact, and in any case were implemented only in limited portions of the state. The rural electrification drive, the creation of agricultural estates to rehabilitate bonded labourers, and the scheme for seasonal labour (in its application rather than its conception) are examples. At least two other initiatives appeared so late as to be little more than election promises.

Those programmes which were in operation for longer periods must also be regarded with caution. With most of them, there were problems in securing their penetration to the local level. There were many reasons for this. Some legislators who might have promoted these schemes allowed themselves to be bought off by wealthy interests in their constituencies. Within the bureaucracy, particularly among minor officials in the *mofussil* (many of whom are drawn from groups threatened by the reforms), there was considerable

---

[27]Interviews with seven Karnataka civil servants, Bangalore, January 1980. Also, D. M. Nanjundappa, 'A New Deal for the Poor: A Position Paper', typescript, 1979.

foot-dragging. To combat this, higher civil servants organised special one-day camps in many local arenas where villagers were granted rights to land, old age pensions and access to other benefits very expeditiously and without recourse to local officials or middle men. But such exercises could only reach a very small portion of the rural population.

The state has not witnessed a rapid erosion of poor (especially illiterate) people's dependence on intermediaries for their dealings with government bureaucrats. A man who votes his own mind may still find it necessary to go to a village accountant or a notable in a neighbouring town for documentation needed to obtain a piece of land or a concession to which he is entitled. These intermediaries often exploit and deceive those who come to them and thereby thwart the penetration of reforms and social services. Civil servants concede that this has impaired and even vitiated the effectiveness of many programmes and has prevented the kind of important, if hardly revolutionary, changes which they might have wrought in the socio-economic framework. And yet in a great many areas some of these programmes are getting through, particularly those most energetically stressed by Urs on his frequent tours: land reforms, pensions for needy people over 60, sites and houses for the poor and, to a lesser extent, the restructuring of co-operatives.

It is impossible to measure the extent to which the programmes have penetrated to the villages. It is thus impossible to say with any assurance to what extent Urs's programmes have wrought changes that will permanently alter the logic of politics. In some areas this has certainly not occurred. In many, and probably most, a substantial beginning appears to have been made.

Urs himself believes that to ensure the durability of both his coalition of less prosperous groups and the socio-economic changes he envisions, he needed another three years in power. This man, who began as a pragmatist sensing that his interest lay in progressive policies but dependent on advisers for guidance, is now clearly in advance of them on one crucial issue. They tend to speak of the government's policies in terms of 'doing good for the poor', in well-intentioned but faintly patronising terms. Urs has sufficient political sensitivity to see that the great weakness of his efforts so far is their failure to foster the *organisation* of the weaker sections of society, for their own defence. He understands that politicisation, which is clearly widespread, is inadequate without organisation.[28] (He had no further opportunity to act on this insight because he died in opposition in 1982.)

In winding up this assessment of the Urs years, we must also take note of the large-scale corruption which marked his regime from early days. Urs developed 'fundraising' into something of a science and is responsible for a huge increase over previous regimes in the role of money in politics. To say this, however, is to be so imprecise as to mislead. It must be emphasised that the money which was raised ('extorted' would perhaps be a more accurate word) came not from the weaker sections of society whom Urs seeks to help but rather from large industrial, planting and urban interests, and from predominantly lower middle class seekers of favours and promotions from government. This is not to say that Urs is a Robin Hood. A great deal of the money obtained ended up in the pockets of his supporters. A great deal more ended up in the coffers of Indira Gandhi's party at the national level until Urs broke with her. But much of this 'fundraising' was forced upon Urs by the Congress (I) high command, and his success at this game bought Karnataka freedom from disruptive interference from above.

It must also be stressed that the money Urs raised, like the many key portfolios he rather undemocratically kept to himself, gave him extra political power which was often necessary to see that reforms were at least partially implemented. This influenced the views of his 'fundraising' among knowledgeable observers. They had earlier reacted with disgust to the money game. But over time, they be-came extremely sympathetic—annoyed by the corruption but seeing much of it as an element in Urs's remarkable successful campaign to force through reforms which are beginning to have a substantial impact.

[28]Interview with Devaraj Urs, 22 March 1981. This of course raises questions about the adequacy of Urs's party organisation to build and integrate grassroots organisations—a topic for another occasion.

It is a measure of this impact that Urs's successors cannot afford to change his polices to any significant extent. The entire front rank of Congress (I) leaders are—like Urs—from small, non-dominant groups. They may ease somewhat the burden on the urban middle class who have been squeezed to fund the reforms.[29] But they cannot seek to reconstruct some variant of the old system in which Lingayats and Vokkaligas dominated. They cannot do so for two reasons. First and most obviously, they and others from similar social backgrounds could be swept aside in the process. But second and more importantly, they could not hope to retain support among the less prosperous groups whom Urs has brought together if they attempted an accommodation with the Lingayats or Vokkaligas. The idea of the new alliance of weaker groups has taken root and will not be easily abandoned.

Before we can assess the historical importance of the Urs experiment, we will need to know not only how things go in Karnataka and India over the months and years ahead, but also how things have gone already in other regions of the subcontinent. Detailed studies of other regions suggest that such reforming regimes can only be built and sustained by politicians possessing both an acute intelligence and an aggressive, audacious temperament. Urs has both, but most leaders do not. More to the point, only leaders who lack such gifts are likely to be given the opportunity to wield power in the regions under Indira Gandhi. It may also be true that such an experiment can only succeed in a state with officials of high calibre in the upper and middle echelons of the bureaucracy, a productive agrarian sector, a well-developed technological infrastructure—and in a state which is also relatively free of destructive inter-communal and inter-regional strife. Most crucially, perhaps this sort of experiment can only succeed in a state where traditional disparities between rich and poor are comparatively less acute. Perhaps Urs and Karnataka are as much cases apart from mainstream India as are Kerala and West Bengal. Only time and research on other regions can answer these questions. But for the moment, this writer holds that Karnataka is not as eccentric as all that. The Shekhawat government

---

[29]See for example, *The Times of India*, 23 January 1980.

in Rajasthan—surely one of the last places one might have expected a reformist government to appear, let alone succeed—suggests that conditions in other states may soon be right for the emergence of pragmatic progressives at the state level.

— twelve —

INDIA'S CHIEF MINISTERS AND
THE PROBLEM OF GOVERNABILITY

This paper, which appeared in 1995, focuses on anxieties—often expressed at the time—about India becoming ungovernable. It considers this theme by looking 'over the shoulders' of chief ministers in various states, where most of the actual governing occurs. The picture that emerges is ambiguous. Weak and unruly party organisations, scarce government funds, mounting demands from awakened interests, and the immense complexity of their tasks forced many chief ministers into constant fire-fighting, and piled excruciating pressures upon them. But we also encounter here one example (among several others, see chapter thirteen for one more) of an adroit chief minister—Bhairon Singh Shekhawat in Rajasthan—who largely overcame these difficulties. Numerous chief ministers performed poorly, but managed enough to provide reasonably adequate governance to ease worries about ungovernability. Readers who turn to chapter fourteen which analyses chief ministers since the turn of the millennium will find certain striking contrasts with the present chapter. Two are especially important. A surge in government revenues since 2003 has enabled them to achieve far more than their predecessors in the 1990s. And changed conditions have made it possible for many chief ministers to centralise power within their states—radically or substantially. That makes their lives less fraught, but it may not be good for democracy.

It has never been easy to govern India. The country is huge, its society is the most diverse on earth, and it is beset by poverty, scarce resources, and marked inequalities. Over the past two decades, India's voters have become increasingly sophisticated and impatient. People in every section of society—including the poor and least educated—have become more aware of their collective strength and self-interest, more insistent in demanding responses from politicians, and more willing on election days to punish those who fail to respond. This has made India a more genuine democracy than in the first phase after Independence in 1947, when prosperous groups dominated politics and poorer people settled for tokenism, but an even more difficult country to govern.

Politicians have found it harder to meet these rising demands because political institutions—the instruments through which they govern—have undergone decay. Political parties have been plagued by mounting corruption, indiscipline, and factional squabbling. The autonomy, flexibility, and resources of formal institutions of state have deteriorated. This decay gathered momentum under Indira Gandhi in the 1970s, which witnessed an orgy of dein-stitutionalisation. After the confused and fragmented Janata government collapsed, the process of decay resumed in Mrs Gandhi's last premiership (1980–84).

It is hardly surprising, then, that many commentators have asked whether India is becoming ungovernable by democratic means. Their concerns take various forms. Some focus mainly on the potent social forces that have emerged. They question the capacity of this democracy to contain and respond creatively to conflicts among classes, castes, and religious and ethnic groups, and between those groups and the state. Others fix mainly on the decay of political institutions, especially political parties. Still others worry that those in authority depend so heavily on the use of coercion against discontented groups that the democratic process may be subverted or abandoned. While their emphases differ, they agree that something close to a crisis is at hand.[1]

[1]See, for example, P. R. Brass, *The Politics of India Since Independence. The New Cambridge History of India*, 2nd ed., part 4, vol. 1 (Cambridge

How anxious should we be about all of this? This chapter examines a key group of politicians—chief ministers who preside over state-level governments in India's federal system. Since state governments oversee the implementation of most national government programmes, and since the states have immense powers of their own, chief ministers are much more intimately involved in the day-to-day dilemmas of governance than anyone in New Delhi.[2]

They have to wrestle incessantly with concrete manifestations of institutional decay. They struggle to maintain political legitimacy in the face of demands from voters. Far more than India's national leaders, they grapple with both the painful adjustments and the opportunities that follow from economic liberalisation. Since the composition and character of society vary greatly from state to state, they are far more thoroughly enmeshed in state-society relations than any prime minister. So it is mainly their decisions that determine how, and indeed whether, the institutions of state are integrated with society. They make the key judgements about the distribution of government resources among various interest groups, about the pursuit of political accommodation or the use of coercive force. Most of the actual governing in India takes place at the state level and below, and at those levels, chief ministers are crucial.

The Constitution arms state governments with formidable powers. It gives them exclusive control over a long list of subjects

---

University Press, New York, 1994); J. Manor, 'The Electoral Process amid Awakening and Decay', in P. Lyon and J. Manor (eds), *Transfer and Transformation: Political Institutions in the New Commonwealth* (Leicester University Press, Leicester, 1983), pp. 87–116; J. Manor, 'Party Decay and Political Crisis in India', *Washington Quarterly*, vol. 4, no. 3 (Summer 1981), pp. 25–40; F. Frankel, 'Introduction', in F. Frankel and M. S. A. Rao (eds), *Dominance and State Power in Modern India: Decline of a Social Order*, vol. 1 (Oxford University Press, Delhi, 1989), pp. 1–20; and A. Kohli, *Democracy and Discontent: India's Growing Crisis of Governability* (Cambridge University Press, Cambridge and New York, 1990).

[2]This is apparent from several of the studies in J. Manor (ed.), *Nehru to the Nineties: The Changing Office of Prime Minister in India* (Viking Penguin/ University of British Columbia Press, New Delhi/Vancouver, 1994).

including public order, local government institutions, public health and sanitation, agriculture, land, animal husbandry, and fisheries. State governments also share responsibility with the Central government for much else: the administration of justice, forestry, industrial disputes, social security, family planning, education, and the provision of electricity.

State influence has been eroded by the authorities in New Delhi over the last 20 years or so. The Central government has encroached into areas supposedly reserved for the states and has taken a larger role in areas of shared responsibility. It has also denied state governments essential funds. But despite this, state governments and chief ministers have actually become more important in recent years. The opening of India's economy to market forces since mid-1991 has in many respects increased their autonomy. Intrusions from on high have declined since the national election of 1989 ended the Indira/Rajiv Gandhi dominance over the political system. The hung parliaments that emerged in 1989 and 1991 made prime ministers less inclined and less able to intervene at the state level.[3]

To understand the role of chief ministers, we need to begin where they do. Their overriding preoccupations are to ensure their political survival and extend their influence. This is not a criticism but a statement of fact. India rightly takes pride in having produced this century's greatest political moralist—Mahatma Gandhi—but his saintly legacy is often used as an unfair basis for judging (and condemning) the behaviour of chief ministers and others. We need to consider objectively what they have done to tackle the daunting array of problems that they face.

Chief ministers loom large because nearly all of them lack strong party organisations that would enable them to interact systematically with other forces in their states. This leaves them badly exposed and compels them to wheel and deal frantically in order to

[3]The Congress government of Prime Minister P. V. Narasimha Rao took office in June 1991 with slightly less than half the seats in the Lok Sabha (the dominant lower house in India's Parliament). By late 1993 it had enticed enough members from other parties to support it that it had achieved a working majority.

survive politically. Their performance becomes disproportionately important to the fate of their states.

This is a relatively recent development. During the first two decades after 1947, chief ministers from the Congress Party ran nearly every state, and the Congress organisation in those days had both sinew and reach. In the various states, it operated political 'machines': a disciplined network of skilled political managers coordinated the distribution of government-controlled goods and services to a large number of key interest groups. It extended from the state capitals down to district, sub-district, and local levels. Chief ministers thus had instruments of governance that were usually more than adequate to their task.

But the Congress organisation was systematically crippled by Indira Gandhi, who saw it more as a threat to her personal dominance than as a tool to help her govern well. In most states, the parties that have arisen to challenge Congress have also failed to develop strong organisations penetrating to the grassroots. This makes it difficult for chief ministers from those parties to govern effectively—though they are partly to blame for inadequate party building. This chapter explains how they try to cope in these unhappy circumstances.

'The Job Makes You Crazy Sometimes'

In the last few weeks of 1990, Hyderabad, the capital of Andhra Pradesh, witnessed fierce rioting between Hindus and Muslims. The security forces had great difficulty imposing order, partly because dissidents within the ruling Congress Party were fomenting violence in an (eventually successful) effort to undermine the position of their *own* Chief Minister, Dr M. Chenna Reddy. At the height of the crisis, an exhausted and traumatised Dr Reddy held a press conference to try to reassure the public. When a reporter asked him to comment on the use of automatic weapons by both sides, he astonished his audience by saying, 'This only shows that the people of Andhra do not lag behind in this respect'.[4]

---

[4]*The Indian Express*, 29 November 1990.

This bizarre remark was all the more remarkable for being uncharacteristic. Chenna Reddy was a highly intelligent leader. After taking command of the Congress Party in his state when it was in opposition and disarray, he had mounted a series of protests that galvanised the party organisation and carried it to victory at the next state election.

Several months after being ousted, when Dr Reddy was in temporary retirement, a visitor asked him how he came to make that remark. He paused and then said quietly, 'The job makes you crazy sometimes'. He explained how much more difficult the job of chief minister was in the early 1990s than in the late 1970s, when he had previously held this post. Earlier, conflict had been more manageable, voters had been more patient, resources had been more plentiful, and the party organisation had been more formidable.[5]

By the 1990s, many more interest groups had become politically active. They came into conflict with one another earlier and more aggressively, so that managing conflict was now harder. They had grown more strident in their demands, and it took more resources to satisfy them. Poor, low-status groups that once settled for a few crumbs now insisted on substantial benefits. The electorate had become sophisticated enough to throw out the Congress Party in 1983. As a result, here and in every other state, Congress now faced a powerful opposition with experience of government. In short, Reddy was describing the cumulative effects of a political awakening which—alongside decay—had been developing among ordinary people for decades.

He went on to say that the resources available to his and other state governments had shrunk as a result of mounting corruption among politicians and bureaucrats. The Congress Party's organ-isation was wracked by feverish factionalism that would have been unthinkable 20 years earlier. To placate various factions, and to prevent individual legislators from becoming dissidents, Reddy had to commit huge amounts of resources and time to flattering them and buying them off. This left him exhausted, undermined his health, and denied him the time to deal with matters of high policy.

[5]Interview, Hyderabad, 11 February 1991.

The effectiveness not only of the Congress Party, but of many formal political institutions had declined, so that it was difficult to meet soaring demands and to prevent social conflicts from spinning out of control.

In other words, Reddy was painfully aware of the dangers posed by the combination of political awakening and institutional decay. It so undermined his position that he was eventually forced by dissension within his own party to resign. Even while he had held office, his life had been unpleasant, even desperate. The job hardly seemed worth having—although he clearly mourned his loss of power.

Chenna Reddy's experience is reasonably typical. Conditions vary from state to state, but nearly all chief ministers to some degree face the problems Reddy encountered. This is worrying, especially since few chief ministers are as intelligent as Reddy. Yet some have coped more impressively than he did. Consider one recent example. (There are others—for example, Sharad Pawar in his three terms as chief minister of Maharashtra, 1978–80, 1988–91, and 1993–95.[6]) Shekhawat's methods will tell us more about the chief ministers' troubles as well as their powers and opportunities.

Bhairon Singh Shekhawat of Rajasthan

In November 1993, voters in Rajasthan elected a legislature in which the Hindu nationalist Bharatiya Janata Party (BJP) held the largest number of seats, but fell just short of a majority. It duly formed a government. A few days later, a woman legislator from the Congress Party (the main opposition) was surprised to be contacted by the Chief Minister, Bhairon Singh Shekhawat. He invited her to explain the needs of her constituency. She rattled off a list of development projects and other benefits, and Shekhawat astonished her by saying that he would see to it that most of them were delivered by the end of his five years in office. The legislator left feeling elated, since she

---

[6]The original version of this chapter contained an extended analysis of Pawar's adroit approach chief minister.

had feared that, as a member of the opposition, she would be cut off from government goods and services.[7]

There were good reasons for the chief minister to feel satisfied too. He could now depend upon this woman (and numerous others in opposition with whom he had had similar chats) to refrain from attacking the government, lest she jeopardise her access to resources. He would allot a small number of benefits to her constituency in the first few months, to give the impression that his promises would be kept. He could decide later about whether to deliver further concessions, depending on her behaviour.

By mid-1994, it was apparent that Shekhawat would not need to maintain the flow of spoils to all of the opposition legislators whom he had met. He had engineered the defection of enough opposition members to the ruling party to give himself a majority. He had promised them sizable benefits, but once they had joined his party, he handed over only a few of these—knowing that these new recruits were locked in. That was because India's anti-defection law requires that a group of defectors constitute at least one-third of the legislators in the party they wish to leave. It was easy for Shekhawat to entice one-third of a tiny opposition party to join his, but once they were members of the huge BJP delegation, they could not defect out again without taking dozens of others with them—an impossibility.

This chief minister was clearly a devious (or if you prefer, ingenious) master of *realpolitik*, but he is more complex than that. For example, he was by turns tough and generous. On the one hand, he often sought to get things done by threatening to reveal compromising information about politicians or bureaucrats. One civil servant said, 'he can be a bit if a terror'. On the other, when confronted with pressure for benefits, he tended to promise more than he could deliver to spare himself the embarrassment of saying

[7]The section of this chapter on Shekhawat is mainly derived from daily newspapers and research in Jaipur during February 1994, when I interviewed numerous politicians, journalists, civil servants, academics, and others. I am especially grateful to Sanjeev Srivastava, G. K. Bhanot, and Rob Jenkins.

no, even though his failure to live up to commitments caused more resentment than would an initial refusal. One sympathetic observer, referring to this habit, described him as 'often a liar in little things'.

At times, however, Shekhawat remained generous when he need not have been. Even after securing a legislative majority, he continued to provide patronage to numerous opposition legislators. He did so partly because it muted criticism of his government, but also because it sustained the amiable relations between ruling and opposition parties that have always existed in Rajasthan (though not in most other states). Those in power cultivate members of the opposition, and when chief ministers and opposition leaders spar in the legislature, they restrain themselves from going for the jugular.

Shekhawat learned this kind of politics during a long spell in opposition, observing a great Congress Chief Minister, Mohanlal Sukhadia, who offered him and his colleagues the same enticements that Shekhawat now provides to opponents. A senior aide insisted that he did this not just because it made political sense, but because he was 'essentially a kindhearted person'. He often went out of his way to assist adversaries who were in personal difficulty or distress. This won him much grudging affection.

His observance of old fashioned courtesies (which include a tendency not to seek excessively partisan behaviour from bureaucrats), and his pragmatic approach to politics, have often set Shekhawat at odds with some members of his own party. This was particularly true of his relations with the zealots from the Rashtriya Swayamsevak Sangh (RSS), an assertively Hindu nationalist association that looms large in the BJP organisation everywhere.

Two things helped him to maintain the upper hand. The first was the widespread and accurate belief that Shekhawat was indispensable—that no one else in the party in Rajasthan could match his deft skills and experience (he had been chief minister twice before). The second was the small size of his legislative majority. This enabled him to persuade his legislators that the party's grip on power was tenuous, and that undisciplined behaviour could upset the delicate balance. A larger majority would have provided him with certain advantages, but it would have allowed legislators to relax so that dissidence in the party would increase. This was why he and many other chief ministers prefer small majorities.

The RSS group was strong enough to give ministers who belonged to it considerable autonomy from the chief minister, and freedom to pursue policies dear to the Hindu right. Shekhawat, who is (or some say, poses as) a liberal, handled this in two ways. He placed some of these people in posts where their rightist views made little difference: as one wag put it, 'What is the Hindu theory of road repair?' He also leaned leftward on certain issues, to compensate for their biases. This was vividly apparent when he created the *antyodaya* programme to target the five poorest families in each village for special benefits.

This was an example of Shekhawat's uncanny ability to devise initiatives that are inexpensive, but touch a sympathetic chord at the grassroots. Another example was his 'your village, your work' scheme, which enables local communities to complete small projects that meet their most urgent needs. Recent research suggests that such programmes, which respond to a ferocious popular appetite for long-neglected micro-level development projects, hold great promise of popularity at little cost and risk.[8] They assisted Shekhawat in being the only BJP chief minister, out of the four whose governments were toppled after the destruction of the Babri Masjid at Ayodhya, to be returned to power at state elections in November 1993.

Shekhawat was intensely preoccupied with gathering information. He was acutely aware that the organisational weakness of his and other parties prevented them from delivering reliable intelligence to leaders. Many chief ministers content themselves with what they learn from party colleagues, who often tell them what they think they want to hear, and from the police and a cursory perusal of the press. Shekhawat went beyond that, actively seeking out well-informed people beyond his party. Reporters say that he frittered away far too much time chatting with informants, but they acknowledge that he is immensely knowledgeable—'the best journalist in Rajasthan'.

[8]This emerges in R. Crook and J. Manor, *Democracy and Decentralisation in South Asia and West Africa: Participation, Accountability and Performance* (Cambridge University Press, Cambridge, 1998).

He had long meticulously maintained an extensive private set of files on policy issues and people—politicians, bureaucrats, journalists, and others. The files contained his notes, official documents, and clippings from the daily press. In the legislature, these enabled him to wear down opponents by citing details and statistics they lack. The files were also widely presumed to contain compromising information on many people. It was exceedingly unusual for Shekhawat to make public use of this material—insofar as it actually existed—but that was seldom necessary. The mere presumption that the chief minister possessed such information was enough to deter people from causing trouble.

Like most chief ministers, he maintained exclusive control over civil servants' postings. He understood that legislators wished to collect sizable payments from bureaucrats seeking agreeable transfers, and thus that he had to tread carefully here. He could not ignore legislators' wishes entirely, but if he gave too much ground, he could dilute his authority and demoralise the bureaucracy—which he was loath to do. He therefore invested much time and effort in finding a balance, and he was unusually adroit at this fiendishly difficult game. He placed talented senior civil servants in high posts within departments run by less dependable ministers—to monitor their actions and correct their mistakes.

Two other things enabled him to avoid Chenna Reddy's fate. First, neither corruption in general nor a market in transfers had developed in Rajasthan to the extent that they have in most other states—thanks in part to the resistance that nearly all chief ministers had offered to these tendencies. Second, he and his party were less corrupt than their Congress opponents. Many chief ministers own fleets of Mercedes, but the only extravagance people mention about Shekhawat was that he has 'a very nice jeep'.

As comments above indicate, he dominated his government. Although this has many advantages, close observers said that he tried to manage too many things. Delays and mistakes sometimes followed. He was prepared to delegate authority to a few ministers and bureaucrats whose competence he trusted, but he does less of this than is good for overall performance.

On the other hand, Shekhawat ensured that his governments were reasonably effective, imaginative, clean and stable. Perhaps most crucially, he created an environment in which the very large number of skilled political activists, who exist at all levels of this and nearly all other states' political systems, were able to operate constructively. This was essential if goods and services were to be delivered efficiently to interests of all kinds, if government programmes were to work reasonably well, and if the politics of bargaining was to adapt to change. These skilled people are a huge political and developmental asset that India possesses in far larger measure than other less-developed countries (see chapter ten of this book).

The Complexity of the Chief Minister's Task

The range of problems faced by chief ministers is even more complicated than the comments on Shekhawat and Pawar indicate. Many wish to centralise power, but only a very few (mainly film stars), whose vote-getting ability exceeds that of their parties, can manage this. (To see how times have changed, see chapter fourteen in this book.) Others who attempt it provoke rebellions from potent factions that can destroy them. If they are sensible, they adopt a dual strategy of playing factions off against each other while decentralising some power and resources in order to forge ties to powerful subordinates. Those who decentralise in this way often grasp a crucial subtlety—that leaders at the apex of complex political systems in India make their influence penetrate downward more effectively by means of bargaining than by *diktat*.

Many decentralisers find, however, that their underlings are so undisciplined that factional strife rips apart carefully constructed transactional networks. They then spend much of their time and political capital patching up deals with contending groups. A great Indian political scientist, G. Ram Reddy, after seeing many ruling parties at the state level overtaken by infighting, suggested that destructive factionalism is a dangerous 'national trait'.[9]

[9]Interview, New Delhi, 11 December 1994.

Chief ministers must also decide how to handle corruption. Some centralisers seek to deprive subordinates of moneymaking opportunities, but this inspires immense resentment from underlings, many of whom are in politics mainly for profit. Others decentralise such opportunities, on the assumption that legislators who are busy enriching themselves will seldom rebel. This strategy sometimes backfires, however, since legislators' appetites tend to exceed what a chief minister can offer, and dissident leaders may promise them greater gain.

Many chief ministers resort to actions, postures, or promises intended to have mass appeal, especially among the poor. Some of these are downright reckless. The movie star / politician N. T. Rama Rao won an election and became chief minister of Andhra Pradesh in late 1994 by promising two things: total prohibition of alcohol and heavy subsidies on rice. Either of these measures would nearly cripple the state financially—the first because almost half of its revenues come from taxes on drink, the second because the proposed subsidies would cover more than 80 per cent of the cost of rice. Rama Rao must either break his pledges or bankrupt his government—not a happy choice. (Soon after this was first published, Rao's son-in-law Chandrababu Naidu ousted him in a palace coup.)

Some populist gestures, however, are carefully designed not to imply specific promises, and they often work well. When Lalu Prasad Yadav of Bihar had himself photographed milking a cow, he reminded members of his cowherd caste that he delights in his and their humble origins. When Biju Patnaik, septuagenarian chief minister of Orissa, rode a bicycle to the office to dramatise the need to conserve fuel, he got a useful point across and reminded citizens of how extraordinary he is.

Still other gestures go at least partly wrong. The same Patnaik invited citizens to 'beat up' errant officials (providing he gave prior approval), in order to deflect resentment about ineffective government onto bureaucrats. It worked for a while, but then he was embarrassed by requests for permission to thrash him for failing to fulfil commitments, and eventually angry civil servants assaulted him as he left the office.

Some chief ministers try to insulate bureaucrats from lobbying by legislators and others—a favourite device of centraliers. But it makes them seem dangerously unresponsive and undemocratic, and it often provokes anger and rebellion among their subordinates and leaders of powerful interests.

Others go to the opposite extreme by allowing legislators and political allies to browbeat bureaucrats into permitting illegalities. This wins support from those who are corrupt profiteers, but it demoralises the bureaucracy, and chief ministers who try this often lose credibility and control over events amid runaway corruption. Cannier leaders seek a balance between these extremes, but that is an exceedingly tricky task that calls for constant shifts of emphasis that overburdened politicians are often unable to make.

All chief ministers try to channel patronage (funds, favours, goods, and services) to social groups from which they hope for votes at future elections. But this time honoured practice has recently undergone important changes. During the first two decades after independence, the Congress Party maintained its dominance in nearly every state by distributing resources, in a largely successful effort to keep *every* conceivable interest group happy. Prosperous groups got the lion's share, but there were at least token gestures for everyone.

Since the late 1960s, other parties have often gained power by targeting not 100 per cent, but 60 to 70 per cent of the population—whether the Hindu majority, clusters of disadvantaged castes, or other groups. Rising political awareness, even among the poor, has made it more difficult to paper over divisions between high castes and low, industry and labour, urban and rural dwellers. Congress too has sometimes given way to this trend. But using patronage distribution to forge majority coalitions has become increasingly difficult for all parties, for several reasons.

Slow economic growth has meant that the resources available for distribution have not kept pace with rising demands from interest groups. (See chapter fourteen of this book on how this changed after 2002.) Mounting corruption among politicians means that money that might have been allotted as patronage has been skimmed off by individuals. Growing indiscipline within ruling parties has made them less capable of distributing resources effectively. And since mid-1991, economic liberalisation has reduced the funds available to state governments. (That also changed after 2002.) So while most chief ministers try to make the most of patronage politics, it yields fewer advantages than it used to.

Some chief ministers make extensive use of their coercive powers. This can entail threats of unwanted transfers or disciplinary action against civil servants to dragoon them into cooperating. Or it can mean the use of the bureaucracy, the police, or even gangs of toughs to intimidate or brutalise interest groups, civil society organisations, opposition parties, and even opponents within one's own party. Other chief ministers use both sticks and carrots in subtle combinations. While this often enhances their power, it is difficult to avoid contradictions between these two approaches. Those who depend mainly on tough tactics usually pay a heavy price at election time.

In recent years, chief ministers have had to face difficult new choices in their pursuit of economic development. Economic liberalisation has forced them to devote more attention to attracting private sector investment and less to patronage distribution. But even more important has been the need to choose between huge development projects like dams, irrigation systems, or major hospitals and small-scale schemes at the village level—wells for drinking water, the building or repair of schools, medical dispensaries, rural roads, and the like. After years of emphasising the former, governments in a few states have become enormously popular by stressing long-neglected smaller projects that bring direct, highly visible benefits to villagers.[10]

The issues discussed above include only a few of the tactical choices that confront chief ministers. They also need to decide whether to try to mobilise comparatively dormant social groups to

[10]This was vividly apparent both from the 1985 re-election of the Janata government in Karnataka after it had stressed such projects (most notably, 60,000 village tube wells), and from evidence gathered in a study of decentralisation in that state: Crook and Manor, *Democracy and Decentralisation in South Asia and West Africa*.

broaden their base, or to divide, intimidate, or otherwise demobilise certain groups—or both at once. They must find a balance between fomenting social conflict and mitigating it; between dramatising politics and lowering the political temperature and popular aspirations (as Prime Minister Narasimha Rao did systematically); between generous responses that assuage grievances and a hard line in the face of pressure from interests; between making themselves easily available and remaining aloof; between leftist and rightist policies—and much more. With so many things to consider, their task is excruciatingly difficult. G. Ram Reddy has said that if a chief minister is not suffering from heart trouble, hypertension, or a nervous disease after just one year in office, he is not doing his or her job properly.[11]

Most chief ministers tend towards moderation in most of the tactical choices listed above. There is, of course, no correct set of postures to adopt in all situations. The appropriate choice will depend on the personality and proclivities of the chief minister, the condition of his/her party and of the opposition, the socio-economic milieu, and many other things. But most of those who have been at least partially successful share a few traits.

First, they have frequently adjusted their postures on these various issues to respond to changing circumstances. They have been compelled to do so by the volatility of Indian politics. This means that relations—within parties, between different parties, between parties and interest groups, and among various interest groups—tend to change quickly, often, and unexpectedly.

Second, relatively successful chief ministers have made these adjustments in a measured manner. It is usually unwise to make drastic changes, since this can give the impression of panic and earn a leader a reputation for wild inconsistency. Continuous fine-tuning is essential.

Finally, chief ministers understand that if they shift their position on one issue, they may need to make adjustments on others—either to maintain consistency or to balance interests.

[11]Interview, New Delhi, 11 December 1994.

To succeed even partially at all of this is obviously difficult. To say that a chief minister is involved in a game of chess is to understate the complexity of the task. It is more accurate to see him or her as a frantic performer in a circus act, rushing back and forth along a long table, keeping 15 or 20 dinner plates spinning—and doing all this from the saddle of a unicycle.

As if this were not enough, in recent times, chief ministers have found the ground shifting beneath them. The process of opening the economy to market forces is changing the fundamental logic of Indian politics.[12] In the past, governments at the national and state levels have succeeded or failed at winning reelection on the basis of their effectiveness at distributing the resources they control. In the future, they are likely to stand or fall mainly on the basis of their effectiveness at enabling market forces to generate growth. (This also changed after 2002—see chapter fourteen of this book.) This change requires politicians to make huge adjustments in their thinking and tactics, and compounds their problems still further.

Assessing the Performance of Chief Ministers

Despite the extreme complexity of their task, a significant number of chief ministers have performed well enough to get reelected. Major Indian states witnessed 51 state elections between 1980 and March 1995, and 19 of these were won by incumbent governments. The defeat of the other 32 reminds us of the inadequacy of many chief ministers. But when we consider the immensity of their problems and the volatility of Indian politics, those 19 victories (37 per cent of the total) are reasonably impressive.

How did this happen? This important question brings us to the heart of the debate over India's governability. The explanation is complicated. In part, it has to do with the quality of the people who have served as chief ministers. Few can match Shekhawat for adroit leadership, but—crucially—few have been such wretched leaders that they were bound to fail.

[12]J. Manor, 'The Political Sustainability of Economic Liberalization in India', in R. E. Cassen and V. Joshi (eds), *India: The Future of Economic Reform* (Oxford University Press, Delhi, 1994), pp. 339–63.

Fortunately, incompetent chief ministers have done limited damage to institutions, for two reasons. First, Indian voters are perceptive enough to have thrown such leaders out on every occasion when they presented themselves for reelection, and replaced them with less destructive figures and parties. Second, the electorate has been able to do this because India's multiparty system, despite much decay, is creative enough always to have produced at least one alternative who—while he or she may not always have been particularly impressive—was at least a significant improvement on the incumbent regime.

What else explains the ability of a large minority of chief ministers to get themselves reelected? Most neither sink to the level of incompetence mentioned above nor rise to the ingenious heights represented by Shekhawat. Most of them have muddled along in the job, often in confusion and distress. So their own political skills clearly do not explain the electoral success of so many. If, however, we look beyond these leaders—or rather below them, to the people whom they lead—we find enough vitally important skills to provide much of the explanation.

Compelling evidence has recently emerged to indicate that India's long experience with open, competitive politics has played a key role by enabling a huge number of activists—local-level political entrepreneurs or 'fixers'—to develop these skills. (For details, see chapter ten of this book.) One study of the political implications of economic liberalisation since mid-1991 found that political operatives in state-level ruling parties have been remarkably successful at adapting political skills acquired before liberalisation to the new circumstances. They have shown themselves as able to forge political bargains, to share out both benefits and pain among key groups, to negotiate with varied interests, and to build coalitions; all of these skills have important uses in preventing liberalisation from damaging the interests both of their parties and of most key interest groups. They have therefore been more adept than politicians in many other countries at coping with the political strains that liberalisation brings.[13]

---

[13]For details, see R. Jenkins, *Democratic Politics and Economic Reform in India* (Cambridge University Press, Cambridge, 1999).

Even the factionalism that bedevils most parties in India has—to a limited extent—been creative. Factions sometimes play positive roles, like those which parties used to play. They serve as instruments for the distribution of resources in ways that cultivate support from important interest groups and integrate state and society. They represent the desires and grievances of interests within the political process, and they mobilise voters at election time. They sometimes promote stability by restraining senior leaders who might otherwise move too fast or too far. When circumstances change rapidly and unexpectedly, factions often adjust swiftly to them and thus contribute to the flexibility of the political system. These positive contributions are far outweighed by their damaging doings, but they are realities nonetheless.

Another study comparing attempts at democratic decentralisation in India, Bangladesh Ghana, and the Ivory Coast, found the experiment in India to be far more successful than in the other three countries, where democracy has enjoyed an intermittent existence at best. A crucial factor in India's achievement was the ability of political activists there to accomplish things that most people in the other countries found impossible.

When elected councils were created near the grassroots, a sizable army of political operatives in India knew how to develop creative relationships between elected councillors and low-level civil servants—because they had seen how it was done at higher levels over several decades. They knew how to maintain contact with constituents, how to articulate constituents' views to elected councils, and how to ensure that councils and bureaucrats would respond to those views. They knew how to make adversarial relations between rival political parties within councils work in ways that were civilised but nevertheless ensured that a lively opposition acted as a check on the excesses of the majority party. They knew how to communicate with representatives of India's free press, to keep citizens informed on council affairs, and to reveal and thus restrain excesses by those in power. They also found it easier to make democracy work at lower levels because both politicians and citizens shared a belief that elected representatives had heavy obligations to voters—an idea that was largely absent in the other three countries.[14]

All of this evidence provides a further explanation for the ability of such a large minority of chief ministers to gain reelection. These political skills are found in abundance at all levels of the political system in India, and in nearly all states and parties. They tend to enable organised interests (which India has in abundance) to exert pressure on state institutions and to extract concessions. They facilitate frequent adjustments and renegotiation in state-society relations to respond to change. They permit many (though not all) conflicts between caste, class, religious, and other groups to be fought out in semi-civilised ways. They tend to enhance the authority of those in power and the legitimacy of open politics.

Chief ministers who can maintain a minimal amount of rationality and order in the political process—as a sizable minority have done—create conditions in which activists can deploy their skills to deliver reasonably adequate governance. There are numerous ways in which chief ministers can help to achieve this. It is usually possible for them to prevent corruption from soaring out of control and to avoid committing huge proportions of the government's resources to giveaway programmes such as subsidies on foodstuffs.

Those who achieve these things should have enough funds available to help skilled activists at lower levels to arrange a politically advantageous distribution of goods and services to key social groups. It is usually possible for chief ministers to structure their daily routines in ways that leave time for consultations with ministers and bureaucrats on matters of policy and political strategy. If they do that, there is every chance that their governments and the activists at lower levels who assist them will remain focused on a manageable number of programmes that address citizens' needs. Chief ministers with theatrical skills (and that includes most) can use oratory, slogans, symbolic acts, and the like to dramatise and clarify their aspirations and achievements. This is a way of cultivating popular support, but it also gives political activists a

[14]Crook and Manor, *Democracy and Decentralisation in South Asia and West Africa*.

clear understanding of the government's main aims and of the social groups that government is targeting for benefits in its effort to develop a solid social base.

Among the many other things that chief ministers can do to facilitate the work of lower-level activists, one is often crucial. By containing and managing factional conflict within the ruling party, they can limit its potential damage and enable activists working within various factions to play constructive roles.

If s/he can manage this and some of the other things mentioned above, a chief minister can go a long way towards creating conditions for skilled activists to work constructively. Some of them have been sufficiently skilled to ensure the reelection of their governments and to suggest that India is governable through its existing democratic institutions. When chief ministers fall short, another democratic institution—the electoral process—rids the system of the failed regime and produces an alternative government that may be more successful.

There is no denying that corruption, brutalisation, and institutional decay are serious problems in India. But that is not the whole story. The accommodative skills of political activists are capable of repairing some of the damage that institutions have suffered, and of restoring minimally civilised social relations after periods of severe conflict. Under even mediocre chief ministers, decay can be checked and this kind of rebuilding can occur. (For more details, see chapter four of this book.)

So commentators who have voiced alarm at the disintegration of party organisations in India have overstated the problem. To have exceedingly good government, strong party organisations are essential. But such organisations are lacking in nearly all Indian states and are very difficult to re-establish. And yet, reasonably adequate governance is often possible in their absence if chief ministers create congenial conditions for the skills of lower-level activists to operate constructively.[15] Those skills are a major national resource that India

---

[15]In an important article written several years later, Merilee Grindle provided a thorough explication of this theme: 'Good Enough Governance: Poverty Reduction and Reform in Developing Countries', *Governance*

has in far greater abundance than most other Asian and African countries.

The picture of India's politics that emerges here is ambiguous. This is not a full-throated anthem of praise to chief ministers or the system in which they work. But while the sense of crisis in many writings on India is not to be dismissed lightly, the country is less ungovernable than many have suggested. Enough has been achieved there to warrant appreciation for the practical utility of Indian democracy, and to discourage despair about its prospects.

(October 2004), pp. 525–48. See also her 'Good Enough Governance Revisited: Poverty Reduction and Reform in Developing Countries', *Development Policy Review* (2007), pp. 553–74.

— thirteen —

BEYOND CLIENTELISM

Digvijay Singh in Madhya Pradesh

Here we encounter another 'pragmatic progressive' in the mould of Devaraj Urs (see chapter eleven), who held office in the years after the chief ministers discussed in chapter twelve. His was a decade (1993–2003) when financial constraints on state governments were tight—before government revenues began to surge in 2003—but he still found ways to achieve constructive outcomes which deepened democracy. He was also one of many chief ministers who understood that the old politics of patronage distribution (clientelism) was insufficient to ensure reelection. He therefore supplemented patronage politics with 'post-clientelist' initiatives— programmes that were largely protected from those who wanted to divert resources for patronage distribution.

The literature on development, in and beyond India, has— astonishingly—paid too little attention to senior politicians, even though they make most of the crucial decisions. It thus offers us Hamlet without the prince. To give 'political agency' its due, this chapter considers an example of an imaginative, adroit and constructive politician, Digvijay Singh, chief minister of Madhya Pradesh between 1993 and 2003.

It examines the ways in which he sought to cultivate popular support, to implement policies, and to achieve important goals. The material presented here is drawn from a book which compares him in greater detail to leaders in Brazil and Uganda who—like Singh—machinated in ways that eased poverty, and which argues that poverty reduction and other progressive outcomes can *serve the interests* of politicians who achieve them.[1]

Digvijay Singh recognised that politics as usual—in his state and in India more generally—was not working. It mainly stressed clientelism, the distribution of patronage (goods, services, funds and favours) through networks of clients to selected social groups in the (often vain) hope of winning their votes. He therefore developed a new strategy and a new type of politics which supplemented and, over time, displaced the old to a significant degree. It entailed the generous devolution of powers and resources to elected councils at lower levels and an imaginative array of new policies and programmes intended to promote 'development' (the main theme that he stressed) in a participatory manner. He also sought to broaden the dangerously narrow base of his Congress Party by mounting initiatives to benefit poor people—some of which were quite successful.

In recent years, many chief ministers in Indian states have seen the need to supplement clientelism with something extra. The 'somethings extra', the varied post-clientelist strategies that they have developed, have caused states to be governed in an extraordinary (and possibly worrying) diversity of ways. In this context, the choice of Madhya Pradesh is important. It is one of the more underdeveloped states, but it is not untypical—so the achievements that occurred there under Singh can also happen in other states. Those achievements are therefore far more important than what has been accomplished in Kerala or West Bengal—of

---

[1] The other two politicians are former President Fernando Henrique Cardoso of Brazil and President Yoweri Museveni of Uganda. The book is: M. A. Melo, N. Ng'ethe and J. Manor, *Against the Odds: Politicians, Institutions and the Struggle against Poverty* (Hurst/Columbia University Press, London/ New York, 2012).

which we have heard much but which is not replicable because they are explained by the efforts of a progressive party that cannot gain power in other states. Singh's approach deserves special attention because—among the post-clientelist strategies which are widely replicable—his has the greatest constructive potential.

Digvijay Singh—more than any other Congress Party leader since Devaraj Urs in Karnataka a generation earlier (see chapter eleven of this book)—demonstrated that the party could reap substantial rewards by adopting left-of-centre policies. Like Urs, he was largely oblivious to ideological tenets or labels. They were both distinctly '*pragmatic* progressives' who undertook redistributive programmes mainly because they were politically advantageous.[2]

It is worth noting that his left-of-centre approach predated and presaged something very similar by the Congress-led government at the national level after 2004. He has received no credit for this. But that was to be expected, since in his party, praise for young leaders is more or less forbidden lest it undercut the dominance of the dynasty (see chapter six of this book).

To legitimise these new programmes and to foster popular awareness of them, he commissioned a United Nations-style *Human Development Report* for Madhya Pradesh which called attention to the state's problems and failings—the kinds of things which most other chief ministers sought to hush up. One key aim of this was to make 'development' the most salient issue in the public sphere—more salient than factional squabbles, or religious and caste issues.

Early in his time in office, Singh provided greater powers and resources to elected *panchayats* at district and lower levels than almost any other government in India or elsewhere. The result was one of the four most robust experiments with democratic decentralisation in India, and one of the six most robust in Asia, Africa and Latin America.[3] On its own, however, this would not suffice to redistribute resources—because, as he well knew, elected

[2]Foremost among them was the Congress chief minister of Karnataka between 1972 and 1980 (see chapter eleven of this book).

[3]A curious paradox stands at the core of this story. Policy-making at the apex of the political system was kept tightly *closed*, but the policies that

local councils are often dominated by the non-poor.[4] So he had to go further, since redistribution was essential if he was to offer poor people more than the patronage politics that his ministers and legislators were assiduously pursuing—and if he was to tackle a further, deeply urgent political problem to which we now turn.

Broadening the Congress Party's Social Base

His party's social base had been contracting since the 1960s when Congress enjoyed pre-eminence in Madhya Pradesh. A political *awakening* had gradually been occurring among ordinary, even poor people. They had become more politically aware, independent and skilled, more impatient with tokenism, and more demanding of politicians. As this happened, the instruments through which politicians might respond had been undergoing *decay*. Both the formal institutions of state and, crucially, informal institutions like the Congress Party's organisation had lost substance, reach, autonomy and flexibility. The confluence of these two trends posed serious dangers to politicians, ruling parties and the democratic process. An imaginative response was required which would promote renewal and political regeneration (see chapter four of this book).

What follows is a rough picture of the traditional caste hierarchy (the potency of which has been seriously eroded even in under-developed states like Madhya Pradesh[5]), plus the Scheduled Tribes (STs) and Muslims. The groups whose names are italicised below are those which Singh made special efforts to cultivate.

---

emerged did much to *open up* the political and policy processes to bottom-up influence from ordinary people at the grassroots.

[4]However, an immensely important recent book argues very authoritatively that democratic decentralisation in India has assisted in reducing poverty: H. K. Nagarajan, H. P. Binswanger-Mkhize and S. S. Mennakshisundaram, *Decentralization and Empowerment for Rural Development* (2014).

[5]This is based on discussions with Adrian Mayer.

Brahmins (5.66 per cent of total population)
Rajputs and other higher castes (7.24 per cent)
Intermediate castes (1.11 per cent)
'Other Backward Castes' (41.44 per cent)—[Singh sought to
   cultivate *some* of the groups in this rather artificial category.]
Scheduled Castes—ex-Untouchables or Dalits (14.05 per cent)
Scheduled Tribes or Adivasis (21.62 per cent)
Muslims (3.85 per cent)[6]

Digvijay Singh is a Rajput. The 'Other Backward Castes' (OBCs) is a highly fragmented category. He knew this and thus reached out to some of them, while ignoring others. He also mounted a serious initiative to cultivate Dalits. This alienated the STs to some extent, but he took steps to reassure them. Muslims were so alienated from his principal opponent, the Bharatiya Janata Party (BJP) that they could be depended upon to lend the Congress Party strong support.

There are social tensions between higher- and lower-status elements of this diverse coalition—and among groups on the lower rungs of the old hierarchy. He knew that, but he believed that he could do enough to prevent that from wrecking his social coalition.

He felt compelled to construct it by two challenges which previous Congress chief ministers there had not encountered. A historic change had occurred in Indian politics in 1990. Two new themes were brought ferociously to the fore which carried huge implications for his party all across the country and for the politics of his state.

First, a non-Congress, secular government in New Delhi, headed by V. P. Singh, committed itself to reserving a substantial proportion of places in educational institutions and government employment for members of the OBCs. Many of them were 'poor' or close to it. This commitment triggered both a significant popular response among those who stood to gain and angry, often violent opposition from those who did not. It also touched off competition for the votes of the large OBC bloc, in which the Congress Party would need to be involved.

[6]I am grateful to Christophe Jaffrelot for these figures.

Second, the Hindu nationalist BJP reacted by launching an agitation for the destruction of a mosque at Ayodhya, allegedly built on the birthplace of the Hindu god Ram. This evoked another substantial popular response which cut across the caste-based appeal of the first issue, and made strident Hindu chauvinism a major force for the first time.

In Madhya Pradesh, Hindu nationalism had long had a potent presence. Then as now, the state had a two-party system in which the Congress faced the BJP. Congress leaders like Singh needed to redouble their efforts to resist the BJP. Far less had been done by rival parties in the state to mobilise the OBCs or other numerically powerful groups of poor people. These latter groups were the Dalits who stood below the OBCs at the bottom of the traditional hierarchy, and the *Adivasis* or STs, impoverished groups who stood largely outside the Hindu social order. Singh recognised that his party had to offer these groups many more tangible benefits if it was to prevent other parties from ending their traditional support for the Congress. The old reliance on the rural dominance of his Rajput caste and political bosses mainly from other high status groups would not suffice for long.[7]

This impelled him, when he became chief minister in 1993, to give 'development' huge emphasis, as the core issue in the state's politics. Previously, it had preoccupied politicians less had patronage distribution, faction fights and other mundane matters. By stressing 'development', he could respond to both of the twin challenges that had emerged without giving ground to either.

He then followed this up with an array of specific programmes to promote 'development', which included several pro-poor initiatives (two of which are examined late in this chapter). This was his response to the twin threats of Hindu nationalism and caste-based appeals to disadvantaged groups, and it marked him out as a new kind of Congress leader. His energetic pursuit of this approach eventually led to his being identified in a national fortnightly

---

[7] Interview with Digvijay Singh, New Delhi, 16 May 2004.

magazine as one of two chief ministers who were sufficiently imaginative and dynamic to qualify as 'Wow Guys'.[8]

Making His Influence Penetrate Downward into Society

How did Digvijay Singh seek to make his influence penetrate downward into society—which was essential to constructing a constituency for himself and his party? There were, broadly speaking, three possible strategies available, which were not mutually exclusive. They were:

- to develop ties to civil society organisations;
- to enhance the penetrative capacity of his Congress Party organisation; and
- to extend the downward reach of the formal institutions and agencies of state.

He depended almost entirely on the *last* of these options. To understand why, let us consider each in turn.

Cultivating civil society. Civil society in Madhya Pradesh was weaker than in many other parts of India, but some development- and rights-oriented organisations had gained strength in the main urban centres, and a small number had forged links to similar organisations at intermediate levels and even some local arenas. Two quite formidable organisations had emerged. The first, the *Ekta Parishad*, was a Gandhian organisation that worked among disadvantaged groups and pressed the government on injustices, especially land issues. It was often very critical of Singh, but he eventually developed an understanding with it. The second, the internationally known *Narmada Bachao Andolan*, sought to resist the Narmada dam project, and to represent the large numbers of people who would be displaced by it.

Digvijay Singh was the first chief minister of this state to reach out to civil society organisations to any meaningful extent. In his

---

[8]*Business World*, 7–21 March 1999, pp. 22–34. The other 'Wow Guy' was Chandrababu Naidu of Andhra Pradesh.

first term, he sought advice on policy issues from enlightened, development-oriented civic groups, and involved a small number of them as partners in development programmes. He also sought to develop an understanding with the *Narmada Bachao Andolan*. One early encounter with its members offers an insight into his style, throughout his time in power, of personal engagement. A sizeable body of demonstrators from the *Andolan* once gathered outside his official residence. Instead of ignoring them—which would have been the response of most chief ministers—he invited them in. When he saw that there were too many of them to take seats even in his large reception room, he suggested that he and they sit together on the front steps and talk—and then he himself sat on one of the *lower* steps. He spoke to them—as he spoke to everyone—in a relaxed and thoroughly courteous manner, as if they were equals. This kind of behaviour is highly unusual in Indian politics, and many of those who encountered it were substantially disarmed by it.

Despite this, however, the *Andolan* was unwilling to make any significant compromise. As he later put it, 'they insisted on "no dam", and it was beyond my power to deliver that'. What he could offer was money to enable displaced people to purchase new lands—his only option, since the state did not possess enough suitable and conveniently located land for redistribution among them. He also promised to encourage governments in neighbouring states to follow suit.[9] Their response was to sustain non-violent but quite energetic protests.

This persuaded some of Singh's cabinet colleagues that he had been naïve to assume that civil society organisations would make useful partners, and they put this view forcefully to him. This and his exasperation over dealing with the *Andolan* appear to have persuaded him to distance himself—unnecessarily and unwisely—from many other organisations, which were not at all confrontational. The main exception was the *Ekta Parishad*. So the option of cultivating civil society was largely set aside.

Building a penetrative party organisation. The most obvious approach to making his influence penetrate downward would have been

[9]Interview with Digvijay Singh, New Delhi, 16 May 2004.

to strengthen the Congress Party's organisation. It had not recovered from the severe damage wrought when Indira Gandhi had abandoned intra-party democracy, radically centralised power within it, systematically inspired factional conflict in all state-level party units, and ruthlessly cut down any state-level leader who appeared to gain significant strength.

But if Singh had sought to revive it, he would have run two risks. He would have opened up space for factional infighting (lurking under the surface). And he might have begun to look even more powerful than he already was, and that might have invited punitive intervention from national leaders of his party. So he wisely avoided party building—a sad, painful necessity.

Extending the downward reach of the formal institutions and agencies of state. This left him with only one choice—to implement imaginative programmes through formal state institutions and agencies. It is remarkable that, in an era in which the state was supposed to be shrinking (and in which his government was indeed cautiously downsizing[10]), major progress should have been made under this chief minister in extending the downward reach of the state. But that is what happened.

During his first term in power (1993–1998) he concentrated on two main approaches which—taken together—were intended to improve the lives of ordinary people at the grassroots. First, he sought to enhance the capacity of state agencies to deliver goods and services downward. Second and more crucially, he generously empowered elected councils at lower levels to give villagers in this predominantly rural state new opportunities to exercise some influence from below over the political and policy processes.

His 'Presentation' of Himself and His Policies

Anyone who has seen Digvijay Singh address crowds or speak on television will know that he is extremely persuasive at delivering

---

[10]A fiscal stabilisation programme, funded by the Asian Development Bank, partly entailed a reduction in the number of 'Class IV' government employees—that is, those performing largely menial, unskilled tasks.

cogent messages and at presenting himself as a shrewd, eminently reasonable and attractive leader. (This has made him one of the most visible and persuasive television spokesmen for the Congress Party—in Hindi and in English.) It is thus rather odd that as chief minister, he made only limited efforts to publicise himself and his policies, and that he was extraordinarily reticent about stressing his efforts at poverty reduction which were a central element of his overall project.

At least a little of the explanation for his reticence is personal, not political. He had clearly concluded—from the courtly manners that he learned within his family, and perhaps from his years at Daly College, a school for the elite—that it was bad form to blow his own horn and inflate his own importance. Instead, he developed a habit of unfailing courtesy, which entailed a degree of self-effacement. One example from his years in power will illustrate the point. When he became chief minister, as a result of discussions within his family and especially with his mother—a woman who was serious about a commitment to public service, but also to restrained manners— he concluded that he should give something up while he was chief minister. He therefore decided to become a vegetarian during his time in office. He stuck to this for a decade, and on the morning in 2003 that election results began coming in, suggesting that his party might be ousted, his wife and children teased him by saying that but sundown, he might cease to be a vegetarian. The most remarkable aspect of all of this is that he was too reticent to announce his decision to give up meat eating—even though it would have pleased many voters. That would have been bad form, a distasteful exploitation of a private decision for public benefit. To this day, it remains unknown to most people in and beyond Madhya Pradesh.[11]

Like all senior leaders in India, he had a publicity machine. But he invested comparatively little in it—far less, for example, than the vast sums spent (largely on myth-making) by another prominent chief minister in his day, Chandrababu Naidu of Andhra Pradesh. His reticence is explained in part by his knowledge (i) that his party's organisation lacked the capacity to penetrate effectively below the

---

[11]Interview with Digvijay Singh, New Delhi, 24 May 2005.

district level, so that it could not help him to deliver his message to most voters, and (ii) that he had to avoid organisation-building because it would lift the lid on serious factional tensions within the Congress Party in his state. The explanation for his reluctance to speak explicitly and often about 'poverty' takes some explaining.

Digvijay Singh made greater attempts to tackle poverty than did senior politicians in most other Indian states and in most other less developed countries. And at least in the case of one initiative, the Education Guarantee Scheme (discussed below), he also achieved more than most others did. *And yet* he made very few references to 'poverty' in his public statements.

His reticence is not explained by an anxiety to avoid alienating non-poor voters. Many people, in Madhya Pradesh and in India, who are not 'poor' by any objective measurement nevertheless consider themselves to be 'poor'.[12] So there is potential political mileage in stressing the issue. His reticence was largely explained by his belief that voters had grown sceptical of such talk—and needed to be persuaded by action in the absence of such rhetoric. His most recent predecessor as Congress Party chief minister had made a habit of *speaking* often and loudly about poverty, while actually *doing* precious little about it. This placed him squarely in the tradition of Indira Gandhi who in 1971 gained an election landslide with a promise to 'abolish poverty' ('*garibi hatao*'), but who had also done little thereafter to follow up with action. This is not the sort of thing that Congress Party leaders dare say, but Singh was well aware that many voters felt sceptical of promises to tackle poverty—so he chose, probably wisely, not to make much use of that word.

The key theme that he stressed was not 'poverty' but 'development'. There was something for everyone in 'development'. He (and his modest publicity machine) also spoke of people's empowerment through decentralisation. That gets closer to 'poverty', but it is still some distance away from it.[13]

[12]I am grateful to Yogendra Yadav for stressing this point.

[13]This is based on several interviews with Digvijay Singh in Bhopal and New Delhi between 2002 and 2005.

The Education Guarantee Scheme

For a better understanding of how Digvijay Singh sought to cultivate popular support by pursuing pro-poor policies, let us consider his most successful initiative—the Education Guarantee Scheme (EGS). Its success was intimately linked to his prior empowerment of *panchayats* (elected councils at lower levels). Democratic decentralisation—a major element of Digvijay Singh's policy agenda—sometimes fails to serve the interests of poor people at the grassroots. But this programme was shrewdly structured to ensure that, in this instance at least, it could advance poverty reduction.

The Scheme, which began in 1997, was preceded by and grew out of a major literacy campaign to tackle one of the most severe problems affecting poor people. That campaign was pushed hard from the top by the chief minister. It mobilised a huge number of literates at the grassroots to teach others to read, and awarded them a 'bounty' for each person successfully taught—an inexpensive way to accomplish this in an era of tight fiscal constraints.[14]

This, together with the EGS, led to a spectacular increase in the official literacy rate between the censuses of 1991 and 2001—of 22 per cent among females, and 20 per cent overall. Comparable gains have been achieved in only one other Indian state over recent decades. The figures appear to be somewhat inflated, but not excessively so.[15]

During the literacy drive, it had become apparent to Singh and two of the bright civil servants who worked with him that one reason for the state's low literacy was that many remote villages did not possess primary schools. (It may seem surprising, but this ghastly fact has not fully registered with previous chief ministers.) Students had to walk long distances to reach the nearest school— and many did not do so. This led those two civil servants to ponder how schools might be provided to those villages.

[14]For Indian chief ministers (and governments at the national level), those constraints eased after 2002 when government revenues surged (see chapters fourteen and seventeen of this book).

[15]This comment is based on a detailed assessment of the methods used to estimate the rise in literacy, in discussions with two education specialists, Bhopal, 4 and 7 December 2004.

They eventually hit upon an idea that formed the basis for the EGS. Any village with 40 children (25 in 'tribal' hamlets) without a nearby school would be given the right to demand one, and to hire a literate person (usually from within the village) to teach local students up to grade five.[16] These new teachers were given three months of training and they were at first paid much less than teachers in conventional government schools. Later, their remuneration was increased substantially—partly in response to demands by them, but mainly as a result of their positive performance.

This programme was an example of the government stimulating demand from below, from poor people, even though demand overload was already a serious problem. It was nevertheless undertaken because Singh believed that insufficient demand had arisen from the state's poorest villages, and because he was (rightly) confident that the government would be able to respond adequately.

The scale of the demand was remarkable, and it surprised Singh himself. Before Madhya Pradesh was bifurcated in 2000, 26,000 villages demanded and got new schools where none had existed before. Twenty-one thousand of these were in districts that remained in Madhya Pradesh. After the bifurcation, the state added still more schools, bringing the total in late 2003 to 26,571. Fully 1,233,000 students were enrolled in them.[17] Of these, 90 per cent were drawn from poorer groups—the OBCs, SCs and STs.[18]

The state government disbursed the funds for this programme, but its day-to-day management was placed in the hands of elected village councils. This was crucial. Since the new teachers were accountable to the councils, and since local residents were quick to inform councillors of slack performance by teachers, absenteeism among them (a severe problem in other schools right across north India) was very low. Absenteeism also declined because the teachers

[16]Interview with Digvijay Singh, *The Hindu*, 11 July 2003.

[17]Interview with Amita Sharma, the civil servant who administered the Education Guarantee Scheme, Bhopal, 4 December 2003.

[18]Interview with Amita Sharma, Bhopal, 4 December 2003; and R. Gopalakrishnan and A. Sharma, 'Education Guarantee Scheme in Madhya Pradesh: Innovative Step to Universalise Education', *Economic and Political Weekly*, 26 September 1998.

in these schools lived locally—they did not commute in from urban centres, as did many teachers in conventional village schools. During the rainy season, which lasts many weeks, those commuting teachers find it impossible to reach a huge number of villages where their schools are located, because roads are impassable. The new schools, like the village *panchayats*, were intended by Singh to show villagers that a shift had occurred from *rajniti* (governance by the state) to *lokniti* (governance by newly empowered ordinary folk, and 'owned' by them). Or to put it slightly differently—he wanted them to see that at the local level, the 'government' now consisted of the people themselves.[19]

Who opposed the EGS? Singh himself says 'no one',[20] and he is almost entirely correct. Legislators and ministers welcomed it because they could claim credit for the new schools, even though they had little to do with founding them. Interests who did not benefit offered little objection, because few funds were diverted to the programme which they might otherwise have captured. Nor did higher castes in rural areas oppose it, for two reasons. Since many of them could pay private school fees for their children, they were unconcerned with what was happening in the public sector. Many others who sent their children to conventional government schools were pleased because the programme meant that low caste or 'tribal' children who had previously (to their dismay) trekked long distances to sit beside their children now had schools of their own. The only group that felt unhappy were the teachers in pre-existing government schools—and they were neither sufficiently discontented (their lives changed little) nor powerful enough to make much impact.

---

[19]Interview with Digvijay Singh, New Delhi, 16 May 2004. For more evidence on the Scheme, see R. Srivastava, *Evaluation of Community Based Primary Schooling Initiatives in Madhya Pradesh: Education Guarantee Scheme and Alternative Schools—Bilaspur and Dhar* (Centre for Education Research and Development, New Delhi, 1998); V. Vyasulu, 'MP's EGS: What are the Issues?', *Economic and Political Weekly*, 12 June 2000; and S. Singh, K. S. Sridhar and S. Bhargava, *External Evaluation of DPEP-I States: Report on Madhya Pradesh* (Indian Institute of Management, Lucknow, 2002).

[20]Interview with Digvijay Singh, New Delhi, 16 May 2004.

Some others were understandably anxious about the quality of the education provided in the new schools. One response is to argue that schools of indifferent quality are an improvement on no schools at all. But the government did not content itself with this. It took steps to ensure as much quality as possible in the new schools. It injected considerable rigour and substance into the three-month training course provided to teachers in them, and then instituted a further nine-month correspondence course based on the Diploma of Education syllabus, through which roughly 21,000 passed over a two-year period.

Fresh legislation—which is harder to rescind than executive action—was then passed requiring regular assessments of the quality of *all* types of schools in every constituency in the state, to be conducted and placed before the legislature every six months. The aim of this was to embarrass legislators whose constituencies yielded low ratings into committing themselves to take action to improve matters. (The tactic worked. For example, ministers whose constituencies showed poor results were quietly laughed at by their colleagues when reports were presented at cabinet meetings, and corrective action swiftly ensued.[21]) The government then decided to hire not one but two teachers for each new school, one of which had to be a woman—partly to attract more female pupils, and partly to ease the burden on solo teachers.[22]

These efforts had an impact. Comparisons of pass rates in examinations for fifth-year students in conventional schools and the new EGS schools tell their own story.

Year	Conventional Schools (per cent)	EGS Schools (per cent)
2001–02	68.29	72.38
2002–03	71.50	72.60[23]

[21]Interview with Amita Sharma, the civil servant who supervised the EGS, Bhopal, 4 December 2003.

[22]*Ibid.*

[23]*Ibid.*

This owed much to lower rates of teachers' absenteeism in EGS schools (and to lower drop-out rates among students in them). It was lower mainly because teachers in those schools were *accountable* to village *panchayats*, unlike teachers in conventional schools.

One set of numbers noted above is worth reiterating, since they tells us something important, both about underdevelopment in the state and about the impact of this Scheme. There were roughly 52,000 villages in undivided Madhya Pradesh, and this Scheme brought new schools to 26,000 of these before the state was bifurcated—and still more thereafter. In other words, *half* of the state's villages lacked schools, and the EGS provided them. These are both extraordinary numbers which indicate both how serious the neglect of rural development had been before Singh, and how much was achieved under him.

We learn three other important things from all of this. First, although the grassroots suffered from severe underdevelopment, the state's pre-existing institutional structures were in certain important ways reasonably well developed. They possessed the capacity (i) to transmit the information downward to remote villages that they had the right to demand schools and (ii) to transmit demands for schools upward to relevant authorities. Second, over half a century, the democratic process had inspired a sufficient political awakening even among people from severely deprived social groups living in exceedingly poor villages to ensure that the demand for schools both existed and would be voiced. There was nothing half-hearted about the response to the Scheme—it was massive. Third, once that demand emerged, the constructive potential of India's state institutions became still more apparent. The EGS reoriented existing administrative institutions so that they responded to this democratic demand, and supplemented the efforts of those institutions by incorporating new ones—in the shape of elected local councils—into the political and policy processes.

* * *

Many chief ministers in India's states have come to recognise that the old politics of patronage distribution no longer suffice to win re-election. Many of them have responded with post-clientelist experiments—with 'something extra' to supplement the old politics. But there are marked variations among the 'somethings extra' that chief ministers have introduced—and as a result, different Indian states have lately been governed in astonishingly different ways. For example, Narendra Modi in Gujarat has used social polarisation along communal lines as his 'something extra', while Lalu Prasad Yadav in Bihar polarised society very differently—between haves and have-nots. Chandrababu Naidu in Andhra Pradesh undertook an energetic drive for 'development' in a top-down, exceedingly illiberal manner which smacked of Malaysia-style control-freakery (and he explicitly identified that country as his model). Digvijay Singh also pursued 'development', but in a very different, far more liberal way—through devolution, bottom-up participation, and major programmes targetted on poorer groups. His brand of 'post-clientelism' is more constructive and more exportable to other Indian states than are those other three—although little has been explicitly made of it by his party which reserves its fulsome praise for just one family.

In order to broaden his party's base, Singh felt compelled to cultivate popularity not informally, through his party, but formally—by mounting new government policies, and by creating new structures, especially genuinely empowered *panchayati raj* institutions. The policies included some that addressed poverty, and some of those met with considerable success.

He neither thought nor spoke in 'ideological' terms. But he did more than nearly all other chief ministers to experiment with promising new *ideas* from two overlapping sources:

(i) a new development paradigm being created within international and (not least) Indian civil society organisations and research centres, which stressed bottom-up, demand-driven development, and
(ii) the Gandhian tradition.

And yet even though he did more than most to tackle poverty, he was remarkably reticent about referring to it explicitly—because his Congress predecessors had over-used that word and inspired popular cynicism about governments' commitment to it. Instead he stressed

'development'—a word which offered something for everyone—
and he had some success on that broad front.

This got him re-elected once—something that only about 10
per cent of chief ministers outside West Bengal have achieved since
1980. Digvijay Singh also miscalculated on certain key occasions,
and his first priority—like that of all other leaders across India—
was his own political interest. So he, like the rest, is attended by
ambiguities. But he also managed to achieve more to facilitate liberal
practices and to deepen democracy—and to address the needs of
poor, socially excluded groups—than any leader in a state where
achievements can be replicated elsewhere. And he demonstrated
not just that progressive strategies are practicable, but that they can
serve the interests of the leaders and parties that pursue them.

— *f o u r t e e n* —

INDIA'S STATES

The Struggle to Govern

This paper follows on from the three preceding chapters in Part IV which focus on chief ministers. It brings readers into the new millennium when conditions— and thus the strategies pursued by many chief ministers—have changed. (Note the contrast with chapter twelve.) For them, governing is still a struggle, but it is less daunting than in the 1990s. Since 2003, government revenues have surged, so that chief ministers can deploy far more resources than before. Economic growth—and the discretionary powers that they retain, thanks to India's limited economic liberalisation (by international standards)—have provided them with unprecedented opportunities to assert themselves. Many chief ministers have seized upon these to centralise power within their states—a process discussed in great detail in parts III and IV. Anxieties about India's governability have receded, and the importance of patronage distribution has declined in favour of programmatic initiatives that are shielded from patronage bosses. But the democratic process has perhaps become less open and robust.

This chapter analyses the difficulties and opportunities that senior politicians and political parties in India face as they seek to govern. It examines leaders' and parties' efforts to connect with, respond to, cultivate support from, and perhaps control *citizens* and *society*. A focus on those two words draws our attention mainly to the states in this federal system. It is at the state level and below that most of the actual governing occurs in India. It is there that governments and society mainly interact.

There is another reason to focus on states. Yogendra Yadav and Suhas Palshikar have argued, 'The 1990s could easily be called the decade of the states: as the theatre of politics shifted to the states...', a decade which saw 'the emergence of the state as the principal arena of political choice'.[1] That has remained true since 2000. State-based parties have participated in ruling, multi-party alliances in New Delhi over the last 18 years, but their cabinet ministers at the national level have often focused less on governing than on milking their ministries for benefits and funds (legitimately and illicitly) to be used within the individual states which form their power bases. They are inordinately but understandably preoccupied with the state level. All national elections since the early 1990s have been 'state led', an expression used privately by a leading Congress Party strategist.[2] Or as Yadav and Palshikar put it, 'National election outcomes do not mainly reflect a "national mood" that prevails at that moment; rather they reflect an equilibrium of political forces that happens to obtain at the state level at the time when national elections are held'.[3]

This is partly the result of fundamental changes in the Indian political system since 1989 when it became impossible for any single party to gain a majority in the Lok Sabha (the lower house of Parliament). That has triggered a very substantial redistribution of power away from the Prime Minister's Office (PMO) which had been dominant for most of the period between 1971 and 1989. Power has flowed to other institutions at the national level, but also to parties,

---

[1] Y. Yadav and S. Palshikar, 'Revisiting the "Third Electoral System"': Mapping Electoral Trends in India, 2004–9', in S. Shastri, K. C. Suri and Y. Yadav (eds), *Electoral Politics in Indian States: Lok Sabha Elections in 2004 and Beyond* (Oxford University Press, Delhi, 2009), pp. 394 and 401.

[2] Interview, New Delhi, 5 August 2005.

[3] Yadav and Palshikar, 'Revisiting the "Third" Electoral System', p. 395.

governments and forces at the state level. (That change and its partly ironic implications are considered in detail in Part I of this chapter.)

Many important policy (and political) initiatives have emerged at the state level since 1989. State governments often adapt, manipulate and re-package centrally sponsored schemes to a greater extent than their argument implies. Even before 1989, this writer argued that most of the actual governing in India took place at and below the state level. But the redistribution of power since then has made that comment more valid than it was then—even though centrally sponsored schemes loom larger today.

Two other things draw our attention to India's states. First, in recent years, state governments have been changing. As we shall see in Part I, power within many of them has been greatly—and in some cases radically—centralised. Second, in the wake of the post-1989 redistribution of power in favour of parties and governments at the state level, variations between state governments (and states' political systems and cultures) have remained at least as strong as ever, and have probably become more marked. So to understand India, comparative analyses of different states are more important than ever. (This theme emerges again in chapter seventeen of this book.)

Much of the discussion in this chapter focuses on the thinking and actions of senior politicians—mainly the chief ministers of states. This is partly because many of them have become far more important in recent years since they have centralised power in their own hands. But senior leaders have also had less attention than they deserve from many social scientists who study India and other developing countries. They hold centre stage here because they usually make most of the key decisions about how their states will be governed. There are certain exceptions to that statement. Some senior leaders operate within parties that have considerable institutional substance, and that curtails their personal influence. But there are few such parties in India—the main example is the Communist Party of India-Marxist.[4] In most states, senior politicians

---

[4]The Bharatiya Janata Party (BJP) also has institutional substance, but as chapter seven in this book indicates, this has been somewhat overestimated.

are largely unconstrained by party institutions, and are reasonably (and in many cases, very) adroit. Despite this, many analyses pay them little heed. They give us Hamlet without the prince—and indeed, without *The Prince*, the book by Machiavelli which should never be far from our minds.

In other words, much of the literature underestimates the importance of *political agency*. Many studies concentrate on the social underpinnings of politics, on economic forces and trends, on formal political institutions, etc. These things are important and need to be examined, but they are not the whole or even the main story. Some analysts treat politics (and even the most potent politicians) as epiphenomenal. Many see part dependency as the central theme in the recent history of political and policy processes.

The credibility of these analyses has been undercut by recent changes in state politics, discussed below. This writer is currently participating in a study of significantly increased efforts during the last decade to tackle poverty and inequality by governments in four countries: Brazil, India, China and South Africa. Except in Brazil, those governments increased their efforts *despite* unhelpful legacies which they had inherited. They experimented[5] and innovated. Political agency overcame those legacies and broke free of path dependency.[6] At the state level in India, we find numerous examples

---

In Gujarat at least, we have seen that an adroit BJP chief minister who is bent on establishing personal rule can undermine and overcome institutional constraints from the BJP and its allied organisations. The Dravida Munnetra Kazhagam (DMK) in Tamil Nadu once had institutional substance, but it has been severely eroded by a drive for dominance by its leader and his family.

[5]For a discussion of the process of political and policy experimentation in India, as it contrasts with a very different process in China, see chapter sixteen of this book.

[6]This three-year project, which is being conducted by an 18-member international team, only began on 1 October 2012. For a further study of three senior leaders who were remarkable innovators, see M. Melo, N. Ng'ethe and J. Manor, *Against the Odds: Politicians, Institutions and the Struggle against Poverty* (Columbia University Press, London/New York, Hurst, 2012). The three leaders were a former Brazilian President, the

in recent years of chief ministers who introduced important innovations.[7] This makes it possible to see India's federal system as a laboratory for political and policy experimentation—hence the emphasis on senior leaders here.

This chapter is divided into five parts. Part I discusses the implications for state politics of the massive redistribution of power since 1989, away from the once-dominant PMO—horizontally to other institutions at the national level, and vertically downward to the state level. It also analyses the centralisation of power that has, paradoxically, occurred in many states in recent years. Part II considers another crucial trend, the surge in the revenues of state and Central governments since 2003, which has enabled state governments to spend (and thus to achieve) more. It explains how this has helped to produce in a key change in recent years: state (and Central) governments have usually been reelected since December 2008, in contrast to the preceding thirty years in which most of them were rejected by voters. Part III examines numerous devices— legitimate and illicit—that senior politicians have used to centralise power in many states. Part IV discusses other devices that have been used—by centralisers and others—in the struggle to govern at the state level. Part V recapitulates.

---

current Ugandan President, and Chief Minister Digvijay Singh in Madhya Pradesh.

[7]A remarkable array of innovations has originated at the state level over many years. Consider just a few examples: West Bengal's land reforms; the experiments with *panchayati raj* in West Bengal and Karnataka (which helped to inspire similar policies not just at the national level in India in 1993, but also across much of Asia and Africa); M. G. Ramachandran's mid-day meals scheme in Tamil Nadu; Bhairon Singh Shekhawat's *antyodaya* programme in Rajasthan; Digvijay Singh's Education Guarantee Scheme in Madhya Pradesh. Those initiatives were introduced by leaders from a diversity of parties, in an era when budgets were tight. The revenue surge since 2003 (discussed in Part II of this chapter) has enabled a great many further and more expensive innovations at the state level.

I. The Redistribution of Power since 1989—And Its Ironic Implications

In a recent discussion in London, research students who work on Indian politics expressed surprise when this writer emphasised the fundamental importance of a transition that began in 1989. Since then, it has been impossible for any single party to win a majority of seats in the Lok Sabha, so that India has been governed by minority governments or by coalition governments that include large numbers of parties, many of them state-based. That has triggered the crucial transition. Power has flowed, very substantially, away from the PMO which was vastly powerful during most of the period from 1971 to 1989, to other institutions at the national level and to governments, parties and forces at the state level. This has made it impossible for the PMO to sustain its dominance at the national level and over the federal system. The research students were too young to have lived through that earlier era, and as a result, they tended to underestimate the importance of this change. It is worth stressing here, partly because (at this writing in May 2014) a new prime minister has just taken office who has long been a determined centraliser.

The redistribution of power since 1989 has enabled many institutions at the national level—and the federal system which bridges national and state levels—to be regenerated after they had withered and suffered assaults during the era of PMO dominance.[8] They have regained a great deal of substance, autonomy and power. Indira Gandhi in particular sought to weaken nearly all of these institutions—and a key informal institution, her own Congress Party's organisation—in the interests of person and dynastic rule. (The only institutions which she ignored were, curiously, the Election Commission (EC) and the armed forces.) Since 1989, abuses of power by actors at the apex of the system, which were common when the PMO dominated, have largely ceased to occur because other, regenerated institutions have checked them.

---

[8]See chapter four in this book.

However, this decentralisation of power away from the PMO has been attended in a startling irony. While power has been dispersed and deconcentrated at the national level and within the federal system as a whole, it has in the same period become more concentrated and centralised in the hands of chief ministers within many individual states in the federal system. This has triggered not a regeneration of institutions but *de*generation—something akin to the deinstitutionalisation that occurred at the national level during the years of PMO dominance (1971–1989). And in an era in which abuses of power by prime ministers in New Delhi have markedly diminished, the centralisation of power in many states has led to an increase in abuses of power by some chief ministers there—although as we shall see in Part III, some other centralising chief ministers have not been illiberal and abusive. A small number of Indian states— extreme cases—have begun to resemble 'authoritarian enclaves', although the Constitution imposes some checks on that trend. (A major opportunity awaits researchers who seek to explain both the trend towards 'authoritarian enclaves' and the restraints upon it.)

Table 14.1 below crudely sorts most of India's larger states into three categories: (A) in which one leader dominates state politics, (B) in which a leader exercises near-dominance, and (C) in which no single leader dominates. (States in the table followed by question marks may belong in different categories.) At this writing in May 2014, 40 per cent of Indians live in Category A states, and nearly 20 per cent more live in Category B states—so that most Indians currently live in states where power is rather (or very) highly centralised.

TABLE 14.1:   Concentrations of Power within State Governments in Large States

---

A. Dominance by one leader (total population, 448.7 million = 40.6 per cent of the Indian total)

> West Bengal (population, 91.3 million)
>
> Gujarat (60.4 m)
>
> Tamil Nadu (72.1 m)

(contd.)

Table 14.1 (contd.)

> Uttar Pradesh? (199.5 m)
>
> Haryana? (25.4 m)
>
> Odisha (41.9 m)

B. Near-dominance by one leader (total population, 218.7 m. = 18.1 per cent of the Indian total)

> Bihar (103.8 m)
>
> Madhya Pradesh (72.6 m)
>
> Chhattisgarh (25.5 m)
>
> Delhi (16.8 m)

C. No leader dominates (total population, 387.9 m. = 34.7 per cent of the Indian total)

> Maharashtra (112.4 m)
>
> Rajasthan (68.6 m)
>
> Punjab (27.7 m)
>
> Jharkhand (33.0 m)
>
> Uttarakhand (10.1 m)
>
> Andhra Pradesh (84.7 m)
>
> Karnataka (61.1 m)
>
> Kerala (33.4 m)

Three comments on this table are needed. First, over time, some state governments have moved from one to another of these categories—in different directions. For example, between 1995[9] and the untimely death of Chief Minister Y. S. Rajashekhar Reddy in

[9]It was in 1995 that Chandrababu Naidu seized power in a palace coup from his father-in-law, Chief Minister N. T. Rama Rao. It is arguable that Rama Rao had personally dominated the state government before his ouster, but Naidu proceeded far more systematically and effectively in radically centralising power. When he was defeated by the Congress Party at a state election in May 2004, the new Congress chief minister (Y. S. Rajashekhar Reddy) sought to exercise personal dominance over the state government in much the same way that Naidu had done. That was more difficult to achieve from atop the Congress Party, but Reddy succeeded

September 2009, Andhra Pradesh was located in Category A, but since then it belongs in Category C. By contrast, West Bengal was a Category C state until the election of May 2011, but since then, it should be placed in Category A.

Second and more crucially, there are important differences between state governments that are grouped in each of the three categories listed above. These are the products of several sets of variations across states, including: traditions of state-society relations and modes of governing; the configurations of powerful interests within any given state; the condition of the bureaucracy (relatively undamaged and thus reasonably effective in some states, but crippled by abusive mistreatment from politicians in others); the state government's revenue base; levels of development; natural and human resources, etc.

Third, in states where power has been centralised, the influence of party organisations and legislators has waned. We have already seen that most state-based parties have long had weak organisations, but when chief ministers achieve dominance or near-dominance, their party organisations lose influence and atrophy still further. (Even the two national parties have experienced this in some states—witness the Congress Party in Andhra Pradesh under Y. S. Rajashekhar Reddy, and the Bharatiya Janata Party [BJP] in Gujarat under Narendra Modi.) Members of ruling parties in state legislatures—and even ministers other than the chief minister— often find themselves unable to lobby bureaucrats on behalf of constituents or powerful allies, to influence policy implementation, to obtain transfers of officials within their bailiwicks, to enrich themselves by selling influence, etc.

We need to consider how power has been centralised in many states. But before we turn to that, it is necessary to examine another key development in recent years. It is mightily important in its own right and in some states, it has contributed to the process of centralisation.

---

to a considerable degree. The two chief ministers who succeeded Reddy have been unable to maintain centralised control.

II. The Surge in State and Central Government Revenues since 2003

If the redistribution of power since 1989 has changed the rules of Indian politics, so has another more recent change. Since 2003, the revenues of state and Central governments have increased markedly. This has enabled governments and ruling parties at both levels to spend far more than before on initiatives that are aimed at easing the problem of demand overload and at attracting popular support. Many of those initiatives have proved successful.

Before 2003, disappointing revenues meant that all state governments faced serious and often crippling resource constraints. Senior politicians were forced to devise ways of cultivating popularity which were not particularly expensive (see the previous chapter in this book). Most of them found this next to impossible, so that failure to win reelection was the norm in that period. In interviews, leading politicians who held power in those years at the state (or indeed, at the national) level wistfully remark upon how much more they could have achieved—and how much more likely reelection would have been—if they had enjoyed the higher revenues available to their successors. Table 14.2 below indicates how substantial the revenue surge has been since 2003.

TABLE 14.2:   Gross Revenues of Central and State Governments (in billions of rupees)

Years	Central Government	State Governments
2002–03	2,162.66	2,577.07
2003–04	2,543.48	2,899.61
2004–05	3,049.58	3,291.53
2005–06	3,674.74	3,824.58
2006–07	4,735.12	4,561.84
2007–08	5,931.47	5,218.44
2008–09	6,052.99	5,483.18
2009–10	6,245.28	5,628.97

(contd.)

Table 14.2 (contd.)

Years	Central Government	State Governments
2010–11	7,868.88	7,358.20
2011–12	9,324.40	8,620.01

Source: Reserve Bank of India, 'Direct and Indirect Tax Revenues of Central and State Governments', Table 116, at: http://dbie.rbi.org/DBIE/dbie.rbi?site=publications, accessed 20 August 2013.

These figures need to be adjusted for inflation, but even if that is taken into account, the steep increase in revenues is vividly apparent. When we consider that a significant portion of Central government revenue is distributed among state governments, we can see that in recent years, ruling parties at the state level have had several times more money to spend than in the period before 2003 when the surge began.

This has made a major difference in their capacity to achieve popularity. Clear evidence of this emerges from a reliable CSDS/ *Lokniti* poll taken in 2009. The data in Table 14.3 show that pervasive *pro*-incumbency sentiments existed towards *both* state *and* Central governments. Respondents were asked whether they were 'fully satisfied', 'somewhat satisfied', 'somewhat dissatisfied' or 'very dissatisfied'—first with the performance of the Congress-led UPA government in New Delhi, and then with that of their state government.[10] The table aggregates responses by 'fully' and 'somewhat' satisfied voters into one figure, for states which elected at least four Lok Sabha members.

[10] At the national level, during the first five years of UPA rule between 2004 and 2009, the government in New Delhi committed in excess of $57.04 billion (or Rs 271,840 crores) to programmes which were intended to tackle poverty and inequality. This was a vastly greater sum than any previous Indian government had spent for this purpose. This figure actually *underestimates* expenditure on poverty initiatives since it does not include several initiatives which entailed hefty outlays. For more detail, see J. Manor, 'Did the Central Government's Poverty Initiatives Help to Re-Elect it?', in L. Saez and G. Singh (eds), *New Dimensions of Politics in India: The United Progressive Alliance in Power* (Routledge, London and New Delhi, 2011).

TABLE 14.3: Satisfaction with Central and State Governments

State	Satisfied with Central Government	Satisfied with State Government (in per cent)
Andhra Pradesh	58.0	63.2
Assam	66.9	63.7
Bihar	75.6	87.9
Chhattisgarh	60.4	72.4
Delhi	73.6	71.3
Gujarat	67.8	64.9
Haryana	63.3	64.1
Himachal Pradesh	73.9	71.6
Jammu & Kashmir	64.9	61.4
Jharkand	42.6	43.1
Karnataka	76.5	61.6
Kerala	66.3	61.1
Madhya Pradesh	74.6	82.3
Maharashtra	62.1	61.5
Orissa	55.4	73.7
Punjab	63.9	56.7
Rajasthan	66.9	63.2
Tamil Nadu	73.8	71.7
Uttar Pradesh	66.5	57.9
Uttarakhand	67.5	62.8
West Bengal	61.2	57.9

Note: I am grateful to Sanjay Kumar for providing this material.
Source: CSDS/*Lokniti* post-poll.

Every state government, except Jharkhand which has witnessed serious political disarray, enjoyed a better than 50 per cent satisfaction rating. Seventeen of 21 achieved over 60 per cent. The Central government could also take comfort from this evidence. It had a better than 50 per cent satisfaction rating in every state except Jharkhand—and in 18 of 21, it scored more than 60 per cent. This evidence of pro-incumbency sentiments owed much to the surge in state and Central government revenues.

A crucial result of this change in the rules of politics has been evident in the outcomes of state elections since December 2008. Before that, the norm over nearly three decades had been the rejection of ruling parties at the state level. Since then, most state governments have been re-elected.

III. How Power is Centralised: Two Sets of Devices, Legitimate and Illicit

To understand what has been happening (and changing) in state-level politics, we must examine the strategies that have been used by some chief ministers to centralise power in their own hands. In some cases, they do not dominate their parties when they assume office, so they must pursue centralisation in order to *achieve* dominance over both their parties and their governments. In other cases, they already dominate their parties when they take power, so that they pursue centralisation in order to *sustain* their pre-existing dominance. In all cases, two sets of devices are available to centralisers. The first entails actions that are legitimate; the second involves illicit machinations. Most chief ministers engage in both strategies at the same time, and vary only in the emphases which they give to one or the other, but for analytical clarity, let us consider each separately.

Legitimate devices: The recent surge in state governments' revenues is extremely important here. It provides those governments, ruling parties and the chief ministers who head them with opportunities to undertake new programmes, and to increase spending on existing programmes—in efforts to cultivate popularity. Three sets of 'legitimate' devices are available to them. Some readers may (understandably) question the legitimacy of the first two of these—populism and clientelism. They are included here because they are 'legitimate' inasmuch as they are not—for the most part, and strictly speaking—unlawful.

The term *populism* has been used in different ways, but it refers here to actions by senior politicians which are intended to have mass appeal, and to dramatise (often rather theatrically) the benevolence of a leader, a ruling party and a state government. Populist schemes include subsidies on services and other public goods (for everyone, or for specially selected sets of beneficiaries), and 'giveaways'. Chief ministers who use populism in attempts to centralise power associate themselves personally with these schemes. An example of a subsidy is the current chief minister's special fund to provide grain at greatly reduced prices in Madhya Pradesh. When giveaways are provided, chief ministers often personally bestow items upon beneficiaries, with cameras present—as when colour television sets were distributed by M. Karunanidhi in Tamil Nadu.

Second, funds may be used to support networks that distribute patronage—that is, resources from government programmes which patrons in the ruling party provide to clients who may then distribute them to their own clients still further down, and perhaps to key interests. Political scientists describe such practices as *'clientelism'*. This term is used here in a somewhat broader sense than in some analyses—which tend to concentrate on the delivery by patrons of material goods in exchange for electoral support.[11] In this analysis, it may entail the delivery of a wider array of things: funds and goods, but also services and favours. It is also important to note that patronage is not only delivered in order to attract electoral support, although that is important. It may also serve as a means of bringing some order to party organisations which are, for the most part, undisciplined and disorderly—by binding clients to patrons and thus to the parties to which they belong.[12]

In recent years, however, many chief ministers and their close associates have become increasingly disenchanted with clientelism because it lacks political efficacy. They see that during the years between 1980 and 2008 in which leaders relied mainly on it,

[11]This is most clearly set out in S. C. Stokes, 'Political Clientelism', in C. Boix and S. C. Stokes (eds), *The Oxford Handbook of Comparative Politics* (Oxford University Press, Oxford and New York, 2009).

[12]The resources or patronage distributed through clientelist channels may derive from one or both of two sources. They may flow from government programmes. Or they may be—or be purchased by—funds raised illicitly by demanding bribes. (Note the discussion later in this section, on 'Illicit Devices', of the increasingly huge kickbacks which chief ministers have received in recent years.)

voters ousted ruling parties at a large majority of state elections. This happened partly because nearly all party organisations lack the strength to distribute patronage effectively. (For more detail see chapter seven of this book.) They also recognise that because party organisations are ill disciplined, patronage networks have haemorrhaged resources—as subordinates have instead pocketed resources or demanded exorbitant payments in exchange for largesse. Patronage is also sometimes misallocated, so that the intended recipients do not receive enough to maintain their loyalty. To make matters worse, clientelism has been unable to keep pace with soaring demands from a great (and increasing) diversity of interests. The financial burdens imposed on profligate governments by clientelism have also persuaded senior leaders to de-emphasise it.[13]

These realisations have led many chief ministers to adopt a third approach: programmatic efforts to deliver goods and services, improve livelihoods, and promote development (including poverty reduction)—which are largely or entirely protected from those who wish to divert resources to patronage networks. These programmes are intended to conform to Weberian norms—so that they are implemented in an impersonal manner through disciplined and relatively impartial bureaucratic channels, according to policy criteria, rules and sometimes laws established by senior leaders. These programmes may be described as '*post-clientelist*' initiatives.

A remarkable diversity of such initiatives have emerged in various states in recent years: new insurance and pension schemes, scholarships, ambulances, health care provisions, training programmes to equip young people for the job market, new employment programmes, new schools, road improvements, water harvesting, irrigation schemes, agricultural extension schemes, etc. Centralising chief ministers seek to identify themselves personally with these new offerings. Some of these initiatives are 'centrally-sponsored schemes' which have emerged from New Delhi. When the party in power at the state level is in opposition to the ruling

---

[13]See for example, 'Why Punjab Can't Afford Pork', *The Indian Express*, 16 October 2010.

alliance at the national level, those schemes or elements of them may be re-labelled, in the hope that citizens will associate them with that party. Other new initiatives are entirely the creations of state governments.

When chief ministers seek to insulate such programmes from subordinates who manage patronage networks, they almost never curtail *existing* patterns of patronage distribution. Such actions would anger groups of clients who receive patronage, and undermine the ruling party's popularity. They would also alienate powerful subordinates within ruling parties who preside over patronage networks, and who might then challenge the chief minister. Those subordinates are permitted to continue with their clientelism. Indeed, they may even be encouraged to do so, and given some new opportunities to divert resources from certain government programmes, in order to distract them from the chief minister's attempts to dominate the formulation of new policies— and not incidentally, to take most of the credit for them. But the amounts of government money spent on 'post-clientelist' initiatives have tended to increase significantly, while the amounts spent on patronage distribution remain constant or increase more slowly. So 'post-clientelist' initiatives tend to gain in importance in relative terms—relative to clientelism. Since chief ministers usually control 'post-clientelist' initiatives, this shift in the balance strengthens the hands of chief ministers and facilitates their efforts to centralise power.[14]

It should be stressed that not all centralising chief ministers who introduce 'post-clientelist' initiatives seek to achieve top-down control and to create aggressively illiberal political regimes. Some do so, and such initiatives can serve their purposes. But in some states, the centralisation of power within ruling parties and state-level cabinets—and the 'post-clientelist' programmes which facilitate that—have instead made governments more inclusive,

---

[14]For a fuller analysis of the post-clientelist theme, see J. Manor, 'Post-Clientelist Initiatives' in K. Stokke and O. Tornquist (eds), *Democratization in the Global South: The Importance of Transformative Politics* (Palgrave Macmillan, London, 2013), pp. 243–53.

responsive and in another way, decentralised. That has occurred where chief ministers have devolved substantial powers and resources onto elected councils (*panchayats*) at lower levels, thus creating participatory processes, and encouraging the emergence of demands and popular preferences from below.[15] In other words, we need to be aware of an irony: the promotion of democratic decentralisation requires strong support from leaders at the apex of power in whose hands substantial powers have been concentrated.[16]

When chief ministers use the legitimate devices discussed above in efforts to centralise power—whether they do so in pursuit of illiberal control from above or to promote more open, participatory processes from below—there are no guarantees that they will succeed. To achieve that, they must also operate shrewdly, subtly and adroitly—to gain and then keep control of the political and policy processes. That is a tall order. Some who have briefly succeeded in achieving dominance have then been so extravagantly and guilelessly autocratic that they have alienated most interests (including many within their own parties) and destroyed themselves. Two examples are former Chief Ministers Ajit Jogi in Chhattisgarh and Vasundhara Raje in her first term in power in Rajasthan. Still others such as former Chief Minister B. S. Yeddyurappa in Karnataka[17] have been so inept that they never achieved dominance in the first place. More often, however, centralisers have flourished and won re-election.

Partly because it is difficult to achieve and sustain dominance, most chief ministers who seek to dominate their parties and governments have also resorted to additional, illicit devices.

Illicit devices: Several years of high economic growth have caused urban land prices to soar and have created opportunities for industrialists to make immense profits—not least in mining, given high prices for raw materials (iron ore, coal, sand, bauxite, etc.).

[15]In India, we have seen this, some or all of the time, in several states—notably Karnataka, Kerala, Madhya Pradesh and West Bengal.

[16]This is discussed in much more detail in J. Manor, *The Political Economy of Democratic Decentralization* (World Bank, Washington, 1999).

[17]For details, see J. Manor, 'The Trouble with Yeddyurappa', *Economic and Political Weekly*, 13 March–1 April 2012, pp. 16–19.

But since India's economic liberalisation has been cautious and limited—and, despite much comment to the contrary, far from neo-liberal—senior politicians retain powers of approval that are crucial to entrepreneurs. Centralising chief ministers have taken advantage of this to extract massive illicit 'contributions' from industrialists in exchange for licences, approvals and other support. One chief minister demanded and received bribes from industrialists in excess of US$1 million on more than 100 occasions[18]—and he is by no means an exception. Chief ministers' also acquiesce in illicit land deals worth vast sums, again in exchange for kickbacks, and some of them have been actively involved as participants in such deals.

Illicit 'contributions' usually go directly to chief ministers. As a consequence, they possess ill-gotten resources that dwarf those of even their most corrupt predecessors in earlier periods. They also dwarf the funds that can be raised by their subordinates or by politicians in rival parties. How does this help chief ministers to centralise power? As we shall see in detail in Part IV, the main targets for the money are not voters (who cannot be bought) but other politicians. Some subordinates in the ruling party need to be supported, while others need to be reined in. Politicians in rival parties can sometimes be induced into restraining themselves. Money can also be used to undermine them and their networks of support.

Some (but certainly not all) centralising chief ministers also develop links to organised crime. They do so partly to raise further money, but since the bribes noted just above usually provide vast sums, those links are often used to provide the ruling party with what one politician described to this writer as 'some muscle'—which can be used for intimidation. Some chief ministers even facilitate already energetic efforts by the criminal underworld to penetrate into booming urban centres. In South India in the early 1980s, only one city had a serious organised crime problem—not Chennai,

---

[18]This is based on an analysis of one state government by this writer and three extremely knowledgeable colleagues.

Hyderabad or Bangalore, but Vijayawada in Andhra Pradesh.[19] Today, all of those cities are afflicted.

IV. Other Devices Used in the Struggle to Govern

The discussion in Part III above on centralising chief ministers' use of populist, clientelist and 'post-clientelist' approaches does not exhaust the repertoire of devices available to them. We must consider three others which are used by leaders who seek to centralise, and by those who do not.

Cooptation, Intimidation, Coercion: Chief ministers and other senior politicians at the state level may use favours and inducements to coopt important actors and groups. They may deploy threats ('intimidation'), and in some cases use coercion to intimidate adversaries. It is unnecessary to explain these things to most readers, but they are noted here because we need to pay attention to them. Some analysts do not.

We must ask a crucial question about leaders in any state government: how do they view and treat *alternative power centres*? How do they deal with the media, civil society organisations and formal institutions of state which are alternatives to the executive— including the state assembly, its committees and Speaker; the courts; the police and the Intelligence Bureau; *Lokayuktas* (ombudsmen); the state Election Commission; regulatory agencies; various state-generated corporations; the Governor; the bureaucracy; *panchayati raj* institutions, etc.?

In some Indian states where chief ministers have achieved dominance or near-dominance, alternative power centres have been treated with great hostility. That has been true, for example, in Andhra Pradesh under Chandrababu Naidu and Y. S. Rajashekhar Reddy, and in Gujarat under Narendra Modi. But in some other states, less hostility has been evident, and in states where no leader has achieved even near-dominance, the treatment of alternative

[19]J. Manor, *Power, Poverty and Poison: Disaster and Response in an Indian City* (Sage, New Delhi, London and Thousand Oaks, 1993), pp. 62–65.

power centres has usually been more liberal than in nearly all of Asia and Africa.

Dividing and Uniting: Senior leaders in state governments obviously make efforts to unite as many social groups behind them as possible, and to divide groups that tend to support their rivals. Identity politics, involving religious and especially caste groups, come into play here. These things help to decide election outcomes, but their importance should not be overstated. Consider the reelection of Nitish Kumar's government in Bihar in 2010. Some commentators rashly announced that it showed that 'development' (which that government had pursued) had finally trumped caste. But they were as mistaken as those who argue that in state elections, identity (or less helpfully, 'ethnic'[20]) politics are decisive. More subtle and authoritative analyses showed that in that Bihar election, both factors were important. Sanjay Kumar used CSDS/*Lokniti* polling data to demonstrate that while 'development' programmes— including some 'post-clientelist' initiatives—gave the government broad appeal, the chief minister's shrewd targeting of most 'lower' caste Dalits referred to as 'Mahadalits' and of 'lower' castes among Muslims referred to as 'pasmanda Muslims' had also been essential. The business of dividing and uniting has become more complex, requiring politicians to disaggregate more than before.[21] (For a further dimension, see item *v* in the list.)

The Deployment of Money: In recent years, as noted above, massive funds have been illicitly raised by senior politicians at the state level. Little of the money is used in attempts to buy votes, since it is well known that Indian voters have the sophistication to accept funds and gifts and then vote as they please. Most funds are used by senior

---

[20]This unhelpful word is examined in detail in chapter eight of this book.

[21]See for example, *The Indian Express*, 7 December 2010. See also Yadav and Palshikar, 'Revisiting the "Third" Electoral System', p. 400, where they write that 'Political mobilization has reached beyond big blocs like the Other Backward Classes (OBCs) or the Scheduled Castes (SCs). Lower OBCs, *maha*-Dalits, and pasmanda Muslims are beginning to acquire a political clout.'

political leaders to pay political actors of various descriptions, for various purposes. The list below covers several such areas.

(i) *Enabling candidates from the leader's party to run lavish election campaigns.*

(ii) *Buying off key personnel in rival parties' organisations as elections approach.* For example, before the 2008 state election in Karnataka, the BJP used funds from mining interests to make huge payments to key Congress Party leaders in numerous districts of the state. This crippled the Congress organisation and was one important reason, among others[22] for the BJP's victory.

(iii) *Inducing legislators and activists from opposition parties to behave agreeably towards the ruling party inside and outside the state assembly.* There are perfectly legal ways to do this which do not entail the use of illicit funds, as Bhairon Singh Shekhawat demonstrated when he was Rajasthan chief minister (see chapter twelve in this book). But the inducements noted here are outright bribes.

(iv) *Inducing legislators from opposition parties to defect, resign their seats, and seek re-election on the ruling party's ticket.* The ruling BJP in Karnataka engaged in such a manoeuvre, in what was called 'Operation Lotus', soon after the 2008 state election.

(v) *Inducing candidates from small parties and/or key social groups (usually castes) to conduct energetic election campaigns in constituencies where they will take votes from the main rival to the leader's party.* In some states, candidates from minor parties have been given substantial sums to persuade them to campaign aggressively (and to cover some of their campaign expenses). They are told that if they gain 'x' number of votes, they will receive a further payment greater than the initial sum. In one state, a party adopted what it called a 'one plus two' approach— meaning that it would pay the candidate twice the initial amount if 'x' number of votes were gained. In that state, a rival party which would lose votes to such candidates considered countering with a 'one plus three' offer to the same people, to

[22]J. Manor, 'Letting a Winnable Election Slip Away: Congress in Karnataka', *Economic and Political Weekly*, 11 October 2008, pp. 23–28.

do little or no campaigning. In the end, however, it decided not
to do this—and lost the election.

The various devices listed just above can be used simultaneously—
along with populism, clientelism and 'post-clientelist' initiatives.
Indeed, that is the usual practice.[23] However, some of them do not
sit comfortably alongside one another. Senior politicians' strategies
for governing Indian states therefore often amount to incongruous
hybrids in which a certain dissonance—and in some cases, outright
contradictions—exist between different components. In analysing
ruling parties and state governments, we must ask how manageable
these incongruities are, and how (if at all) they are managed.

V. Recapitulation

States in India's federal system have always been important political
arenas. It has always been there that most of the actual governing
occurs. It is there that state and society mainly interact. But since
1989, they have become even more important, as substantial powers
have flowed downward from New Delhi to governments, parties
and forces at the state level.

This has created both problems and opportunities for politicians
at the state level, but (so far at least) the latter greatly outweigh the
former. A surge in central and state government revenues since 2003
has made it possible for ruling parties and governments in the states
to spend and achieve more. Many senior politicians have seized this
opportunity by devising new initiatives that have enabled them to
reverse a trend that had prevailed over the previous three decades,
whereby ruling parties were thrown out by voters at most state
elections. Those new initiatives have been popular enough to gain
most state governments re-election since late 2008.

If economic stagnation were to reduce or reverse the increase
in revenues, state governments and ruling parties would face serious

[23]See for example, the links between either 'clientelist' or 'post-
clientelist' initiatives and efforts at 'dividing and uniting' which are
discussed by Badri Narayan in *The Hindu*, 5 June 2012, and Sanjay Kumar,
in *The Indian Express*, 7 December 2010.

dilemmas. Funding the new initiatives that have been created in recent years—some of which are expensive—would become extremely difficult. If belts were tightened, popular discontent might re-emerge. But at this writing in May 2014, that has not yet happened. As Table 14.2 indicates, revenues during 2011–12 (a year of slowing economic growth) continued to rise impressively.

The decentralisation of power from New Delhi to the states has been attended, paradoxically, by a centralisation of power within many state governments—a trend that has largely been overlooked by scholars. Nearly six in ten Indians now live in states where chief ministers have achieved dominance or near-dominance. That centralisation has undermined the influence and substance of formal government institutions and of ruling parties (which are informal institutions) at the state level. This change makes it imperative that political analysts focus on chief ministers—and on the immense importance of political agency, a theme which (again) has been seriously under-researched.

Any study of them must examine two other recent changes. The first is the massive increase in the illicit profits which chief ministers can reap from two main sources: bribes from industrialists, and land deals—both of which have contributed to the centralisation of power in many states. The second is the increasing emphasis given at the state level to 'post-clientelist' initiatives—another trend that has been largely ignored by scholars.[24] Chief ministers have promoted such initiatives out of frustration with the inadequacy of populism and clientelism to ensure reelection. The increasing importance of 'post-clientelist' initiatives—which are mainly implemented through bureaucracies—has reduced the influence of parties and party organisations at the state level. But again paradoxically, it has also helped to make ruling parties reelectable. This chapter has suggested various research strategies that may help colleagues to explore these changes, so that parties, leaders and governments at the state level may be better understood.

---

[24]For an exception to this statement, see A. Wyatt, 'Combining Clientelistic and Programmatic Policies in Tamil Nadu, India', *Commonwealth and Comparative Politics* (January 2013), pp. 27–55.

— fifteen —

As Caste Hierarchies Wane

Explaining Inter-Caste Accommodation in Rural India

Most other papers have mainly focused on India's politics and state-society relations. By contrast, this paper deals mainly with society, and with caste. It considers a change of fundamental, historic importance which has received far less attention than it deserves: the declining acceptance of caste hierarchies by disadvantaged groups in rural areas where most Indians live. We saw in chapter two that caste hierarchies were one of the two main sources of order in India during the first phase after independence in 1947. It has now largely disintegrated in most parts of the country. This paper summarises findings that will appear in a forthcoming book on the implications for local-level power dynamics of this change. It also explains why we have seen less violence and more accommodation between castes that might have been expected as hierarchies are increasingly rejected. But it also suggests that some of the changes discussed elsewhere in this book (for example, in chapter ten) may make accommodations more difficult in the future.

I. Introduction

This chapter considers a fundamentally important social change that has become apparent over the last generation in most rural areas—and its implications. The change is a decline in the acceptance of caste hierarchies by members of disadvantaged caste groups. Since the mid-1990s, we have had solid evidence of this trend from village-level studies conducted in several different regions of India.[1] As Dipankar Gupta has put it,[2] caste is increasingly coming to denote 'difference' more than 'hierarchy'. Investigations by this writer in nine regions of India between 2011 and 2103[3] clearly indicated that this change is—with inevitable variations in its strength and in matters of detail—a widespread reality.

The change is of monumental importance because caste hierarchy was long a central element in the rural social order. Indeed, in this writer's view, this is one of the two most important changes to occur since Indian independence in 1947—the other being the establishment of a socially rooted democracy.

The old caste hierarchies[4] posed threats to the security and well being of so called 'lower' castes. But their increasing—and

---

[1]See for example, G. K. Karanth, 'Caste in Contemporary Rural India', in M. N. Srinivas (ed.), *Caste: Its Twentieth Century Avatar* (Penguin, New Delhi, 1996), p. 106; A. Mayer, 'Caste in an Indian Village: Change and Continuity', in C. J. Fuller (ed.), *Caste Today* (Oxford University Press, Delhi, 1997), pp. 32–64; G. K. Karanth, *Change and Continuity in Agrarian Relations* (Concept, New Delhi, 1995); S. R. Charsley and G. K. Karanth (eds), *Challenging Untouchability: Dalit Initiative and Experience from Karnataka* (Altamira Press, London, 1998); D. Gupta, *Caste in Question: Identity or Hierarchy?* (Sage, New Delhi, London and Thousand Oaks, 2004); S. S. Jodhka, 'Caste and Untouchability in Rural Punjab', *Economic and Political Weekly*, 11 May 2002, pp. 1813–23; and S. S. Jodhka and P. Louis, 'Caste Tensions in Punjab: Talhan and Beyond', *Economic and Political Weekly*, 12 July 2003, pp. 2923–36. See also, J. Manor, 'Prologue', in R. Kothari (ed.), *Caste in Indian Politics*, second edition (Orient BlackSwan, New Delhi, 2010), pp. xi–lxi.

[2]Gupta, ibid.

[3]The author is grateful to the Harry Frank Guggenheim Foundation for a grant to make that research possible.

[4]The plural is used here because not one but a great many different hierarchies exist within India. For example, crudely speaking, every linguistic region possesses its own caste system—which contains sub-regional variations. It had largely confined members of various castes to their traditional occupations—the least remunerative and respectable of which rendered poorer groups dependent on local elites.

increasingly open—refusals to accept those hierarchies have generated new and potentially more severe threats, since so called 'higher' castes may react against the change and seek to enforce the old inequities by force, by violence. This chapter examines processes—accommodations between 'higher' and 'lower' castes—which have eased this danger across much of rural India. Given the limitations on space, it focuses not on accommodations between *all* 'higher' and 'lower' caste groups, but on only the most important set of accommodations—those that have been reached between the formerly dominant landowning castes and Dalits (ex-untouchables).[5]

The discussion below is just one part of a much longer and more complex analysis which will require a book-length treatment. To give readers a sense of the overall picture, here are a few comments to set the scene.

This analysis focuses only on rural areas. It does so partly because that is where roughly two-thirds of Indians still reside, but also because villages have long been the main bastions of traditional caste (and hierarchical) interactions. Society there has undergone less change than in towns and cities, but now quite fundamental changes have become apparent in rural arenas too.

Readers should not conclude from this discussion that caste is becoming weaker. If we consider one meaning of the word 'caste', *jati*—an endogamous groups (into which people marry their children)—then it remains extremely strong. Indeed, *jati* appears to be the most resilient and durable pre-existing social institution in Asia, Africa and Latin America. It is not caste (*jati*) that is in decline, but the acceptance of hierarchies among *jatis*.

---

[5]This chapter therefore omits discussion of conflicts and accommodation between Dalits and the 'Other Backwards Classes' (OBCs) when the latter constitute the main group with which Dalits must interact. In villages where that is the case, the formerly dominant landed castes—for example, Marathas in Maharashtra, Kammas and Reddys in Andhra Pradesh, Lingayats and Vokkaligas in Karnataka, Jats in much of north India, etc.—are either absent or present in very small numbers. For complex reasons, it is usually more difficult for Dalits to forge accommodations with OBCs than with the landed castes.

Nor should anything in this chapter should be taken to imply that Dalits no longer suffer humiliations, abuses and violence. Such outrages persist in strength. But this analysis seeks to show that other important things are also happening. If we focus only on outrages, we miss this crucial point. Since our concern here is with *inter*actions between Dalits and others, it is necessary to consider the dilemmas faced by those 'others', and their reactions to them. That is why this chapter discusses the recent experiences and perceptions of the formerly dominant landowning castes.

India is the most complex and heterogeneous society on earth, so we should not be surprised when we encounter variations. The declining acceptance of caste hierarchies has become increasingly evident, across most of rural India, but to differing degrees. In some sub-regions (and even within certain districts within sub-regions) the old social order has stubbornly resisted change. In such places, challenges to it by 'lower' castes are especially dangerous and thus more muted—though not absent.

It is also worth stressing that on present evidence, it is impossible to quantify the changes that are noted here. For example, we cannot measure with any precision the degree to which refusals to accept caste hierarchies have increased in different places, or the number and character violent incidents and of other abuses based on caste that have occurred in India or in parts of it. But it is clear from an extensive enquiry by this writer in numerous regions that, across most of the country, inter-caste accommodations outweigh violence—to a greater extent than we might have expected, given the momentous nature of the declining acceptance of caste hierarchies.

It is impossible in a single chapter to give adequate attention to the numerous, diverse causes of the waning of the old hierarchies. In brief, they include micro-level economic changes, increasing occupational diversity among Dalits and others, and the spread of education. These and other things have eroded the old *jajmani* system[6] and the material bonds of dependency which once locked 'lower' castes into relationships of subordination.

[6]It had largely confined members of various castes to traditional occupations—the least remunerative and respectable of which rendered poorer groups dependent on local elites.

The causes also include changes that flow from the wider political system: reservations for 'lower' castes in educational institutions, government employment and posts in elected bodies; the recognition by political leaders that members of 'lower' castes vote in vast numbers, that they possess immense numerical strength, and that nowadays their support can only be obtained if they are offered real substance and not just empty promises; plus the resulting proliferation of government programmes, some of which address caste and other inequalities. As we shall see, one response from politicians—the Atrocities Act of 1989—has facilitated both the increase in open refusals by Dalits to accept caste hierarchies, and the emergence of inter-caste accommodations when those refusals stoke social tensions. Other changes outside formal state structures which have also had a causal impact are briefly discussed below—such as the increasing penetration of rural areas by Dalit organisations, other enlightened civil society organisations, and the media.

The rest of this chapter is divided into three parts. Part II surveys a broad array of actions taken by Dalits in recent years—all of which indicate their refusal to accept the old caste hierarchies. Part III examines increasing difficulties faced by many members of the formerly dominant landed castes, and their perceptions of them. The trends discussed in Parts II and III generate inter-caste tensions, but in Part IV we shall see that despite this, accommodations between these two sets of castes (Dalits and landed castes) have nonetheless emerged as the predominant trend in rural areas.

II. Rejecting Hierarchies: A Repertoire of Dalit Actions

Dalits have always harboured doubts and dissenting views about caste hierarchies,[7] but in recent times they have made their increasingly strong rejection of them increasingly apparent. To illustrate how that translates into action—and impinges on inter-caste relations—let us consider a diverse repertoire of devices which Dalits have used. There

---

[7]For an interesting way into this topic, see D. Gupta, *The Caged Phoenix: Can India Fly?* (Penguin, New Delhi, 2009), chapter nine.

is only room here for a tightly compressed survey of these devices, but it will convey a sense of how social interactions have been changing. Dalits' actions fall into two broad categories—those which mainly or entirely entail *dis*engagement from other castes, and those through which they engage with them. The discussion below of each category proceeds from the least to the most assertive actions.

Modes of disengagement: Dalits in villages sometimes interact—to varying degrees—with Dalit organisations or activists. This may only entail listening to activists' ideas or to stories which reinterpret Dalit history by telling of struggles and heroes.[8] Or they may interact with pro-Dalit civil society organisations which are not exclusively Dalit. Such actions usually lead rural Dalits to think and to act more independently, and thus to disengage somewhat from interactions with other castes—and from those castes' interpretations of history and their belief in caste hierarchies.

Dalits may take action (and make sacrifices) to ensure that they or their children obtain some education because (following the iconic Dalit leader, Dr B. R. Ambedkar) they see that it can make them less dependent upon 'higher' castes. This often enables them to disengage from those castes.[9]

They may take advantage of education, and/or caste reservations to obtain good jobs or to develop small enterprises which provide them with greater material autonomy and enable them to leave behind their traditional (and often degrading) occupations.[10]

---

[8]For a valuable discussion of this trend, see Badri Narayan, *The Making of the Dalit Public in North India* (Oxford University Press, New Delhi, 2011).

[9]In some localities in various parts of India, Dalit efforts to obtain education have made them more qualified for employment in good jobs than OBCs and even formerly dominant landed groups in their localities. This is advantageous to Dalits, but it can also be a source of social tension.

[10]They may obtain such employment partly as a result of connections with other Dalits, or with state institutions, or independently. In all of those cases, they become less dependent on other castes, and therefore disengage somewhat from them. Occasionally, however, they find such jobs as a result of contacts with members of other castes—and in such cases, they may not become less dependent upon and less engaged with members other castes.

Dalits may convert to a religion other than Hinduism—usually to Buddhism, as advocated by Ambedkar—in part because that helps them to disengage with the traditional caste hierarchy that is associated with Hinduism.

Dalits sometimes change their lifestyles in ways that emulate those of higher status groups—sanskritization.[11] They sometimes do so in order to claim higher caste status. This does not entail a disengagement from caste hierarchies, but it may enable Dalits to disengage somewhat—in their thinking, and perhaps in their actions—from other castes in a locality.

Individual Dalits increasingly migrate out of villages for extended periods to find work elsewhere, or commute daily to nearby urban centres for work. This enables them to disengage from other castes in their villages in two ways. Their physical absences remove them from often stultifying local environments and hierarchies. And the wages earned from work elsewhere often reduce or break their dependence upon other castes within their villages—by (again) providing them with a degree of material autonomy.

Some enterprising Dalits travel back and forth between their villages and government offices at higher levels in the political system in efforts to obtain benefits for their villages.[12] Such benefits may be shared only among fellow Dalits or among multiple castes. In the latter case (which of course entails engagement with them), they tend to gain esteem in the eyes of members of other castes. But in both cases, they break the monopoly which members of the formerly dominant castes once exercised over links to higher levels— which enables Dalits to disengage somewhat from relationships of dependency on other castes.

Modes of engagement: There is abundant evidence from many regions of India to indicate a significant increase in refusals by Dalits—including some who are quite vulnerable—to accede to the

---

[11]M. N. Srinivas, 'A Note on Sanskrization and Westernization', *Far Eastern Quarterly* (1956), pp. 481–96.

[12]See the discussion of 'fixers' or *naya netas* (new leaders) elsewhere in this chapter.

wishes or demands even of powerful members of 'higher' castes.[13] There are marked variations in the precise manner in which people say 'no', and in the frequency of refusals. In many places, Dalits are not in a position to say 'no' to every possible demand, but in many others, they routinely refuse to defer to individuals from formerly dominant castes—so that the old 'order' that existed in their villages has substantially or entirely disintegrated.[14]

We have already seen that in many localities, Dalits have managed—in a diversity of ways—to achieve a significant degree of material autonomy. This tends strongly to embolden them to demonstrate that autonomy more defiantly. There is for example evidence from Bihar of Dalits earning enough from the Mahatma Gandhi National Rural Employment Guarantee Act (MGNREGA) to provide them with enough autonomy to make possible open acts of defiance of a local landlord—by refusing to work on his lands, even though they remain in the village, something that would have been unthinkable until quite recently.[15]

---

[13]For example, during an extensive exercise in field research in different parts of Maharashtra, Gopal Guru—who has a healthy scepticism about happy stories of change for the better—found abundant evidence of this trend. Interview with Gopal Guru, New Delhi, 7 April 2010.

[14]For a telling account of this, see G. K. Karanth, V. Ramaswamy and R. Hogger, 'The Threshing Floor Disappears: Rural Livelihood Systems in Transition', in R. Baumgartner and R. Hogger (eds), *In Search of Sustainable Livelihood Systems: Managing Resources and Change* (Sage, New Delhi, London and Thousand Oaks, 2004), pp. 265–74.

[15]A landless labourer in Bihar told Roy that even though they could earn more money by migrating to Punjab for work, they preferred to stay at home because NREGA had made it possible for them to 'desist from working the *jamindars* (landlord's) land even if we stay in the village'—a choice that both reflected and hastened the erosion of status-based dependence. Another low-caste worker stated,

> Before this program, we were ... subservient to the *jamindar*, and to the 'high' caste. With the NREGS, we can live in the village without having to adhere to the village rules, of working the *jamindars* land. By seeing us in the village, without us begging him for work, he understands that we are human beings too, capable of a dignified life.

When inter-caste disputes and tensions arise, Dalit elders/ leaders often negotiate accommodations with their counterparts from 'higher' castes. This topic is hugely important, so it is discussed in detail in Part IV of this chapter.

Dalits occasionally mount boycotts of other castes. Such episodes are rare, but for example, in a village in southern Karnataka, the formerly dominant Lingayats selected as their informal leader a man who behaved offensively towards Dalits. Outraged Dalits resolved collectively to impose a total boycott on Lingayats until this leader was changed. Over several days, the Lingayats realised how dependent they were upon their Dalit neighbours for various things and—remarkably—they agreed to replace their leader with a more agreeable person.[16] (Thus, alongside bonds of dependence which force Dalits into positions of subordination, there are sometimes bonds of *inter*-dependence.[17])

Also on rare occasions, Dalits lash out violently in response to (or in anticipation of) violence from other castes. For example, Dalits in parts of Tamil Nadu who have suffered brutal attacks from 'higher' castes have occasionally hit back violently in return, in order

---

Emboldened by this display of assertiveness, another labourer added, 'His [the landlord's] economy be damned'. Indrajit Roy, 'Guaranteeing Employment, Forging Political Subjectivities: Insights from the NREGS', unpublished paper, June 2012, p. 26.

[16] I am grateful to A. P. Kripa for an account of this incident.

[17] Often, bonds of interdependence between 'higher' castes and Dalits no longer exist. If landed castes use machines for cultivation and harvesting, or hire agricultural labourers from outside the locality to till their plots, the old bonds which tied *local* labourers into relationships of dependency are broken. A near total discontinuity separates 'higher' castes from Dalits, especially (as is common) when the latter inhabit separate hamlets or parts of a village which stand at one remove from the main settlement. Little or no social interaction occurs between the two groups. Paul Brass found numerous examples of this in rural Uttar Pradesh in 2013, and this writer saw this in several other regions (or districts within regions) in 2012 and 2013—for example, in Mandya District (but far less often in neighbouring districts) of southern Karnataka.

to deter further outrages.[18] Those counterattacks proved effective enough to persuade other castes to abandon violence for several years.

III. The Dilemmas and Perceptions of Formerly Dominant Landed Castes

Let us now turn to certain key changes experienced in recent years by members of the landowning castes who formerly dominated life in India's villages. Many of them have faced increasingly harsh realities. To understand how inter-caste accommodations occur, we need to consider these changes, and their perceptions of them.[19]

For them, agriculture and the control of land are not the sources of prestige, prosperity and satisfaction that they once were. Many families have had to divide their landholdings into smaller and smaller plots, as they parcel out shares among children—or at least male children. These shrunken plots are less economically viable than the larger ones that were the norm a generation or two ago. To this must be added what has often been called India's agricultural 'crisis'—which has led 40 per cent of farmers to conclude that they would abandon cultivation if an alternative emerged.[20]

Farming since the early-to-mid-1990s has yielded less abundant livelihoods than in former times. Growth rates for agricultural output have declined, and the availability of credit is a problem for many farmers, in part because of the 'gradual collapse of the cooperative credit system'.[21] Subsidies on some inputs have been cut. Government investment in the sector has declined, most damagingly in the key areas of irrigation and infrastructure. Agricultural extension services have been substantially wound down in many

[18]I am grateful to Hugo Gorringe and A. R. Ventakatachalapthy for information on this trend. For evidence from Tamil Nadu of hitting back, see for example *The Hindu*, 9 November 2013.

[19]The comments which follow are based in part on discussions with members of these groups in villages in nine Indian regions.

[20]M. S. Swaminathan, 'The Crisis of Indian Agriculture', *The Hindu*, 15 August 2007.

[21]Ibid.

states. Soils have become less fertile in some areas as a result of the excessive use of fertilisers and pesticides, and cultivators in many areas also face what is sometimes termed a 'water crisis'—which often takes the form of chronic shortages of groundwater. Some farmers have experienced financial ruin after taking sizeable loans to cultivate risky cash crops that have not met expectations. That provides much of the explanation for the spate of farmer suicides in recent years. The influence of the once formidable 'farmers' lobby' has declined as caste and religious identities (some of which divide farmers) have become more salient in politics at the state and national levels, and as state and national governments have focused more on the manufacturing and services sectors.[22]

The woes of the landed castes do not end there. The attractions of urban centres and the declining prestige of farming have made their children hanker after lives in cities. To make their daughters attractive as potential brides to members of their castes with good urban jobs, many farmers send them to college in cities where they develop an aversion to returning to the land. (In those colleges, they sometimes develop romantic attachments to young men from other castes—which cause great anxiety among their parents.) Their sons also seek such urban jobs. Many of them who do not obtain enough educational qualifications to gain white collar employment still move to cities, where they seek low skilled jobs. Many fail to find work that conforms to their expectations, born of caste status, and they return defeated to the villages where parents often struggle to support them. Sons who agree to live as cultivators often have great problems finding brides—since young women prefer urban living. In Coorg in Karnataka, this problem because so acute that

[22]See for example, D. Narasimha Reddy and S. Mishra, *Agrarian Crisis in India* (Oxford University Press, Delhi, 2009); B. Posani, 'Farmer Suicides and the Political Economy of Agrarian Distress in India', Development Studies Institute, London School of Economics, February 2009); A. C. Dhas, 'Agricultural Crisis in India: The Root Causes and Consequences', *Munich Personal RePEc Archive*, working paper 18930 (December 2009); and R. S. Deshpande and S. Arora (eds), *Agrarian Crisis and Farmer Suicides* (Sage Publications, New Delhi, 2011).

Brahmin farmers[23] obtained dispensation from a local priest to travel to northern districts to find Lingayat brides—since Lingayats, like Brahmins, are vegetarians. Similar reports have emerged from north India. All of these problems cause elders in the once dominant landed castes intense distress.

Those same elders also find their former influence within the political/administrative system waning. Their old role as the main gatekeepers between the village and higher levels in that system has been ended by local political entrepreneurs—*naya netas* or 'fixers'— who travel back and forth between villages and government offices at higher levels, to obtain benefits for local residents from a wide array of government programmes.[24] These people often come from less exalted castes, and so do leaders and enterprising members of elected local councils (*panchayats*) who also provide links to bureaucrats and elected leaders at higher levels and wield influence within villages. Many senior figures in the landed castes have developed a hearty distaste for involvement in *panchayat* politics since it exposes them to sometimes searing political contestation and to cross-examination by opponents—both of which they regard as beneath their dignity. Many therefore withdraw from *panchayats*, but that further undermines their political influence.

To all of these sources of exasperation, we must of course add one more: dismay among the formerly dominant landed castes over increasingly frequent and open refusals by 'lower' castes—especially Dalits—to acknowledge their supposedly superior status, and the old caste hierarchies. When that is piled atop the numerous frustrations described above, the danger arises that members of the landed castes may lash out violently, with Dalits as the most likely targets.

Such spasms of violence have certainly occurred—although only occasionally—in recent years, and when they do, they tend to

[23]Unusually in Karnataka, Brahmins own and cultivate land in Coorg and other pockets across the state.

[24]For more detail see A. Krishna, *Active Social Capital: Tracing the Roots of Development and Democracy* (Columbia University Press, New York, 2002); and chapter ten in this book. Krishna calls these entrepreneurs '*naya netas*' (new leaders) and I call them 'fixers'.

be more savage than in former times. Thirty years ago, when attacks on Dalits occurred, they were usually calculated and measured—and non-lethal. An individual Dalit who had supposedly violated the informal code of deferential behaviour would be singled out as someone who needed to be 'taught a lesson'. S/he would then be beaten and/or publicly humiliated, as a signal to others not to challenge the hierarchical order. But in those days, such violent outrages tended to stop short of murder. In more recent years, when inter-caste tensions arise, usually after an incident of some kind, and violence ensues, it is sometimes far less measured. The pent up frustrations felt by the landed castes sometimes lead to sudden, heated (not calculated) attacks of great, often murderous severity. These violent acts tend to be committed by *groups*, against *groups* of Dalits, not by or against individuals. They are collective acts in both senses. They are not the result of calculated plans to impart a lesson. Instead, they are frenzied outbursts of deep seated anger at the entire array of troubles which the landed castes face.

But in considering such grotesque atrocities, we need to bear two things in mind. First, when such spasms occur, they tend strongly to be confined to a single village—they *almost never spread* to nearby localities. Visits by this writer to villages close to several places where such outbursts have occurred have revealed far more relaxed inter-caste relations, and a perception among residents there that the strife-torn village (where tensions usually persist over many years) is eccentric and rather puzzling. Second and far more importantly, such savage outbreaks of lethal violence are far less common than accommodations within villages—even where inter-caste tensions clearly exist, and even when incidents that might spark violence occur. We must now consider this predominant tendency—towards accommodation—in more detail.

IV. Understanding Inter-Caste Accommodations

It is worth re-emphasising that thirty years or so ago, acts of violence by the landed castes against Dalits tended to be (i) measured, and based on (ii) calculations by (iii) elders or senior leaders within the 'higher' castes. To understand how in recent years, inter-caste accommodations have become far more common than spasms of lethal violence, we need to consider all three of these things.

When accommodations are forged, senior figures within the landed castes still play key roles along with Dalit counterparts (although as we shall see below, the authority of both within their castes is sometimes in doubt and under threat). In most recent episodes, decisions by members of the landed castes to opt for negotiations and accommodations—that is, for measured, restrained actions—are based on careful tactical calculations by them. Crucially, those decisions are not inspired by a new-found empathy among 'higher' castes for Dalits. Instead, they are the results of a change of *mind* and not of *heart*.[25]

What sort of calculations are made? Senior figures within the landed castes know that any violent act, lethal or otherwise, is very likely to become known in the world beyond their village— for several reasons. Dalit organisations are often shot through with factional disputes, but in most parts of India, they penetrate at least tenuously into many (and usually most) rural areas. Thus, they tend to learn of violent incidents, and the result may be a visit to the village by eminent urban Dalits to investigate and publicise the episode. Other (non-Dalit) civil society organisations which are sympathetic to Dalits may also call attention to a violent event. The media now penetrate fairly effectively into rural arenas as well, so that they often report such incidents. When such reports surface, state governments often respond—because most ruling parties cannot afford to alienate Dalit voters through inaction. Judges may also enter the picture—especially if petitions are filed by public interest lawyers, a common occurrence. And behind all of these potential intrusions into the village looms the Atrocities Act of 1989.[26]

That Act (which Dalit leaders often refer to simply as '1989') is a draconian law which characterises a broad array of actions—many of which stop short of violence—as 'atrocities' against Dalits. It

[25]I am grateful to K. C. Suri for stressing this point.
[26]Its full title is the 'Scheduled Castes and Scheduled Tribes (Prevention of Atrocities) Act, 1989'.

empowers the authorities to jail alleged offenders immediately and without bail, on the strength of an accusation that an atrocity has taken place. It places the burden of proof on the accused rather than the accuser.

State governments vary in the zeal with which they implement the Act. Many are less than assiduous in doing so.[27] Even when a state government seeks to make robust use of the Act, conviction rates for alleged offenders tend to be quite low. But that should not blind us to the fact that even if a member of a 'higher' caste escapes conviction, s/he (usually 'he') faces a very prolonged legal struggle—often lasting years—which is decidedly expensive and excruciatingly inconvenient. It imposes huge opportunity costs since it impedes the accused from getting on with other things that are mightily important: cultivating lands, marketing agricultural produce, developing other enterprises that may yield income, arranging loans, overseeing investments, getting children properly educated and married off, etc. For these reasons, even though convictions are unlikely at the end of the legal process, members of the 'higher' castes view the Atrocities Act with trepidation. In 1999, this writer saw palpable fear in the eyes of members of landowning castes when the Act was discussed even in villages in the Gwalior region of Madhya Pradesh where their social/political dominance and the old hierarchies had undergone little erosion.

All of these considerations weigh on the minds of leaders of the landed castes in most villages. They take them into account when deciding how to proceed when inter-caste tensions arise, often because some sort of incident has occurred. These worries (and other considerations, discussed below) are usually sufficient to persuade them to seek to negotiate accommodations with Dalit leaders. Those accommodations are usually uneasy and grudging, but they (and not violence) represent predominant trend.

What types of 'incidents' occur? There is space here only for inadequate comments on this complex, delicate topic—a full

---

[27]See for example the cover story in *Frontline*, 21 November–4 December 2009.

discussion of which will appear in a book-length study. But let us consider three types of incidents.

Accommodations within villages are sometimes facilitated by a perception among most members of all castes that certain incidents—quarrels and modest ructions, however angry, between members of 'higher' castes and Dalits—are rather minor events that do not threaten the prestige of either group. This is often true of disputes which appear to everyone to involve unusually truculent individuals or households. They are perceived to be rather isolated, private squabbles that do little to disrupt the equanimity of social relations more broadly.

Another set of incidents, which are deeply serious, often trigger not violent conflict but frantic efforts to undo or otherwise resolve them—and to conceal them. That is frequently the response when amorous entanglements develop between individuals from Dalit and 'higher' castes, when individuals from those castes elope, or when rapes occur. All of these three occurrences have one thing in common: if they become known beyond the village, all of the young women there will be viewed by outsiders (unfairly of course) with suspicion—suspicion that loose morals prevail in the village, and/or that young women there may have been molested. Those suspicions will make it difficult to find husbands for *all* of those young women.

Such incidents may trigger violence, but that is not necessarily the most common outcome. Lest suspicions engulf all young women in the village, the first reaction by elders within it is not to resort to violence (which will only call attention to the embarrassment) but to hush things up. If an amorous relationship has developed between members of different castes, efforts are made to separate the two people, and perhaps to buy the silence of one or both. If an elopement has occurred, attempts are made to bring the pair back to the village, to annul a marriage if it has taken place, and again to separate the two and to use threats and/or enticements to break their links.

Rapes, which are obviously acts of violence in themselves, are even more inflammatory events. They require more extensive discussion than is possible here. In some (but certainly not all) parts of India, members of the landed castes have long routinely made free use of the bodies of Dalit women, and this vile practice persists in some areas. But now that Dalit and other organisations and the media have extended their reach into many rural areas, such outrages are more likely to become known—and action under the Atrocities Act may follow. Given that possibility, and given the importance of protecting the reputations of all young women in a given village, efforts are again often made to hush things up, to intimidate those who might reveal that it has happened, and perhaps to compensate the victim.

Finally, let us consider a further set of events which are not trivial squabbles between individuals or households. They are not as salacious as amorous relationships, elopements and rapes, but they pose genuine threats to peace in villages because they are perceived to be serious insults to the dignity of 'higher' castes, and to what remains of the old hierarchical order. By way of illustration, consider two such incidents, both of which occurred in similar areas of south India but which produced contrasting outcomes.

In the first, a few young Dalit men attended a village cinema. They had earned enough money to pay for the most expensive seats—for 'chairs' when the cheaper alternatives were 'benches' and 'floor'. During the screening, they placed their feet on the backs of the seats in the row front of them—a row in which young women from the local landed caste were sitting off to one side. As Indian readers will know, such things are seen as a patently insulting act. When word spread among members of the landed caste in the village, they were infuriated, and a few began violent attacks on Dalits which soon mushroomed into a killing spree that left many Dalits dead. Criminal investigations ensued, and several members of the landed castes were eventually convicted and jailed for long periods.

In the second case, three Dalit boys teased a lone boy from the landed caste which had formerly dominated social life in the village. When this was reported to landed caste elders, they gathered to consider what action to take. Some advocated violence, to teach the three Dalits a lesson. But the more influential elders argued that such action would produce too many lasting problems for the members of their caste, so they organised a meeting with Dalit elders. After some negotiation, it was agreed that the three Dalit boys would apologise to the boy whom they had teased. After that happened, the incident was considered by all to be closed.

The kind of accommodation that was reached in the latter case is far more typical that the savage outbreak of violence in the first. There are, however, reasons to wonder whether such accommodations, which represent the predominant trend in recent years across most of rural India, will remain so. Doubts arise when we delve more deeply into the power dynamics that prevail *within* castes—and more specifically, into the influence of caste elders. It may not prove to be sustainable.

Accommodations are usually negotiated between senior figures from different castes, between elders. They share one common interest. No matter which caste they belong to, they see themselves as custodians of some sort of predictable 'order' in the village (or what is left of it after recent changes)—an 'order' within which they enjoy considerable influence. Violence would threaten not just tranquillity but predictability, which is of great value to all of those senior figures.

Violence can threaten predictability in several ways. Quite apart from the injuries that it would (unpredictably) cause, violence could cause lasting disruption to daily village routines and make them less predictable. It might create longer term resentments that would poison predicable inter-caste relations, and thus the outwardly peaceable 'order' within the village, the maintenance of which is seen by many as the responsibility of senior leaders within different castes. Since that would impair their capacity to fulfil that responsibility, it would undermine their authority—within their castes, and in general. Violence might also invite unpredictable interventions in village affairs by police or other government actors at higher levels, undermining the already limited autonomy of the village—autonomy which serves to make local affairs predictable. Even if no such interventions occurred, a spasm of violence would hand the initiative to those engaged in it—that is, to persons who were at least temporarily beyond the control of local leaders. It might thus have unpredictable consequences which could deprive those leaders of their much prized influence over village life. That might open the way either to challenges by rivals or to a loss of discipline and coherence within their caste.

Accommodations negotiated by senior leaders of different castes are only enforceable if each leader has the authority within his[28] caste to persuade or compel his caste fellows to accept them. But in many localities, that authority faces the threat or the reality of erosion—by several different processes.

Many of the changes, noted earlier, which have contributed to the declining acceptance of hierarchies by members of 'lower' castes also threaten the authority of elders *within* all castes. Education, occupational differentiation and spatial mobility may make individuals within a caste less deferential to their own more senior fellow caste men. The emergence of local political entrepreneurs— 'fixers' or *naya netas*—and of entrepreneurial politicians on elected councils (*panchayats*),[29] may also undermine the pre-eminence of caste elders. The problems that afflict agriculture, and the sagging prestige attached to farming, may weaken the influence of senior figures within landed castes.

Their authority is also sometimes undermined by actions which landed caste leaders themselves have taken. Three themes matter here: withdrawals, exits and distractions. We noted above that some senior figures within the once dominant landed castes have *withdrawn* from *panchayat* politics after becoming exasperated with challenges and cross-questioning that they face there from opponents. Surinder Jodhka has shown that such senior leaders may invest funds in urban centres, and establish second homes there for themselves or their children, where they spend part of their time. Even if they do not undertake part-time *exits* from the village, these things become *distractions* which prevent them from giving enough attention to affairs within their villages and their castes to maintain their influence there.

These and other trends may damage authority structures within castes, and even render castes leader-less. If that occurs, then it will

---

[28]The leaders are invariably men.
[29]For more detail, see chapter ten in this book.

become extremely difficult to arrange accommodations between castes, and to enforce compliance once they are arranged.

This chapter—and the book which will deal more fully with these and related themes—is not intended to provide a final, definitive analysis. Rather, it seeks to open up discussion of several crucial issues which have, strangely, been largely ignored. But at least a start has been made here.

— *s i x t e e n* —

POLITICS AND EXPERIMENTATION IN INDIA

The Contrast with China

This paper contrasts approaches to political experimentation in India with China, and sets the scene for a wider discussion of comparative studies in chapter seventeen. It indicates that experiments in India's open, democratic system are inevitably far more untidy and indeed risky than those in China, but also more ambitious. Experiments in India fail more often than in China, but many also achieve more than in China. The anxieties and calculations of India's senior politicians, who (unlike their Chinese counterparts) must seek re-election after five years or less, loom large here—as they have done in several other chapters.

The literature on politics in less developed countries says too little about 'experimentation' by political actors within governments and ruling parties. But in important recent studies of China, Sebastian Heilmann places 'experimentation' at the centre of his analyses of the political and policy processes. He does so because leaders of the Chinese Communist Party (CCP) and government have long made systematic use of an unusually rigorous type of experimentation. He argues, 'a distinctive policy cycle, experimentation under hierarchy, is the key to understanding the emergence of an unexpectedly adaptive authoritarianism in China'.[1]

An explicit emphasis on experimentation is needed in studies of other—quite different—political systems. The approaches adopted elsewhere often contrast sharply with those used in China, and so do the results. But these contrasts help us towards a fuller understanding of how politics differs from country to country. This chapter uses Heilmann's analyses as a point of departure for an assessment of experimentation in India. It thus considers processes that affect something approaching one-half of humankind. But the issues that emerge here are also meant to suggest new questions to ask about other cases in Asia, Africa and Latin America.

It will become apparent that politicians in both India and China are much more adventurous than readers may expect. In both cases, leaders have a surprisingly strong appetite for innovation, and thus for experimentation. This common characteristic could easily be overlooked here amid a multitude of contrasts between China and India. But it is worth bearing in mind.

The discussion below first examines certain basic differences between the political and policy trajectories of China since 1949 and India since 1947. That is followed by six sections which focus on important aspects of experimentation in these two systems: the methods commonly used, the origins of experiments, their locations, their main aims, and their impact on corruption. The conclusion summarises important findings.

Differences in the Nature of Policy (and Political) Change in China and India

The policy process in India has always differed in important ways from its Chinese counterpart—because the two political processes, which lie at the root of policy change, differ. This analysis of India, like Heilmann's studies of China, straddles a watershed in recent history. He considers experimentation before and especially since

[1]S. Heilmann, 'Policy Experimentation in China's Economic Rise', *Studies in Comparative International Development* (March, 2008), pp. 2–3.

the great transformation which occurred after 1979 when Deng Xiaoping and his colleagues introduced marked changes in politics and policy, using well established experimental techniques. This chapter considers trends both before and especially since a somewhat different transformation in India, in which changes were less marked and abrupt. It occurred in five phases.

It began (i) in the late 1960s when the Congress Party found it impossible in most parts of the country to maintain one-party dominance in that multi-party democracy. It gained momentum (ii) in 1977 when the Congress Party led by Indira Gandhi suffered a crushing electoral defeat after her brutish, hare-brained 19-month Emergency. Then (iii) in 1989, it became impossible for any single party to win a majority in India's Parliament—mainly because regional parties had gained great strength. Since 1989, India has been ruled by minority governments or multi-party coalitions. In 1990, (iv) two new themes emerged with potent popular appeal: the promise by centre-left forces of preferential treatment for disadvantaged 'backward castes', and the pursuit by the religious right of a more aggressive strain of Hindu nationalism. These two themes competed not only with one another, but also with the Congress Party's traditional efforts to draw support from a very broad, diverse array of interests. Then (v) in 1991, a Congress minority government introduced market-oriented economic reforms. They were limited by East Asian standards, but substantial by previous Indian standards—and for a time facilitated a surge in economic growth.

The contrast between the dramatic, comparatively sudden changes in China and the more incremental pattern of change in India is typical of the two political systems. From the late 1940s onward, swings in government policy between left and right occurred in China rather abruptly and with striking clarity. In India, by contrast, somewhat similar shifts in emphasis occurred, but more gradually and in a more cautious, moderate and muddled manner. That is hardly surprising since just one party has always been utterly dominant in China, and it has always possessed a formidable capacity and an inclination to enforce discipline throughout what analysts rightly refer to as the 'party-state'—since the two entities are fused. In India, no party has exercised dominance since the late 1960s, and even before that, the dominance of Congress was based on its appeal to an *un*disciplined welter of competing interests which vied for leverage within the party's internal democracy. The result in India has always been policy-making rooted in compromises among diverse forces—hence the more moderate, democratic but muddled nature of its policy process. Also, India has been a federal system which gives substantial powers and autonomy to state governments. This has enabled parties opposed to governments in New Delhi to capture power at the state level and to pursue policies—and policy experiments—which differ from those of the Central government.

Thus, there are striking differences between the two countries when we consider experimental methods, the locations of experiments, their sources, and their main aims.

Experimental Methods

Chinese leaders' approach to experimentation entails unusually rigorous methods. This is reflected in Heilmann's comments on that term.

> ... Policy experimentation is not equivalent to freewheeling trial and error or spontaneous policy diffusion. It is a purposeful and coordinated activity geared to producing novel policy options that are injected into official policymaking and then replicated on a larger scale....[2]

He explains that in China, most experiments are carried out within small arenas, and those which prove their worth are then incorporated into national policy—a process which, even during the Maoist era, has been formally described as 'proceeding from point to surface'. He argues that in China since 1979, experiments have had a 'transformative' impact, in that they 'alter economic and administrative behaviour and institutions'.[3]

In the period before 1980, a somewhat similar approach was often used in India. Heilmann quotes a study of India published in

[2]Ibid., p. 3.
[3]Ibid., pp. 3–5.

that year which stated that 'the corpses of pilot projects litter the development field'.[4] But since then, Indian policymakers—especially in state governments in that federal system—have increasingly followed a different path. Experimental programmes have tended to be introduced fully formed, without prior pilot studies to test their impact. As a result, it is extremely difficult and often impossible in India to fine-tune promising initiatives, and experiments which misfire cannot be abandoned before they become embarrassing failures. A comparison of China's rigorous approach with these less tidy patterns in India will yield fresh insights into the political and policy processes in both countries.

Policymakers in India would love to test ideas in carefully crafted pilot projects before applying them more broadly. But over the last three decades, they have shunned them for one mundane but compelling reason: they lack the time for such slow processes. They are elected for five-year terms and they are acutely aware that unless they can make a substantial impact for the better within that limited period, they are likely to be thrown out at the next election. Voters have rejected ruling parties or coalitions in New Delhi at five of the last six, and seven of the last nine national elections. At the state level, reelection is even more difficult. In major states since 1980, incumbent governments have been ousted around 70 per cent of the time. These are hair-raising numbers which leave politicians desperate to achieve dramatic successes swiftly, across the entire territories that they govern. They cannot wait a year or two to see if a pilot project succeeds because that would leave them too little time to implement the ideas tested in the pilot scheme across an entire state—or in the case of national leaders, across the whole country. They are therefore forced to devise experiments which are intended, from the start, for universal or near-universal application. So in India, experiments almost always take the form of grand gambles,

---

[4]D. F. Pyle, 'From Pilot Project to Operational Program in India: The Problems of Transition', in M. Grindle (ed.), *Politics and Policy Implementation in the Third World* (Princeton University Press, Princeton, 1980), pp. 123–44.

something close to leaps in the dark. They sometimes fail—which is galling, but an unavoidable risk that must be taken.[5]

When experiments yield positive results, this sometimes comes as a surprise. One of the most constructive experiments in recent years was the Education Guarantee Scheme created in Madhya Pradesh in the 1990s. It gave every village which did not have a nearby school the right to demand a school and a paraprofessional teacher funded by the government. As a result, half of the state's villages demanded and received new schools—which were attended by 1.16 million children, many of whom would otherwise have had no education. When the chief minister approved this scheme, he did not know that so many villages lacked schools, so he was astonished at the massive uptake.

Not all Indian experiments are undertaken on such limited prior evidence. When that same chief minister energetically supported democratic decentralisation, he did not need pilot projects to convince him that it made sense to empower elected councils and to enhance grassroots participation. He had seen such methods generate improved development outcomes earlier.[6]

But however much—or little—prior knowledge underpins Indian politicians' experiments, over the last 30 years most have eschewed pilot studies and plunged headlong into new initiatives. Many have succeeded. This may not be the highest form of experimentation, but it is not to be despised—especially because this is the only option available to leaders in a country where voters routinely reject incumbent governments.

The experiments at the state level in India can be viewed as pilot schemes in only one sense. When a new state government programme proves beneficial and thus popular, leaders in other states and at the national level (who are looking for ideas that will promote development and win votes) often copy it. So the initial

[5]On the care taken in China to confine failures to small arenas, see Heilmann, 'Policy Experimentation in China's Economic Rise', p. 21.

[6]The comments on this leader (Digvijay Singh) are based on numerous interviews with him in New Delhi and Bhopal between 2002 and 2007. He is discussed in detail in chapter thirteen of this book.

experiment may serve as a pilot scheme for governments elsewhere. However, within the state where such programmes were first introduced, there is no time for pilot exercises.

The Locations of Experiments

When we ask where experiments have been located in China and India, we discover sharp contrasts. Most experimentation in China has occurred well below the regional level, in quite small arenas. These have been systematically coordinated, evaluated and either scaled up or abandoned by higher authorities within the party-state—usually at the apex of the national system. But since most have been sited within rather localised arenas, those that misfire do little damage.

In India, the main sites for experiments have been entire states in the federal system—regions which in most cases contain tens of millions of people. But a limited number have originated at or just above the grassroots—in the small minority of states where elected councils at lower levels have been generously empowered and funded. Governments at the national level have also engaged in a certain amount of experimentation—with the whole country as its location, especially between 2004 and 2009. But actions at these two levels are greatly outnumbered by experiments at the state level.

This is partly explained by a feature of the Indian Constitution which has no counterpart in China. It gives state governments in the federal system powers over local government, public health and sanitation, agriculture and animal husbandry, water, land, fisheries, the electricity sector, mining, etc. However, the main explanation for the increasing role of state governments in experimentation is not constitutional but political. State-level politicians have eagerly embraced it, to cultivate popular support at upcoming elections. A distinguished Indian civil servant has stated that the most striking change during his career (from the 1960s through the 1990s) was the proliferation of government programmes[7]—most of which qualify as experiments.

[7]Interview with B. K. Bhattacharya, former Chief Secretary of Karnataka, Bangalore, 12 July 2003.

The Origins of Experiments

When we turn to the origins from which experiments in China and India arise, we encounter certain contrasts, but also surprising similarities. We have seen that in India, the main initiators have been ruling parties at the state level which often seek to show that they are more imaginative than the ruling party or coalition at the national level, which they oppose.[8] So a key source has been the desire to compete against whatever party holds power in New Delhi, and to undermine its legitimacy. The contrast here with China is radical. The CCP is the only party that matters there, so competitive experimentation between parties cannot occur. In China, the party-state has been the sole source of experiments, which are intended to enhance, and not to undermine, the legitimacy of the Central government.

On other fronts, however, we find more similarities than we might expect, given the differences between the two political systems. Consider, the degree to which ideas for experiments have been borrowed from outside these countries—from international development agencies or governments elsewhere. Since 1979, Chinese leaders have made little use of ideas generated by aid agencies. Heilmann attributes their increasing willingness to engage in consultation with ordinary folk (see the discussion of civil society below) to international agencies,[9] but he also stresses that they have resisted 'the imposition of international "best practices"'.[10] It is not entirely clear how much China's leaders have looked to practices used in other countries. Singapore's highly illiberal model may have suggested certain possibilities, especially after 1989,[11] but most approaches used elsewhere appear to have been disregarded.

[8]State governments which support those ruling in New Delhi have also sometimes engaged in experiments—again in attempts to win popular support.

[9]Heilmann, "Policy Experimentation in China's Economic Rise', p. 19.

[10]Ibid., p. 23.

[11]K. Huang, *Capitalism with Chinese Characteristic: Entrepeneurship and the State* (Cambridge University Press, Cambridge, 2008). See also, Heilmann, 'Policy Experimentation in China's Economic Rise', pp. 15–17.

India is similar. Ideas generated by international development agencies have had only a very limited impact there—somewhat more than in China, but far less than in aid-dependent countries. Most bilateral donor agencies were invited to leave India in 2003, and those that remain feel unimportant. A former head of the huge British aid mission there has said in private that he felt 'like a fly on the bum of an elephant'. Donors have tended mainly to support initiatives devised by state and national governments. Indeed, India has done more to influence donors' agendas than vice-versa. For example, the experiments with democratic decentralisation in the states of West Bengal (after 1977) and then Karnataka (after 1983) preceded by several years most donors' discovery of the utility of such policies—and helped to persuade them of it.

Nor have Indian leaders borrowed many ideas from governments in other countries. Many senior politicians are alert to promising official experiments in other parts of their *own* country, but almost none have looked further afield. The main exception was Andhra Pradesh under the Chandrababu Naidu government (1995–2004) when the policies and politics of the illiberal Mahathir regime in Malaysia were carefully analysed for ideas that might be adapted. This writer and two colleagues discovered remarkable parallels between experiments attempted after the late 1980s by progressive politicians in Brazil, Uganda and the Indian state of Madhya Pradesh. But the three leaders had scarcely heard of each other and knew absolutely nothing of the others' policies.[12] That has been the norm in India.

What of the influence of civil society on governments in China and India. Such associations in China—insofar as they exist[13]—have had little influence on official experiments. But Heilmann notes,

[12]M. Melo, N. Ng'ethe and J. Manor, *Against the Odds: Politicians, Institutions and the Struggle against Poverty* (Hurst/Columbia University Press, London/New York, 2012).

[13]'Civil society' here is defined as a domain that stands between the state and the household which is populated by voluntary associations with a significant degree of autonomy from the state. Few associations in China possess such autonomy, and those which do exercise very little influence over the state.

... bringing policy issues to the national agenda through social demands and public criticism ... has become more prevalent in China ... official experimental programmes, aimed at improving the provision of social and public goods, have been complemented by more systematic societal consultation since the mid-1990s.[14]

These exercises appear to have been initiated and coordinated by officials from above, so that the influence from below of non-state, civil society actors is still quite limited. But the Chinese system is now more open.

Civil society in India is far stronger and is flush with constructive ideas. But the pattern there is only somewhat, and not radically, different from that in China. Only a small number of Indian policymakers have paid limited attention to ideas from enlightened civil society organisations.

The word to emphasise here is 'limited'. One state government which, very exceptionally, listened to such groups—the Madhya Pradesh government between 1993 and 2003—illustrates the most that can be expected at the state level. The enlightened chief minister of that state was personally acquainted with a few leaders of civil society organisations in *other* parts of India, and he drew upon their advice when devising some experiments. But he had little interaction with civil society *within* his state—partly because it was less strong than in most other states, and partly because elements of it raised inconvenient demands. On one occasion, he forged an agreement on land rights with one of these organisations, but that occurred because it (unlike nearly all of the others) had a mass base which made it formidable in political terms. Most of the rest were treated with benign neglect, and one suffered some harassment.[15] In other states, little or no listening has occurred.

At the national level, the story has been different, but only since 2004. Until then, Central governments had paid scarcely any heed to civil society. The main exception was the close link which governments led by the Bharatiya Janata Party or BJP (1998–2004)

---

[14]Heilmann, 'Policy Experimentation in China's Economic Rise', p. 19.

[15]For more details, see Melo, Ng'ethe and Manor, *Against the Odds*, chapter three.

maintained with its aggressively Hindu nationalist sister organisation, the Rashtriya Swayamsevak Sangha (RSS). But that association is largely unconcerned with development issues, and many Indians regard it as decidedly 'uncivil'.[16]

However, when a Congress-led coalition government took power in 2004, its coordinator, Sonia Gandhi, established an advisory committee which included several major figures from development-oriented civil society organisations, and gave them considerable influence over the design of certain important initiatives. Their role stands in marked contrast not just to China, but with India itself before 2004. But it remains to be seen whether this approach will be adopted by future national governments.

Finally, we discover some similarities—alongside one startling contrast—when we examine the influence of ideology on experimentation in China and India. Before 1979, China was regarded as intensely preoccupied with ideology, while in India it counted for little. Since then, the two systems have converged. This has mainly occurred because China has changed. Its leaders have largely forsaken ideology. But some of their Indian counterparts have also become a little more inclined to use ideology as a source for experimentation.

Many of the experiments that Chinese leaders have undertaken since 1979 have been intended to accelerate their abandonment of the CCP's traditional ideology, and to justify it by finding ways of producing better results without it. In India, ideology has seldom played a major role in experiments. The main exception has been the land reform undertaken by the Communist Party of India-Marxist (CPI-M) in West Bengal state. It conformed to leftist principles, despite complaints that it failed to address the needs of the poor*est* villagers. But it is notable that the land reform also had pragmatic utility. It solidified popular support among the state's rural majority

---

[16]It qualifies as a 'civil society organisation' if we use the intentionally *neutral* definition set out in note 13. Such a definition is analytically essential if we are to avoid the regrettable tendency in many overly enthusiastic (and thus misleading) writings on 'civil society' to define out of it 'uncivil' voluntary associations.

for the CPI-M, and ensured that despite opposition from some urban interests, the leftist government would be repeatedly reelected.

Some might argue that ideology has mattered in certain other states, but such claims are dubious. In Gujarat, Chief Minister Narendra Modi of the BJP (2001 to 2014) has made aggressive use of Hindu chauvinism to polarise society—in part by facilitating a pogrom against Muslims in 2002. But to attribute his brutish tactics to Hindu nationalist 'ideology' may be to dignify them unjustifiably. It might be said that the Congress Chief Minister Digvijay Singh in Madhya Pradesh (1993–2003) derived some of his experiments from the Gandhian tradition. But Singh himself is hesitant to accept the word 'ideology' to describe that tradition. When he is asked why he undertook what could be seen as neo-Gandhian initiatives, his response is utilitarian: they produce better developmental outcomes, and help to shift people's attention from caste and religious divisions to the more important issues of development.[17]

Several experiments, poverty reduction programmes by the Congress-led government at the national level between 2004 and the present, have been inspired by social democratic ideology. Thus surprisingly, that government has been more ideologically-driven than any government in Beijing since 1979. But for the most part, we are dealing here with 'pragmatic progressives'[18], leaders who adopt progressive policies because they enhance a government's legitimacy and popularity. (Indeed, the same is true of China's leaders since 2003 when they awakened belatedly to the need to address the problems of vulnerable groups—not for votes which they do not need, but to tackle a surge in protests.)

That Congress-led government's victory in the national election 2004 was attributed in many media reports to a revolt of the rural poor against economic growth and increasing inequalities. That was a myth. The Congress-led alliance did better in urban than in

---

[17]For details, see chapter three of Melo, Ng'ethe and Manor, *Against the Odds*.

[18]That term was first used to describe a Chief Minister Devaraj Urs in Karnataka. See chapter eleven in this book.

rural areas, and the rural poor in different states voted in markedly different ways.

Congress leaders knew this,[19] but they did not challenge the myth—because it made them look like saviours of the downtrodden. The poverty programmes with which they experimented after 2004 were not so much ideology-driven as pragmatic attempts to win the votes of the rural poor at the next national election in 2009.[20]

So ideology has served only exceptionally and occasionally as a source of ideas for experimentation in these two countries—or rather in India, since China's leaders have been in determined flight from Marxism-Leninism-Mao-Zedong-Thought. It is astonishing to see ideology counting for more in India than in China. But even in India, the time-honoured generalisation that ideology counts for little remains largely true.

The Main Aims of Experiments

When we consider the aims of experimentation in these two countries, certain similarities and—more crucially—striking contrasts emerge. The predominant aim in China has been to spur economic growth—indeed, 'growth by any means'.[21] In India, such experiments have also occurred, but the main emphases have been in other spheres, all of which have seen significant experiments. These include governance reforms which deepen democracy and enhance participation and government responsiveness to popular preferences; improved service delivery; poverty reduction by means other

[19]This comment is based on interviews with three key Congress election strategists in 2005.

[20]For an analysis of this, see J. Manor, 'Did the Central Government's Poverty Initiatives Help to Re-elect It?', in L. Saez and G. Singh (eds), *New Dimensions of Politics in India: The United Progressive Alliance in Power* (Routledge, New Delhi and London, 2011).

[21]His analysis of experimentation in China rightly focuses mainly on the complex set of processes which have been used to pursue economic reform, with growth as the principal goal. See Heilmann, 'Policy Experimentation in China's Economic Rise', pp. 12–18 and 24. The quotation is from p. 24.

than economic growth; environmental programmes; sustainable livelihoods; etc. So once again, we encounter greater focus, single-mindedness (and narrowness) in the actions of Chinese leaders, and considerable diversity in India.

How do we explain this contrast? It derives from the differing views of political elites in the two countries about the actual and potential sources of legitimacy for their regimes.

China's leaders have concentrated on growth because they believe that it will benefit not just China in general but more specifically, the party-state.[22] After the destructive Cultural Revolution (1966–1975), the long-term survival of the party-state was in doubt. The formidable coercive power of the regime ensured that it was not about to collapse, but it was a matter of urgency to find it new sources of legitimacy. Its old ideology would not suffice, so it was substantially set aside. The capacity to deliver economic growth became the main new source of legitimacy. Indeed, some scholars have argued that it has become the only remaining source.[23]

By contrast, Indian leaders believe that while growth may inspire popular support, much more will be gained from new experiments on other fronts. So they have sought to draw legitimacy from a broader array of sources than do their Chinese counterparts. Electoral mandates are obviously crucial. To obtain them, economic growth has some relevance, but greater emphasis has been given to government responsiveness, the provision of information, openings for popular participation, programmes targeted on important interest groups, poverty initiatives to reach groups left behind amid growth, and identity politics. Some of these concerns are also shared by China's leaders, especially in recent years when they awakened belatedly to the damage which the drive for economic

---

[22]Some Chinese experiments with economic reform have also created opportunities for individuals (usually within the party) to make illicit profits through rent seeking. See section 6 of this paper where we encounter a further, surprising, contrast with India.

[23]This comment is based on discussions with and a communication from A. J. Saich. See, for example, D. Apter and A. J. Saich, *Revolutionary Discourse in Mao's China* (Harvard University Press, Cambridge MA, 1994).

growth has done to vulnerable groups and to the environment.[24] But Heilmann—who analyses Chinese experiments in several different spheres[25]—indicates that the drive for growth has always been (and remains) paramount.

Like China's leaders, India's have experimented in pursuit of legitimacy, but they have been much less united in their views of how to achieve that. So they have devised a great diversity of strategies and experiments. This owes much to the remarkable variations in the conditions from state to state in India—and to the openness of the political system which permits these variations to impinge mightily on the politics of different states. We find variations in levels of development, human development indicators, per capita incomes, patterns of land control, cultural traditions, relations between social groups, and the very composition of society. As a result, the political traditions and cultures of the various states differ (often substantially) from one another. So it is not surprising that the preoccupations and aims of state-level leaders in India, and the types of experimentation that they have undertaken, have been far more varied than in China.

India's state-level politicians are also a vastly more variegated group than are their Chinese counterparts. Instead of working within a single party, and in pursuit of variations on a single theme which that party had adopted, they stress a diversity of themes in order to distinguish their parties from others. Many are regional parties which need to demonstrate that they are more imaginative and beneficent than the two national parties—the Congress Party and the BJP. So instead of seeking to develop new strategies that would bolster the legitimacy of the ruling party at the national level (as in China), they have often had the opposite intention. Many whose parties were not part of the national government have sought to develop popular experiments in order to *undermine*, by

[24]Heilmann (in 'Policy Experimentation in China's Economic Rise', p. 9) notes that experiments to promote cooperative health care and Central government co-funding of rural health services began in earnest only in 2003.

[25]Ibid., pp. 19–20.

comparison, the credibility and influence of New Delhi. But state-level leaders from the two national parties, when they head state governments, also devise a diversity of experimental programmes—to ingratiate themselves with impatient electorates—which vary from state to state in the conditions that they face, and thus in their concerns. The result is lively inter-party competition to develop the most successful and politically appealing new experiments.

Since the early 1990s, Indian politicians have increasingly understood two key realities. The first was the need to rely less on their ramshackle party organisations and more on official government programmes which could be delivered through administrative (and to a degree, new democratic) structures. Second, they recognised the insufficiency of the 'old politics' of patronage distribution through networks of lieutenants, to cultivate popular support from important social groups—that is, clientelism. Rising demands for spoils from a diversity of assertive interest groups have greatly exceeded leaders' capacity to respond, even in an era of economic growth and rising revenue collections. Many politicians have therefore concluded that a new, 'post-clientelist' politics is required. They must provide something extra, to supplement patronage distribution—which continues—if they are to have any hope of re-election.

Indian leaders have, however, responded to this problem not with one, but with a great diversity of post-clientelist initiatives. Consider a few examples.

- In the late 1970s, the CPI-M-led left front government in West Bengal—and in 1985, the Janata Dal government in Karnataka—introduced strong systems of democratic decentralisation.
- The AIADMK[26] government in Tamil Nadu introduced a mid-day meals scheme in schools which at first appeared to be a grandiose exercise in populism, but which proved to have

---

[26]The All-India Anna Dravida Munnetra Kazhagam (AIADMK), a product of the regional Dravidian movement in Tamil Nadu.

strong positive effects in terms of both nutrition[27] and pupils' attendance rates.

- The BJP government in Rajasthan devised an *antyodaya* programme providing special support to the five poorest families in each village.
- The Congress government in Madhya Pradesh introduced the Education Guarantee Scheme (noted above) which gave any village that lacked a nearby school the right to demand a new school and teacher at the state government's expense. Fully half of the villages in the state received schools, and since teachers were local residents who were accountable to the elected local council, teacher absenteeism—a severe problem in conventional government schools across India—scarcely occurred.

The Telugu Desam Party (TDP) government in Andhra Pradesh launched an aggressive campaign to develop women's self-help groups. The result was that, at the programme's peak, this state contained one-quarter of all such groups *in the world*. The government pressed ahead too quickly with this initiative, so that many of these groups foundered. But enough survived to provide women with substantial new opportunities in the public sphere.

Note that each of these experiments was initiated by a *different* political party. Experiments with post-clientelist programmes have arisen across the spectrum of parties.

Should we see these variations as more constructive than the far more homogenous picture that emerges from China, or less? There are at least two ways of answering this question, both of which have some validity. On the one hand, as we have seen above, it means that the strategy which any Indian state government uses to pursue development and thus popularity is more likely to suit the distinctive conditions and capacities that are found in that state. This minimises the one-size-fits-all problem. On the other hand, the increasing diversity that we see among India's states—in the character of both politics and policy making—gives some cause for concern.

---

[27]Including the nutrition of pupils' families since they were permitted to take some food home.

It has meant that since the early 1990s, when regional parties became able to make a potent impact in nearly all policy spheres, India's various states have been governed in increasingly diverse ways. Consider, by way of illustration, the approaches used by just four state chief ministers in recent times. Both Lalu Prasad Yadav (who dominated Bihar's politics from 1990 to 2005) and Narendra Modi (in Gujarat, 2001 to the present) sought to polarise society in ways that bolstered their influence. But Lalu sought polarisation between 'haves' and 'have-nots' while Modi has sought to cultivate the division between Hindus and others. Both Digvijay Singh in Madhya Pradesh (1993–2003) and Chandrababu Naidu in Andhra Pradesh (1995–2004) stressed 'development'—but again in strikingly different ways. The former did so in a bottom-up, participatory manner while the latter adopted an aggressively top-down, illiberal approach which entailed the marginalisation and harassment of alternative power centres. In most other states, a diversity of other strategies has been adopted.

As a consequence the 'Indian state', as ordinary people experience it, takes quite different forms in different regions. So national leaders find it increasingly difficult to make their policy initiatives penetrate to the grassroots in a consistent manner—because they are (always) filtered through and (often) substantially adapted or (sometimes) ignored by state governments. Thus, Central governments are less able than in earlier years to make a coherent impact on the people who will ultimately determine their political fate. To say all of this is not to argue that India is many different countries, or that it is about to fall apart. Neither of those tired journalistic myths have any substance. But this trend towards variegation—which has been little discussed in India—needs serious consideration.

The Impact of Experiments on Rent-Seeking

One final, arresting contrast between these experiments in India and China is important. As Heilmann indicates, many of the Chinese experiments provide key actors, especially within the ruling party, with 'new channels for profit-seeking *and* rent-seeking opportunities'.[28] He adds, 'Beyond a doubt, generating new sources of income for local elites has been a key driving force behind experimentation'.[29]

This is far less true of India's post-clientelist experiments. They have—to a remarkable degree, given the importance of corruption in India—are intended to *thwart* profiteering. Many seek to promote a 'new' politics that departs from the old politics of patronage distribution—in which rent-seeking flourishes. We sometimes hear of 'wet' government programmes which create opportunities for illicit profiteering and 'dry' programmes which do not. These post-clientelist experiments are, in the main, intended to dry out sizeable portions of the political and policy processes. This does not mean that corruption is vanishing. It proceeds apace in other spheres, but strong efforts have been made to insulate many post-clientelist experiments from it.[30]

This has happened not because India's politicians are morally superior to leaders elsewhere, but because these programmes differ from those in China in one key respect. In China, experiments have mainly been aimed at achieving economic *growth*—and to facilitate that, many have enabled rent-seeking among key actors who must be won over to new practices aimed at promoting growth. The dominant motive behind the Indian experiments is a quest by politicians for *votes*. Since the extraction of rents from these post-clientelist programmes would undermine their capacity to attract votes, care is taken to minimise it.

[28]Heilmann, 'Policy Experimentation in China's Economic Rise', p. 19. The italics are in the original text. See also p. 17 and 21–23.

[29]Ibid., p. 22.

[30]Witness for example the complex set of transparency mechanisms which have been included in India's (and probably the world's) largest poverty reduction programme, the Mahatma Gandhi National Rural Employment Guarantee Act (MGNREGA). This writer's research on that scheme suggests that it possesses the most formidable array of transparency mechanisms in the world. Extensive field research in two key states indicates that these mechanisms are far from fool proof, but it also reveals that it is harder to steal money from this scheme than from most other government programmes in India.

Summing Up

Finally, let us briefly recall some of the ideas that have emerged here. Since the 1940s, changes in policy in China have occurred more swiftly, sharply and with greater clarity and single-mindedness than in India. That pattern has continued in recent years, even though policy agendas have changed—drastically in China, and significantly in India. They changed because in each country, the old politics and political economy were seen not to be working. In India, the increasing number of political parties which capture power at the state level (and which share power in coalitions at the national level), plus the increasing leverage of all state governments since the end of prime ministerial dominance in 1989, have made the policy process more diffuse, complex and muddled than before—but also more variegated and arguably more creative. So policy processes are powerfully shaped by political dynamics and forces. That may not sound like a surprising conclusion, but it is one which technocratic analysts sometimes overlook.[31]

The methods used in China to test policies through experimentation have been far more rigorous than those in India. Nonetheless, many experiments in India have produced constructive results.

When we examine the origins of experiments in the two countries, we find some surprising similarities. Leaders in both countries have largely ignored ideas that originate beyond their borders, and have paid only limited heed to civil society—although on the latter front, the government in New Delhi after 2004 is a notable exception. But when we consider 'origins', we also encounter a startling contrast between the two cases. In recent years, ideology has had greater influence in India than in China. Its importance in India has been limited, but arguably greater than in earlier times.

Important differences also emerge when we assess the principal aims of experiments in the two countries. Both sets of leaders have sought to strengthen not only their countries but also their own political legitimacy and prospects. But while the Chinese have

---

[31]I do not include Heilmann among them.

regarded economic growth as the main means of achieving these things, the Indians have concentrated on winning votes—and growth is seen as less likely to enhance popularity than are new initiatives in several other spheres. This largely explains the greater diversity in Indian experimentation. It also owes much to the greater openness of its political system to the varying conditions and the felt needs of ordinary people in its diverse regions—and to the stronger emphasis on social sector programmes and on responsiveness.

The brief discussion of rent-seeking (corruption) uncovered another arresting contrast. Experiments in China that have sought to spur economic growth—which is to say, most Chinese experiments—have often provided political actors with opportunities to make illicit profits, in order to ensure their compliance with new policies. But in India, post-clientelist experiments—which is to say, most Indian experiments—have tended strongly to close down such opportunities. There are of course other ways to make money illegally in India, but this trend is still important.

India's multi-party system and the rise of regional parties with experiments of their own have made it far more difficult than in China for the Central government to leave a consistent imprint across varied regions. The 'Indian state', as ordinary people experience it, takes somewhat different forms in different regions. This is a potential cause for concern which has scarcely been discussed in India. But this process also protects regions from national initiatives that may be inappropriate or damaging.

Indian leaders are far less capable than their Chinese counterparts to concentrate minds and energies behind highly focused experiments (or almost anything else). Their political system is too open. As a result, many of the impressive outcomes achieved in China through experimentation are beyond them. But there is another way to look at this. India's leaders cannot and do not apply discipline (backed by coercive potential) to regiment, narrow down, and homogenise experimental activity (or anything else). So the remarkable flowering of diverse experiments that we have lately seen in India, on a broad array of fronts, is beyond Chinese leaders.

So too is the strong Indian emphasis on responsiveness—on devising experiments which either respond to the felt needs of numerically powerful groups, or enable ordinary people to trigger responses to their own preferences and demands. Since around 2003, we have seen some of this in China. But it is still something of a novelty there, applied in a minority of cases. National leaders in China still set most of the agendas and pursue experiments within characteristically tight constraints. Such constraints are largely absent—indeed, they are almost impossible to impose—within India's untidy but vastly more liberal system.

seventeen

WHAT DO THEY KNOW OF INDIA WHO ONLY INDIA KNOW?[1]

The Uses of Comparative Politics

As the contrast with China suggested in the previous paper, comparisons of India with other cases are useful. They may reveal important things about the country which those of us who focus only or mainly on India take for granted. We may fail to understand how distinctive and crucial they are. They may even remain invisible. This paper presents comparative insights on certain key themes in the new millennium. In the process, it revisits several of the issues examined in earlier chapters, and provides updates on some of them. It also argues that valuable discoveries may emerge from comparisons of India's varied states—comparisons of the kind which often appear in other papers of this book.

A scrap of pale blue paper is stuck to the wall by my desk. Its edges are curling and to visitors, it looks tawdry. It is a receipt for a cup of coffee from Koshy's, an unpretentious

[1]This title is obviously adapted from Kipling. But to be precise, the actual quotation from his poem 'The English Flag' is: 'And what *should* they know of England who only England know?'

restaurant in Bangalore where I have eaten hundreds of meals. Much of the appeal of Koshy's has to do with its clientele—lawyers from the high court, legislators, a few scholars,[2] and especially journalists. But it also owes much to the quality of the coffee that they serve, coffee grown in the hills not far away—Mysore coffee.

For years, I suspected that my taste for this coffee was mainly explained by my strong identification with this region of India. But then in the 1990s, I was chatting in England with a group of people who made their living analysing trade in commodities, especially chocolate and coffee. I asked them about their ideal cup of coffee. They astounded me by saying that it was a 50/50 blend of Mocha (which comes from Yemen) and—yes—Mysore. I had not known how superior my preferred cuppa was. That only became apparent when it was compared with the alternatives from other parts of the world. Comparison has its uses.

What is true of coffee is also true of politics. We enrich our understanding of political phenomena in India (or any country) when we compare them to counterparts elsewhere—or, occasionally, when comparison reveals that no counterparts exist. Comparisons of politics in India and other countries reveal things about India which we do not fully grasp when we focus only on that country. If we merely consider India, we take many important things for granted. They are so familiar to us as India specialists that we pay them little heed, and when we actually notice them, we assume that they are normal. Some of them may indeed conform to international norms—comparisons often reveal commonalities rather than contrasts. But we can only know that if we undertake comparative analyses. Often, however, comparative studies show that many things in India which at first appear normal to India specialists are in reality unusual and distinctive.

This chapter over-emphasises contrasts and downplays commonalities, for illustrative effect, but it should not be read as an argument for Indian exceptionalism. India is in many ways distinctive, but in many other respects, it is also a lot like other countries. Amartya Sen is especially (and rightly) impatient with

---

[2]They include the distinguished historian Ramachandra Guha.

those who makes claims for one particular type of exceptionalism—
the depiction of India as 'the land of religions, the country of
uncritical faiths and unquestioned practices ... (of) unreasoning
culture'.[3] This chapter repeatedly demonstrates the rationality—
indeed, the canny scepticism and shrewd calculations—of Indian
political actors, be they powerful or obscure. It also seeks to acquaint
readers with several important recent trends in India.

The Radical Redistribution of Power in India since 1989

Power within the Indian political system has been radically
redistributed since 1989. In that year, it became impossible for any
single party to win a majority in the Lok Sabha, the dominant lower
house of Parliament. For most of the period between 1971 and
1989—during the years when Indira and Rajiv Gandhi had headed
governments—power had been highly centralised (indeed, grossly
over-centralised) in the Prime Minister's Office (PMO). That became
impossible once parliamentary majorities eluded single parties—as
they have done at the seven elections since 1989.

Power has flowed away from the PMO horizontally, at the
national level, to a diversity of institutions: to Parliament and
its committees, the courts, the Election Commission (EC), the
presidency (which plays a role similar to the monarchy in Britain), to
other formal institutions of state—and to *informal* institutions such
as the media and political parties in ruling coalitions. Power has also
flowed downward to powerful forces at the state level in this federal
system—to state governments and to important parties at that level
(both regional parties and state-level units of national parties). So if
we compare the India of recent years with its old self between 1971
and 1989, the contrast is marked.

It becomes even more startling if we compare India with
other democratic (and with undemocratic) systems. I have found
little evidence of anything approaching this dramatic change in

---

[3]A. Sen, *The Argumentative Indian: Writings on Indian Culture, History
and Identity* (Penguin, London and New Delhi, 2010), pp. xiii–xiv.

other countries—not just developing countries, but industrialised democracies as well.

Two Consequences of this Redistribution: Political Regeneration and a Decline in Abuses of Power

This change has immense consequences. Consider two. The first is political regeneration. When the Gandhis governed from an over-mighty PMO, the strength, autonomy, integrity and agility of other political institutions were undermined. Indeed, Indira Gandhi set out, proactively and systematically, to weaken every alternative power centre—including (unwisely) her own Congress Party—in pursuit of personal and dynastic rule. After 1989, most of these institutions (although not the Congress Party) have been revived so that they are able to perform many of the tasks assigned to them by India's Constitution and expected of them by democratic theorists. (For details, see chapters four and six of this book.)

People who focus only on India sometimes underestimate how extraordinary this is. If we consider other cases in Asia, Africa and Latin America, we find a few parallels—Brazil after 1992 and Ghana after 2002 are examples. But nowhere else has institutional regeneration occurred to the same degree. This suggests that in India, we find human resources, political skills, and habits of mind which equip it unusually well to achieve constructive changes of this kind.

The second consequence is a marked decline in abuses of power by leaders at the apex of the political system. Between 1971 and 1989, such abuses were common—indeed, they reached outrageous levels. Since 1989, abuses have been extremely unusual. I can identify only one occasion in that period when an Indian prime minister has committed an abuse of power—the bribery of Members of Parliament (MP) from a regional party in the mid-1990s to secure the survival of the Congress Party's minority government. One abuse in 21 years is far fewer than in India before 1989—and far fewer than the United Kingdom (UK) experienced under either Margaret Thatcher or Tony Blair. It is only when we compare India with other polities that we fully realise how remarkable this change has been.

Getting Re-Elected: Clientelism, Post-Clientelism and a Revenue Surge

Between 1980 and mid-2008, ruling parties or alliances at the state level in India's federal system were thrown out by voters more than 70 per cent of the time. If we remove West Bengal (where the ruling Left front has won every election from 1977 to 2011) from that calculation, the rejection rate nears 90 per cent. At the national level, ruling parties or alliances were ousted at five of the six parliamentary elections between 1989 and 2004.

These are hair-raising statistics for politicians. They become even more remarkable when they are compared with data from other polities. Winning re-election in India between 1980 and mid-2008 was far more difficult than just about anywhere else. This was true partly because Indian elections are free and fair which is not always true elsewhere. But it also owes much to India's sophisticated, assertive voters. Fewer of them may be literate than their counterparts in many other countries, but they are more alert and discerning.

India's politicians were acutely aware that their usual strategies for winning re-election were inadequate. They had long depended mainly on the distribution of patronage (goods, services, funds and favours) through networks of clients—that is, clientelism—to cultivate popularity. But when they saw that it was not producing positive results, many leaders decided to supplement clientelism by offering voters additional things to win their support. (They seldom curtailed clientelism because that would have alienated powerful allies.) These 'add-ons' were *post*-clientelist initiatives which often sat uneasily alongside systems of patronage distribution. (For more on this, see chapter thirteen of this book.)

Politicians pursued a remarkable diversity of post-clientelist strategies. At the state level, some of them stressed identity politics in efforts to polarise society, but these campaigns varied greatly. In Gujarat, for example, Chief Minister Narendra Modi fomented antipathy between Hindus and others. But in Bihar, Lalu Prasad Yadav stressed the division between 'haves' and 'have-nots'. Other state-level leaders preferred to emphasise development, but again, they did so in different ways. Chief Minister Chandrababu Naidu in Andhra Pradesh radically centralised power and pursued development in a top-down, commandist and illiberal manner. By contrast, Chief Minister Digvijay Singh in Madhya Pradesh pursued it by decentralising power and encouraging bottom-up participation. We find echoes of these various approaches in other parts of Asia and Latin America,[4] and even to a degree in Africa where clientelism still looms very large.[5] But no other country has seen so many variations on the theme of post-clientelism, and in very few or perhaps none does it loom as large as in India.

The search by anxious politicians for ways of ensuring re-election has led most of them to create new government initiatives which deliver benefits to voters whose support they need. But they have a serious problem here. Most of their parties possess only limited organisational strength. In particular, most fail to penetrate effectively downward below intermediate levels to the grassroots. This incapacity is shared even by the over-estimated organisation of the Bharatiya Janata Party. (See chapter seven of this book.) So politicians tend strongly to rely not on their parties but on formal administrative structures to implement these initiatives. We have thus seen, over the last 30 years, a proliferation of new programmes and a growth of state agencies which manage them.

Until recently, politicians who introduced these new programmes faced severe fiscal constraints which often undermined the impact of even the most imaginative new initiatives. But a new

---

[4]M. Melo, N. Ng'ethe and J. Manor, *Against the Odds: Politicians, Institutions and the Struggle against Poverty* (Hurst/Columbia University Press, London/New York, 2012).

[5]One notable example is Tanzania where the ruling party has stressed development programmes while seeking to limit the importance of clientelism. (I am grateful to Ole Therkildsen for insights into that case.) Steven Friedman has detected the beginnings of this trend in other African countries. (Private communications from both of these colleagues.)

trend has changed the rules. The revenues of Central and state governments have surged since 2003—thanks to economic growth and to new approaches to tax collection. This has enabled leaders to spend massively on new programmes. The government in New Delhi committed over $57 billion to poverty reducing initiatives between 2004 and 2009, and it also spent lavishly on programmes for the non-poor.[6] Most state governments have done the same. These outlays have been vastly in excess of anything seen before in India.

It is thus not accidental that in very recent times, governments have found it easier to win reelection. The trend first became evident in December 2008 when three of four state governments in north-central India were re-elected. The exception, Rajasthan, had experienced exceedingly inept governance by an over-centralising chief minister who managed to alienate both the main wings of her own party. Several other state governments have retained power since then, and in May 2009, the ruling alliance in New Delhi won a fresh mandate at a parliamentary election. Reliable polls conducted during that election indicated, astonishingly, that both the national government *and* the state governments in all but one major state enjoyed strong approval ratings from voters.[7] A new political logic applies, for the time being at least. Reelection has become the norm.

Small-Time Political Entrepreneurs

In every country, there are people at the local level who are politically ambitious. But the actions that they take to pursue their ambitions vary, somewhat or enormously, because the political environments in which they operate vary. We can learn a lot about

[6]J. Manor, 'Did the Central Government's Poverty Initiatives Help to Re-elect It?', in L. Saez and G. Singh (eds), *The Indian General Election of 2009* (Routledge, London, 2010).

[7]These polls were conducted by the National Election Study, coordinate by the Centre for the Study of Developing Societies (CSDS). For more detail on all of the topics discussed in the preceding paragraphs, see ibid. By contrast, a similar poll a few weeks before the 2014 national election found Central government approval ratings to have plummeted in most states.

those environments and political dynamics within different systems by studying the actions of small-time political entrepreneurs.

In some systems, they have few opportunities—because power is highly centralised, because political systems are rather closed to newcomers, or because pursuing political ambitions is a dangerous business. But most systems these days offer at least some openings, so small-time entrepreneurs often have enough opportunities to become active.

It turns out that, on the evidence from comparative investigations, India is an extreme case—and it is extreme in being encouraging. A minority of state governments there (perhaps four to six) have generously devolved powers and resources onto elected councils at lower levels—*panchayats*. In those places, political entrepreneurs at the grassroots tend to become active mainly within the formal structures of the decentralised system since they offer significant opportunities. But in most states, elected councils have only limited powers, so ambitious local residents pursue their ambitions through informal channels.

There is usually a compelling need for them to do so. It arises from a hugely important change in rural India (where two-thirds of the population still resides) which has become evident since the mid-1990s from studies by anthropologists. The power of caste hierarchies has declined quite markedly (see chapter fifteen of this book.) As a result, the castes which once dominated village life no longer enjoy the deference they need to persuade others to join in collective efforts to 'get things done' using only the resources available within the locality.[8] This forces people who want to 'get things done' to reach beyond the village—upward to higher levels in the political system—for resources, goods, services and advice. Local political entrepreneurs—'fixers'—are the ones who engage in such efforts, shuttling back and forth between villages and sub-district or

[8]This quotation is drawn from a case study which elegantly illustrates this point, G. K. Karanth, V. Ramaswamy and R. Hogger, 'The Threshing Floor Disappears: Rural Livelihood Systems in Transition', in R. Baumgartner and R. Hogger (eds), *In Search of Sustainable Livelihood Systems: Managing Resources and Change* (Sage Publications, New Delhi, Thousand Oaks and London, 2004), pp. 265–74.

district headquarters, seeking help from bureaucrats and politicians at those levels. Huge numbers of these entrepreneurs have emerged across India (see chapter ten of this book), and they help to make the democratic process work well. A significant number of these people come from outside the formerly dominant castes, and if they are effective, other villagers (even elites) often turn to them rather than to traditionally dominant caste leaders for assistance and leadership. That in turn erodes the old caste hierarchies still further.

But we only see how remarkable their emergence in India is when we look for similar political entrepreneurs in other countries. I have done this in Zambia, South Africa, Ghana, Cambodia and Bangladesh. In none of those countries (for varying reasons), are local entrepreneurs present in anything like the strength that we see across most of India.

There appear to be two main explanations for this. First, we find few countries in which something like the decline in the power of India's caste hierarchies has occurred. Instead we find:

(a) little diminution in the power of local elites, or
(b) 'social change in fast forward'[9] as a result of rapid economic growth which has triggered substantial social dislocation (seldom seen in rural India), or
(c) the breakdown of old social structures amid conflict and predation.

The other explanation lies in over six decades of democratic government in India—which has next to no parallels elsewhere in Asia, Africa and Latin America. This has made India's political system more open—and more porous for political entrepreneurs emerging from the local level—than other systems. In most of them, efforts to reach upward to higher levels yield little benefit—either because bureaucrats and politicians at slightly higher levels can scarcely be found, or because they do not possess the capacity or the

---

[9] I owe this phrase to a discussion with Anne Booth of the School of Oriental and African Studies. She was referring to parts of East and Southeast Asia where growth spurts have caused rapid social change—and dislocation.

inclination to respond helpfully. In some countries, it is risky to reach upward in this way. The proliferation of government programmes in India (noted above)—which has seldom been matched in other countries—also offers local political entrepreneurs who seek assistance from higher levels an abundance of opportunities.

Comparative studies of these entrepreneurs can tell us much about the character not just of other political systems, but of India's. If we focused only on India, we would take them for granted and would not realise how remarkable their emergence actually is.

The Fluidity of Political Identities

One pattern of behaviour has been extremely important in sustaining the democratic process in India. We find similar trends in some other countries—though not, as we shall see, in all—but it is especially strong in India. In every society, people have available to them a wide range of identities. But because Indian society is unusually complex, people there have an unusually broad range of identities upon which to fix when they engage as political actors in the public sphere. At a minimum, these include three kinds of caste identities[10]; linguistic identities; religious identities (which include broad categories like 'Hindu', 'Muslim' and 'Sikh', but also sectarian sub-identities within those larger categories); urban/rural, class and gender identities; and national, regional, sub-regional and local identities. Indians, like people everywhere else, operate with multiple identities in mind. But at any specific time, they tend to be preoccupied with one (or a very small number) of these identities.

As we saw in chapter eight of this book, Indians have long tended to shift their preoccupations from one to another, and then another of these identities—*often* and with *great fluidity*. They do not fix, permanently and ferociously, upon one of these identities—as for example their neighbours in Sri Lanka have done, with

---

[10]These are *jatis*, *jati*-clusters and *varnas*. I have discussed this in much more detail in J. Manor, 'Prologue: Caste and Politics in Recent Times', in R. Kothari (ed.), *Caste in Indian Politics*, new edition (Orient BlackSwan, New Delhi, 2010), pp. xi–lxi.

ghastly consequences. In India, this fluidity has prevented tension and conflict from building up along a single fault line in society, so that the democratic process has been largely spared the problem of bitter, long-running enmities. People may for a time perceive contradictions between themselves and others who cling to a different identity. But in due course, they shift their preoccupations to another identity and what had looked (to them and to observers) like an insurmountable, permanent contradiction melts away. Thus, no identity has predominated for very long.

To say this is not to argue that all Indians think alike. We are dealing here with predominant patterns. But they are sufficiently predominant—and more predominant than in most other countries—to have prevented severe conflict from developing for long periods along any fault line in society. That has eased the burdens which the democratic process has had to bear. Here, once again, we only discern these things clearly and fully when we consider India alongside other cases.

Finally, a Problem—which is also an Opportunity

The comments above may be well and good, as far as they go. But it would be wrong to end the discussion here because a serious problem remains. Most social scientists in India lack the resources to travel to other countries for comparative studies. Until they can do so, we need to consider alternatives.

Fortunately, two hold promise. The first is to compare India today with its former self, at an earlier period in its recent history. This approach has been used at several points in this chapter, and elsewhere in this book. The second alternative has even more to offer. There are many startling—and only half-explored—variations in the politics of India's diverse regions. Indian scholars can deepen their (and our) understanding of this inspiring, exasperating and vastly complex democracy by doing comparative studies of different states in the federal system. They might also examine different sub-regions within larger states. We badly need fuller understandings of the internal diversity of (for example) Orissa, Bihar, Uttar Pradesh, Madhya Pradesh, Maharashtra and Andhra Pradesh. There is abundant evidence of the dividends that such research can yield,[11] but many more opportunities remain under-exploited. Consider just two examples.

Let us start with bureaucracies. I was once pulled up short when describing a constructive development programme in south India by a senior civil servant from a north Indian state. She said,

> ... what you say may be true, but we can't hope to achieve things like that in ... Uttar Pradesh, Haryana or Bihar [totalling one-quarter of India]. Bureaucrats have been browbeaten, abused and undermined for so long there that we no longer [are] the kind of civil service that you need to do things like that.

She was right, and we urgently need research on how and why things vary so much from state to state—not least because it will indicate what sorts of national programmes are or are not feasible across much of the country. One part of that exercise might be an analysis of why bureaucracies not just in the south, but in some northern states—Madhya Pradesh and Rajasthan come to mind—have largely escaped such damage.

Or consider relations between governments and civil society organisations in different Indian states. In recent times, a number of politicians have recognised that India's civil society organisations have devised an extraordinary array of promising, feasible strategies for the promotion of poverty reduction, service delivery, social justice and much else. Several state governments—and the national government between 2004 and 2014—have reached out to civil society for ideas and partnerships. And yet some state governments have remained cool or downright hostile to civil society. This has,

[11]For a recent example see R. Jenkins (ed.), *Regional Reflections: Comparing Politics across India's States* (Oxford University Press, Delhi, 2004). But see also, M. Weiner (ed.), *State Politics in India* (Princeton University Press, Princeton, 1968); J. R. Wood (ed.), *State Politics in India: Crisis and Continuity* (Westview Press, Boulder, 1984); M. Weiner, *Party-Building in a New Nation: The Indian National Congress* (University of Chicago Press, Chicago, 1967)—plus a revisitation of the same states that Weiner studied in A. Kohli, *Democracy and Discontent: India's Growing Crisis of Governability* (Cambridge University Press, Cambridge and New York, 1990).

predictably been true of ruling parties on the left, given their belief in the constructive potential of the state. But we also see other ruling parties at the state level which are not remotely leftist dealing harshly with civil society—apparently because their appetite for top-down control has inspired a generalised assault on alternative power centres. The prime example was the Telugu Desam Party (TDP) in Andhra Pradesh between 1995 and 2004 which surpassed leftists elsewhere in its antipathy to voluntary associations, but others cry out for analysis, including both film star-led parties in Tamil Nadu.

The internal diversity of India is remarkable. This is partly the result of its size. India has a larger population than North, Central and South America put together. We find plenty of diversity across the Americas, so it should be no surprise that we encounter it in India. There is in one sense less diversity in the subcontinent than in the Americas since the formal institutions of state are the same everywhere. But a vast array of variations—some subtle and some striking—in society, culture, language, religion and political economy emerge as we move from region to region in India. The presence of a common set of formal institutions facilitates comparisons on these fronts because it enables us to hold one thing constant as we explore contrasts.

INDEX